Greenhill Books

CHINA, 1900:
THE EYEWITNESSES
SPEAK

CHINA 1900:
THE EYEWITNESSES
SPEAK

The experience of Westerners in China during the
Boxer Rebellion, as described by participants in letters,
diaries and photographs

Frederic A. Sharf and Peter Harrington

Greenhill Books, London
Stackpole Books, Pennsylvania

China, 1900: The Eyewitnesses Speak
First published 2000 by Greenhill Books, Lionel Leventhal Limited,
Park House, 1 Russell Gardens, London NW11 9NN
and
Stackpole Books, 5067 Ritter Road, Mechanicsburg, PA 17055, USA

British Library Cataloguing in Publication Data
Sharf, Frederic A.
China 1900: the eyewitnesses speak: the Boxer Rebellion as described by
participants in letters, diaries and photographs
1. China – History – Boxer Rebellion, 1899–1901
2. China – History – Boxer Rebellion, 1899–1901 – Personal narratives
I. Title   II. Harrington, Peter, 1954–
951'.035

ISBN 1-85367-410-9

Library of Congress Cataloging-in-Publication Data
Sharf, Frederic Alan.
China, 1900 : the eyewitnesses speak : the Boxer Rebellion as described by
participants in letters, diaries and photographs / by Frederic A Sharf and
Peter Harrington.
p. cm.
Includes bibliographical references and index.
ISBN 1-85367-410-9
1. China–History–Boxer Rebellion, 1899–1901–Personal narratives. 2. China–
History–Boxer Rebellion, 1899–1901–Sources. I. Title: Boxer Rebellion as
described by participants in letters, diaries and photographs. II. Harrington, Peter,
1954– III. Title.
DS770-b.S54 2000
951'.035—dc21   00-024952

Typeset by DP Photosetting, Aylesbury, Bucks
Printed and bound in Great Britain by
Creative Print and Design (Wales), Ebbw Vale

Contents

Illustrations and Maps

All photographs are from the collection of Jean S. and Frederic A. Sharf, except 8, 9 and 31, courtesy of the Peabody Essex Museum, Salem, MA.

Maps

Maps created by Newburyport Press, Newbury, MA.

Acknowledgements

We are grateful to the following people for their valuable help with this book:

Ms Nancy TenBroeck, Salem, MA
Mr William La Moy, Peabody Essex Museum, Salem, MA
Mr Tom Okado, Tokyo, Japan
Ms Hisako Ito, Yokohama Archives of History, Yokohama, Japan
Mr Glen Mitchell, Maggs Bros. Ltd., London, England
Mr Jim Clancey, Maggs Bros. Ltd., London, England
Mr Richard Kossow, London, England
Mr Jeffrey Somers, London, England
Ms Kate Ker, Afold, Cranleigh, Surrey, England
Mr Kenneth, J. Ross, Presbyterian Historical Society, Philadelphia, PA
Dr Harold F. Worthley, Congregational Library, Boston, MA
Mr Norman Brosterman, New York City, NY
Ms Nancy Manley, Lake County Public Library, Leadville, CO
Mr Mitchell Yokelson, National Archives, Washington, DC
Ms Kay M. Bryan, Independence, MO
Mr Frederick J. Graboske, Marine Corps Historical Center, Washington, DC
Mr Dwight M. Miller, Herbert Hoover Library, West Branch, IA
Ms Susan Burroughs, Bowdoin College Library, Brunswick, ME
Mr Eden Juron Pearlman, Evanston Historical Society, Evanston, IL
Ms Mary R. Herr, Davensport Public Library, Davenport, IA
Mr Chester Brummel, Museum of Fine Arts, Boston, MA

Frederic A. Sharf
Peter Harrington
2000

Introduction

The event known in history as the Boxer Rebellion is always identified in the public mind with the 55-day siege of the Legation Compound in Peking, which started on 20 June 1900 and ended on 14 August. In reality, of course, a series of events unfolded prior to the siege and continued to unfold well beyond its ending. This book examines a complex series of overlapping events through the eyes of men and women who witnessed them.

The Boxers

The Boxers were adherents of a secret society committed to expelling foreigners from China. Their Chinese name (*I Ho Chuan*) was translated into English as 'Fists of Righteous Harmony' – an allusion to the strength that could come from a united effort. The Chinese word for 'fists' could also translate as 'boxing'. The movement was peasant-based and combined colourful clothing with exotic ceremonies in which converts were supposedly invested with supernatural powers of invulnerability.

The movement started in the North China provinces of Shantung and Chihli, where severe drought and the resulting famine combined with chronic unemployment to create difficult living conditions. Foreign intrusion into peaceful Chinese life was blamed. The word 'Boxer' first appeared in official western correspondence in May 1898, and by January 1900 there was widespread concern within the western community.

Boxer placards, posted in towns and villages across North China, proclaimed their motto: 'Protect the Empire: Exterminate Foreigners'. Missionaries living in the interior cities were the first to feel the effects of this movement. They saw bands of lawless peasants roaming the countryside, harassing the missions and the Chinese Christian converts. Because the anti-foreign message was also implicitly anti-Christian, the missionaries and their converts were the first targets and the first victims.

The missionaries realised that the Boxer fanaticism and belief in their magical powers gave them courage which made them a very dangerous enemy. They brought this movement to the attention of the foreign ministers in Peking who, in turn, asked the *Tsungli Yamen* (Chinese government office that dealt with foreigners) to take steps to outlaw the movement. No such action was undertaken.

11

Background information: Peking and Tientsin

A traveller who wished to visit Peking early in 1900 would arrive off the coast of China at the open roadstead of the Gulf of Pechihli, where all ocean-going ships were required to anchor. Transfer to lighters and small steamships took place ten miles out to sea. Conditions were normally turbulent, and often made more so by poor weather and high winds. It took two hours to reach the sandbar at the mouth of the Peiho River.

Only small ships could cross this sandbar, after which was found the Chinese city of Taku on the south bank of the river, and the western city of Tongku on the north bank. All passengers disembarked at Tongku, from which the railroad ran to Tientsin, a distance of approximately 30 miles, in two hours. Arriving at the Tientsin terminus, the western traveller needed to cross the river to reach the Foreign Concession, which was totally separate from the enormous walled Chinese city of Tientsin.

Tientsin was an important commercial centre, well situated at the junction of the Peiho River with the Grand Canal. Before the opening of the railroad in 1897 there was enormous traffic to Peking on the river as far as Tungchow, and then over a stone paved road for the 15 miles to Peking.

The Foreign Concession was composed of three distinct western communities at this time: British, French and German. Here were handsome buildings, excellent roads, gas lights, parks, churches, clubs, theatres – in short, an up-to-date, even elegant western community totally separated from that of their Chinese neighbours.

From Tientsin the railroad went on to Peking, a distance of approximately 80 miles, requiring five hours. Its route was via Lanfgang and Fengtai to the Peking terminus at Machiapu, a few miles outside the wall of the Chinese City, a huge oblong-shaped walled city. One wall of the Chinese City served as one wall of the adjacent square-shaped Tartar City. Within the Tartar City was located the Imperial City containing government offices, and the Forbidden City containing royal palaces. Adjacent to the Forbidden City was the Legation Quarter, in which all foreign legations were located, each within its own walled compound. The numerous western missionary societies each had walled compounds of their own, but they were spread throughout the Tartar City, often at some distance from the Legation Quarter.

Most western visitors to Peking at this time found the city very unattractive. They complained especially about the crowded conditions, lack of proper sanitation, and unusual smells; the streets of Peking were overwhelmingly dirty. However, foreigners living within the Legation Quarter were housed in western style, with proper sanitation, and enjoyed a totally separate social life – dinner parties, dances, theatricals, picnics in the countryside, and their own horse racing track.

Both Tientsin and Peking were reputed to have Chinese populations of approximately 1,000,000, though there was no scientific basis for the calculations. By contrast, the foreign populations of each city were minute – perhaps 500 in Peking and double that in Tientsin. In each city, half of the foreign population consisted of missionaries. In Peking, the balance was primarily members of the diplomatic community, while in Tientsin most of the remainder were businessmen and their families.

Such, then, was the setting for the events under consideration. The curtain was now lifting on a drama that dominated the news media and the attention of an international audience for many months. The acts that ensued are summarised in the Chronology which follows.

Chronology

May 1900

30   Allied fleet begins to assemble outside Taku Bar in Gulf of Pechili
       Allied marines and sailors arrive at Tongku and Tientsin
31   Allied marines and sailors arrive at Peking Legations

June 1900

6   Railroad from Peking to Tientsin destroyed
9   Peking race course destroyed by Boxers
       Sir Claude MacDonald wires Admiral Seymour to send troops
10   Telegraph line from Peking destroyed by Boxers
       Seymour Expedition departs from Tientsin
11   Sugiyama Akira, Chancellor of the Japanese Legation, murdered in Peking
7   Allied troops capture Taku Forts following bombardment
       Foreign Concession of Tientsin besieged by Boxers
19   Tsungli Yamen demands all foreigners leave Peking
20   Baron Klemens von Ketteler, German Minister, murdered in Peking
       Legation Quarter of Peking besieged (siege began at 4 pm)
       Roman Catholic Mission at Peitang Cathedral, Peking, besieged
23   Allied Relief Column enters Tientsin, ending the siege
26   Seymour Expedition returns to Tientsin

July 1900

13   Allied army attacks Chinese Walled City, Tientsin
14   Allied army captures Chinese Walled City, Tientsin
17   Truce at Legation Quarter in Peking
25   Firing resumes in Peking for a few days

August 1900

4   Truce ends at Legation Quarter with resumption of heavy firing in evening
       Allied Relief Expedition departs from Tientsin for Peking
5   Allied victory at Peitsang
6   Allied victory at Yangtsun

9 Allied victory at Hosiwu
12 Allied occupation of Tungchow
14 Allied entry to Peking; relief of Legation Quarter
15 Dowager Empress flees from Peking
Allied capture of Imperial City
16 Allies capture Peitang Cathedral
28 Allied victory parade in Forbidden City

September 1900
3 Prince Ching returns to Peking
8 Punitive Expedition departs for Tiu-Liu
10 Punitive Expedition departs for Liang-hsian
16 Punitive Expedition departs for Pa-ta-chal
25 Punitive Expedition departs for Nam-Hung-Men
Field Marshal Alfred von Waldersee arrives at Taku

October 1900
2 Allied troops occupy Shanhaikwan Forts
3 Troop review in Peking to honour departing Americans
10 British troops occupy Summer Palace
German troops occupy Winter Palace
12 Punitive Expedition departs for Paoting-fu
17 Marshal von Waldersee arrives at Peking
20 Allied occupation of Paoting-fu
Sir Ernest Satow, British Minister Plenipotentiary, arrives in
Peking to replace Sir Claude MacDonald
25 Sir Claude MacDonald departs Peking for new posting at Tokyo
26 Dowager Empress arrives at Sian (Xian)

November 1900
6 Return of Paoting-fu Punitive Expedition
10 First coating of ice on Peiho River at Tungchow; river traffic
continues
12 Punitive Expedition departs for Kalgan

December 1900
7 Peiho River frozen over, closed to traffic
9 Train service from Tientsin to Peking resumes
12 Train service from Peking to Tientsin and to Tongku resumes
22 Ministers present peace proposal terms to China
31 Public execution of von Ketteler's confessed murderer

January 1901

1   Parade of Allied troops in Peking

24   News of death of Queen Victoria reaches Peking

27   Troop review in honour of German Emperor

February 1901

2   Funeral Service for Queen Victoria and parade of Allied troops in her honour

19   Celebration of Chinese New Year

26   Public execution of two prominent Boxer leaders

March 1901

6   Parade of New South Wales Naval Brigade prior to their departure from China

10   Bodies of siege victims removed from British Legation compound for burial in the European Cemetery outside the city wall

12   Crisis in Tientsin; dispute between British and Russian soldiers over a railroad siding

19   British Marines arrive at Tientsin railroad siding to replace Sikh soldiers

22   Tientsin railroad siding crisis resolved; all troops withdrawn

27   China offers to pay huge indemnity to Allies

September 1901

7   Peace Protocol of Peking signed by China and Allies; official ending of Boxer Rebellion

NORTH CHINA: THE BOXER THREAT

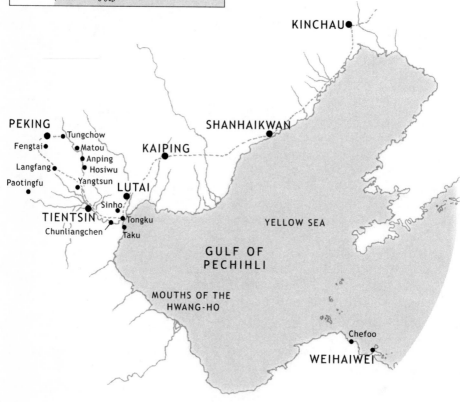

The Area of Operations

Introduction

In the autumn of 1899, people of the western world in general, and British citizens in particular, were preoccupied with events in South Africa. The British Army was suffering embarrassing losses at the hands of a wily Boer enemy and three British communities were besieged: Kimberley (14 October 1899–15 February 1900); Ladysmith (2 November 1899–28 February 1900); and Mafeking (16 October 1899–17 May 1900). The Chinese press reported these events in detail, even down to the numbers of troops involved and the casualties. Western residents of China recognised that any failure of British troops in South Africa might well embolden the Chinese and add fuel to the Boxer fire.

Meanwhile, in China the cry for action to combat the Boxer threat came principally from missionaries; diplomats and businessmen tended to regard the missionaries as crybabies. Even sophisticated observers were often of two minds with regard to the Boxers – feeling on the one hand that a cataclysm was about to take place, but on the other that the entire threat would ultimately collapse. Then, on 31 December 1899, an Anglican missionary, Reverend Sidney Brooks, was brutally murdered in Shantung Province.

Gradually the Boxer movement spread from Shantung into the province of Chihli and by the spring of 1900 Boxers were active on the outskirts of Tientsin and Peking. Tungchow, only 13 miles from the walls of Peking itself, became a centre for Boxer drills, attracting students and bargemen. On 20 May 1900 Sir Robert Hart, the Inspector General of the Chinese Maritime Customs Service, wrote to his colleagues in London: 'The Boxers are busy and mischief is intended. If my wife and children were here I'd move them off sharp to Japan.'

On 28 May the Boxers destroyed the important railroad station at Feng Tai, six miles from Peking, the junction for trains both to Peking and Paotingfu. The British Legation, sensing the gravity of the situation, notified British subjects in outlying communities surrounding Peking that they could seek asylum within the Legation compound if they felt threatened.

The real drama was about to begin.

Account of Charles Davis Jameson, American Mining Engineer

Charles Davis Jameson (1855–1927) was born in Bangor, Maine and graduated from Bowdoin College with a degree in engineering. He specialised in bridge and railroad construction before taking a position as Assistant Professor of Engineering at the Massachusetts Institute of Technology in 1885. In 1887 he was appointed Professor of Engineering and then head of the Engineering Department at the University of Iowa.

Jameson moved to China in 1895 to work for the Chinese government; he reported directly to Li Hung Chang, a senior official and diplomat who was responsible for representing the Chinese government as it intersected with the foreign world. He inspected gold mines in order to suggest new equipment, and studied railway routes from Tientsin into the interior, reporting on coal and iron deposits along the routes. He travelled extensively in North China.

In January 1898 he signed a two-year contract with the Peking Syndicate of London to serve as their Chief Engineer in China. This Syndicate had secured title to rich deposits of coal and iron in the provinces of Shansi and Honan, but some of the sites were so remote that railway lines were needed to reach them. The Boxer rebellion set back their plans. Jameson resigned in the fall of 1900 and returned to the United States.

We first began to hear of the Boxer movement in China in December 1899. During most of the winter business called me to Peking, and through the kindness of our Minister, Mr Conger, I spent nearly three months with him as his guest in the Legation.

The missionaries from the Province of Shantung were constantly writing letters and asking that something might be done in order to afford them protection for the carrying on of their work, that the Boxer movement was not at all a local affair but was spreading through the entire Province of Shantung, and gradually working its way north into Chihli.

Very little credence was given to these cries of 'wolf' by the missionaries, as they were an annual occurrence, and so far nothing had ever materialized.

23

All the people that had lived in Peking for many years and who were supposed to know more or less about things Chinese and the Chinese situation, scouted the idea of their being in danger.

Ministers of the different nations repeatedly requested the *Tsungli Yamen* [Chinese Foreign Office] to exert their authority and have the Society of Boxers suppressed; these requests were always followed by an edict from the Empress Dowager, ordering that the Boxers be suppressed and that all disturbances be put a stop to. The Ministers were satisfied by these pro-testations of friendship and promises of redress on the part of the Chinese Government. And so things were allowed to slide along.

The cause of the uprising which followed cannot in any way be laid to the missionaries; it was an anti-foreign uprising, not an anti-Christian one. The object was to kill all the foreigners or drive them into the sea, and retain China for the Chinese alone. There were undoubtedly a great many Chinese connected with this movement who were solely so connected for patriotic reasons. . .

During the month of May [1900] I received orders from the Peking Syndicate of London to make preparations for a trip to Southern Shansi for the purpose of opening up some coal mines in the territory conceded by the Chinese to this syndicate. There was sent to me from England one young Scotchman as mining engineer and superintendent and a young Welshman as mine foreman. All the preparations for the trip were made, and on the 19th of May I went to Peking in order to take my last orders from the General Agent of this syndicate, and also to get the opinion of various people there as to the expediency of my going west at this time for the purpose of opening up new work by foreign methods.

I interviewed the British Minister, our own Minister and Sir Robert Hart. They were unanimous in their opinion that any trouble which might come from the Boxers or from the Chinese would be purely of a local nature and confined to Northern Shantung and Southern Chihli.

There was no foreigner in China better posted or who knew more about the conditions there than did Sir Robert Hart. He has been at the head of the Imperial Maritime Customs for the past forty years. Neither the British Minister nor the American Minister had been a great many years in China, but, of course, both were supposed to be well posted on the situation.

The Agent of the Peking Syndicate, Mr Henry Bristow, had been in the British Chinese Consular Service for thirty years, spoke Chinese perfectly, and, like the rest of us, thought he knew all about the country. As I said before, all of the above-mentioned were unanimous in the opinion that I would have no trouble and I felt that way myself, as I had travelled for many years through Western China, knew all the towns, people and officials, and did not consider the situation in any way serious. I wished, however, to be backed up by some opinion other than my own, as I was to take two young strangers into Western China.

I returned to Tientsin on May 21st and found everything ready to start the next day. Among all the people that knew of my leaving for Western China there was only one who urged me not to leave, and whose information, as subsequent events proved, was correct. This was Colonel, now General Wogack [or de Wozack], the Russian Military Attaché. He met me on the street and begged me not to think of leaving for Western China, and said that in less than two weeks the whole country would be in uproar, that the trouble would extend to the borders of Thibet, that I would be cut off from the coast and undoubtedly lose my life. That the last of February he had informed his Government of all this but had been laughed at for his trouble, yet that he knew exactly what he was talking about, that he considered the situation most critical, and that he could not conceive of the stand taken by the Ministers in Peking and their continual cry that nothing serious was the matter.

I laughed at his advice, told him that I did not think there would be any trouble, and that I would like to wager that I could go from one end of China to another with nothing but my servants and my riding whip. I have paid that wager several times since then.

On the afternoon of May 22nd I started for the West. My party consisted of twenty-six in all, with myself and my two foreigners, Chinese Secretary, Interpreters, *Wei Yuan*, Chinese Director, servants etc.

The *Wei Yuan* is a Chinese official of about the rank of a magistrate, appointed to attend to all official business required during my trip, to interview all the officials, see that one received the courtesy due to one's rank, that every advantage was given me for the conduct of my work, and that none of the natives in any way were allowed to interfere with me or the members of my party.

Mr Feng, the Chinese Director with me, was the Director of the Chinese part of the Peking Syndicate, or, as it is called in China, the *Fu Kung Ssu*. His business was to see that I had no trouble with local mine owners, and that everything was made smooth with the native gentry.

My official Chinese Secretary was Mr Lo Hsi Luh, brother of His Excellency Lo Feng Luh, Chinese Minister to Great Britain, and, poor fellow, he was sent along, not so much for any work he could do himself, as for the prestige which his brother's name would give to my party.

As will be seen later, he paid with his life for this before the end of the trip.

We left Tientsin in houseboats, and were to go the first 600 miles by the Grand Canal and Wei River. The houseboats used were 40 feet long, 8 feet wide, with 15 feet of dock room in front, the rest of the boat being covered with a small house just high enough to allow one to stand up in, and divided into four small compartments. In one of these I slept and ate. Two others were occupied by my servants, and in the fourth was the captain of the boat with his wives and families. Each foreigner had a boat to himself and also each Chinaman of any importance. In all there were about eight boats. These boats are propelled by means of large sails when the wind is fair, but owing to the sinuosity of the Canal this is never the case for any great distance, and the usual method of propulsion is by pulling them along by trackers who walk on the tow path . . .

From the very beginning an unexplainable something was noticeable in the manner of the boatman and the natives met with at each village. I had been over this portion of the Grand Canal a number of times before, and although unable to explain exactly what this difference was, I felt it to a very marked degree. The country was barren and burnt brown; crops that should have been ready for the market were only a few inches above the ground and shrivelled by the heat of the sun and the lack of water. God knows, the people looked poor enough in this part of the country at any time, but they now seemed absolutely poverty stricken and on the verge of starvation. Vegetables and food of all kinds were hard to buy and had nearly doubled in price. The country swarmed with beggars, and according to report was overrun with small bands of robbers looting the granaries of the rich farmers. There appeared to be no thieving or robbing going on with any other object than to get food.

At every place there were rumors in regard to the Boxers and their intentions, but to me these intentions appeared vastly exaggerated and to be beyond the reach of possibility of execution. It was common talk that the Boxers would march on Peking, drive out the foreign embassies or kill them all, kill all the foreigners at Tientsin and other Treaty Ports and burn all Foreign Concessions. Such reports as these were brought to me every day by my servants, and I simply laughed at them as Chinese fairy tales.

About the 27th of May I reached the town of Techow where there was a telegraph station, and wired to Peking for news. The answer came back that the Boxers had advanced upon Fengtai, which was the railroad station for Peking and the junction point with the Lu-Han Railway; that they had destroyed all the rolling stock and burnt all the buildings; that the foreign Legations had sent for Legation Guards who were expected every day, and that the whole of the country to the south and west of Peking and Tientsin was in open rebellion; that I was to proceed to Ling Ching where there was another telegraph office and await orders there. I proceeded to Ling Ching and arrived there the 1st of June.

At every village I passed immense crowds of natives came down to the Canal side to see the hated foreigner, and their remarks were anything but complimentary or encouraging.

On reaching Ling Ching I found that the General in charge of the Chinese troops there was an uncle of Mr Feng, the Chinese Director. He at once called upon me and stationed a large guard around my boats, keeping a clear space for 500 feet along the river bank. Ling Ching is at the junction of the Grand Canal and the Wei River, and is almost entirely inhabited by boatmen, by far the most disorderly class one meets with in China. There I received the following telegram from Peking:

LEGATION GUARDS ARRIVED YESTERDAY. ALL QUIET HERE. YOU CAN PROCEED WITH YOUR WORK. WILL NOTIFY YOU IF THERE IS ANY TROUBLE.

This telegram shows how little some of the people in Peking, even at that time, realized the seriousness of the trouble by which they were surrounded. This was one of the last telegrams sent out from Peking, and it is needless to say that the sender was not after that in a position to notify me as to any danger until the 14th of the following August.

Beside this telegram from Peking with orders for me to proceed west, I also received advice from Yuan Shih-k'ai's General, Mr Feng, who, as I have said, was stationed at Ling Ching. This advice was given me by order of His Excellency Yuan Shih-k'ai, the Governor of the Province of Shantung. The advice was for me to go west as rapidly as possible; that the whole country between Ling Ching and the coast was in rebellion and that I was cut off from Tientsin; that the Boxers knew of my party and would be on the lookout for it if I attempted any retreat to the east, and that if I wished I could come to the capital of Shantung and His Excellency would do his best to protect me and my party and get us to the coast at Chefoo.

As I was told that the insurrection did not extend into the Western Provinces and as my orders from the General Agent of the Syndicate were to proceed with my work, I decided to continue up the Wei River.

General Feng gave me a guard of eight foreign-drilled Chinese soldiers, armed with modern rifles, whom he had reason to believe would be faithful.

The second night out from Ling Ching, as we tied up to the bank, two houseboats came down the stream containing missionaries. These missionaries were on their way to Peitaho, the summer resort on the sea coast, for a rest, and did not seem to think there was any immediate danger to their Missions, or that there was likely to be any general uprising in that part of the country. They told me that the week before Dr Mitchell and wife (missionaries), in going up the river in houseboats, had been attacked two days farther on, but only by a mob without firearms. We turned over our mail to these missionaries to take to the coast, wished them a pleasant voyage and started on our different ways.

These missionaries in their houseboats never got any further than Ling

Ching, at which point they were obliged to leave the boats and travel overland to Hsinan Fu, the capital of Shantung, guarded by Yuan Shih-k'ai's soldiers. They all got through with safety, however, and I would like to mention here that in all the troubles that followed not one missionary was killed in the Province of Shantung, but at every point perfect protection was given them by Yuan Shih-k'ai, who had them all taken to the coast where they were delivered to an American man-of-war. Considering the fact that Shantung was the birthplace and hotbed of the Boxer Society, and that it is a most rabidly anti-foreign province, no praise can be too great for the magnificent manner in which Yuan Shih-k'ai handled the situation of last summer. And it also goes to prove that, given the right man as an official, foreigners and foreign property can receive protection under any circumstances that may arise in China. That the laborers and ordinary village and townspeople will never take the initiative in any violence towards foreigners, and that no violence of moment has ever been committed without at least the supposed protection of the Mandarins in power.

The next day I stopped in the afternoon at the missionary station of Mr McKenzie, a Canadian Presbyterian. Mr McKenzie came down to the boat and we had a long talk concerning the situation. I found that he took a pessimistic view of the situation. He said that the entire country was ripe for rebellion; that only a spark was needed for it to burst into flames; that open threats were made that all missionaries and foreigners would be destroyed and that all mission property would be burnt; that the local magistrates acknowledged that they had not the power to afford protection and that the missionaries would have to look out for themselves. He also told me that there was not the least doubt but that I would be attacked during the next thirty-six hours – such at least was the common talk among his native Christians. As usual, I smiled at his prophecies and thought I knew more about the country than he did . . .

On the morning of the 9th of June we approached a place called Tutsun. The river at this point is very shallow, less than two feet in depth, and the channel narrow. My boat, leading the procession, went aground under a bluff, just at the corner of the village wall, and swung across the stream, thereby preventing any other boat from passing. I was dressing at the time, shut up in my cabin. As soon as my boat grounded a watchman on the wall fired his gun in the air, apparently as a signal.

My other boats had crowded up behind as closely as possible and were all more or less jammed in, the boatman shouting and everything in confusion. Just at this moment my No. 2 Boy[1] rushed into my cabin and said: 'Oh Master! the Boxers have come.'[1]

I took my revolver and looked out of the window in the next compartment. My boat was against the bluff, but looking down the river along the line of boats I saw a mob of insane-looking Chinamen shouting 'Sha! sha!' ['Kill! Kill!'] and forthwith smashing in the windows of the other boats with bricks and stones and other available material. Among them were a few armed with swords and firearms, who seemed to have gone mad with excitement and were endeavoring to reach the boats. One in particular, who appeared to be the leader, and who, as I afterwards learned, was in full Boxer uniform, was advancing slowly on the boats waving a large naked sword and encouraging his followers to attack the boats.

I had a new English Webley revolver that I had purchased the night before leaving Tientsin, which I had never fired. This appeared to be a good opportunity, and I took five deliberate shots at this man, every shot striking the ground about a foot in front of him, and he calling attention of his followers to the fact that no foreign bullet could hit him. I began to think that this was no fairy tale and reached for my Winchester, which missed fire three times. I then began to get frightened as the man kept coming nearer and nearer, and wondered if there might not be some supernatural power back of this Boxer movement. My Boy, however, at once handed me a shotgun with both barrels loaded with buckshot, which I straightway emptied into the man's legs. He did not do any more advancing on the boats but simply lay down and howled.

By that time I had gotten out on deck where everything was in confusion, the Chinese all howling and crying, my guards firing straight into the air and saying that the Boxers were upon us. In a minute, however, things quieted down a little and six of the guards ran up the bank to see what really was going to happen. The mob took to its heels and soon was nearly out of sight within the walls of the village.

We then got my boat afloat and began up the river. As soon as we passed the village the mob came out again, and it was necessary to land some of the guard and fire on them occasionally. They followed us along for some three miles, when I decided that they were having all the advantage on their side, as the high banks of the river prevented anyone on the boats from seeing across the country. So I stopped the boats and we were all landed and made entrenchments. By this time the whole country was up, and we could see crowds of villagers in all directions hurrying towards a central point. Apparently the natives had but three modern rifles and twenty cartridges, which they very soon got rid of, and without doing any damage, as we simply lay in holes dug in sand or stayed in the boats. They never came near enough for their Chinese guns to be of any use, as they stood in great fear of our rifles.

I sent a native courier off at once for a Magistrate of that district, and then simply sat down to wait for him. We held up a small Chinese gun-boat coming down the stream, and the Captain agreed to stay with us until the magistrate arrived. He amused himself by firing his one cannon every half hour to let the people know he was there. Owing to the height of the bank the shot from the cannon always tore up the earth about one hundred feet away from the gun. The mob fired on us on and off for fourteen hours.

At that time I did not know they were Boxers, and looked upon the whole affair as merely the uprising of an irresponsible mob which was probably hungry.

The Magistrate and General arrived about three o'clock in the morning, and at daylight went through the farce of trying three prisoners we had captured. They were convicted and sentenced to receive 500 blows with the bamboo. The blows were given, the prisoners howled and grovelled in the sand, and not one of the blows would have killed a fly.

After an interchange of Chinese courtesies and the drinking of several quarts of poor champagne by the Magistrate and General, we started on our way rejoicing ... I pushed on as rapidly as possible to the head of the river. Owing to the lack of rain the water was very shallow, and at the end of two days' journey we found it would be impossible to reach Wei Hui, the usual head of navigation, so we were obliged to stop with the boats at a place called Ta Kou, where we left the boats for carts and ponies and started for Hwai King Fu.

At about noon the first day we passed a station of the Canadian Presbyterian Mission. The missionaries here were Mr Slimmon and Dr Mitchell, each of them with his wife and the former with the addition of a little baby girl. I had known the Slimmons for a number of years and had been through this station several times, consequently I stopped there in order to give them what news I could from the coast and find out what they knew of the condition of affairs further west. They were taking the most gloomy view of the situation; they had received a telegram from the coast warning them of the impossibility of reaching there, and advising them to escape west or south as soon as possible, notifying them that all missionaries had been warned by their respective ministers to leave interior China, and that most serious trouble was pending in Peking and Tientsin.

They were most undecided as to what would be the best plan, or which way to try for an escape. Their principal drawback to any movement was their lack of money; none of these missionary stations carry large bank accounts in the interior, and what little they do have is in a Chinese bank. They had just been informed by those banks that they were unable to cash any orders. The whole city was in a state of excitement, and although the magistrate at that time was protecting them and their property, still, it was doubtful how long this protection would last.

These missionaries were in a good position to receive news from the coast and from different parts of the country, owing to their long established system of native couriers, and at this time the Chinese Post Office service had not been interrupted.

It was at last decided that I push on west to see if it would be possible to carry on the work for which I had come to that part of the country. In the meantime Slimmon was to send word to all the missionaries of Northern Honan, notifying them that my headquarters would be in Hwai King Fu and that I had an ample supply of money with me, so that if serious difficulty ensued they were to keep me thoroughly posted, and if necessary I would appoint a day for them to meet me at the crossing of the Yellow River and take them down through Western China. My stop there was about half an hour, but as my guards had blocked the road the whole city was in a state of uproar when we got ready to start.

During the next three days I pushed on as rapidly as possible and arrived at Hwai King. This is a city of about 50,000 inhabitants, situated about forty miles north of the Yellow River and is the governmental city of Northern Honan, which includes all the province of Honan north of the Yellow River. The city itself has its magistrate who has charge of the city affairs and the small district around the city, also the prefect who has charge of the whole of Honan north of the Yellow River, that being included in his prefecture; also the general who has under his command the troops in this section of the country.

I had been at Hwai King a number of times before, and had always occupied the Kung Kuang or official residence. All the large cities in China have these official residences; they are more or less furnished according to the Chinese ideas, and usually capable of accommodating anywhere from 50 to 200 people. None of the natives of the city live in them, and they are simply used as official guest houses for any stranger who may appear, and who, on account of his rank, is more or less the guest of the city. They have one great advantage over the ordinary Chinese inn, which is that they are occupied so little that they are more or less clean, but in the winter the facilities for warming them are so slight, and it may have been a year since they had been warmed, that to use them for two or three days only is most uncomfortable.

The city government had been informed by couriers of the hour at which I would arrive. The change in the attitude of the people was very marked. In the years before I had gone in and out of the city as I chose, with no guard excepting two foot soldiers who always ran in front of my pony. The people were formerly smiling, good natured and had always given me a hearty welcome. This time a guard of some twenty men met me a few miles from the gate, and additional troops were waiting at the gate to escort me through the streets. The side streets were packed with a curious and vicious-looking crowd, their remarks were not complimentary, and the whole thing showed that trouble was brewing for someone, and I began to realize that possibly the time had not been well selected for opening up coal mines with foreign methods.

The General, Prefect and Magistrate called on me within the next two or three hours, each of them bringing the usual tremendous crowd of servants in order to show his importance. The Prefect and General did not hesitate at all in telling me that things were very serious through all that section of the country, and that it would be probably impossible, or at least impracticable, for me to start work. Would I please move slowly and see that my men did nothing that would in any way arouse the prejudices or superstitions of the natives. They told me, and that I well know, that there had been no rain for over two years; the crops of the country were ruined, the people were on the verge of starvation, also the whole country was overrun with small bands of robbers, so that not even the natives could travel with safety from place to place, without going in large bodies and being well armed; that it did little good to send small bodies of troops to cope with these robbers as all the troops were more or less in sympathy with them, and both the Prefect and General admitted that, while they would afford me every possible protection, and, if I followed their advice, could probably guarantee my safety, still, the condition of the country was such, and the anti-foreign feeling was reaching such a point that to a great extent they were in sympathy with it themselves, and that beyond the fact that they would protect me and my party from personal violence, they would not make any great efforts to facilitate the opening up of new work.

Both the General and the Prefect were old friends of mine and I had known them for a number of years. They were among the few Chinese officials for which I have the utmost respect and in whom I have the greatest confidence, and their honesty and frankness in explaining the situation to me and their future conduct has done nothing to lessen this feeling.

I agreed to make no move outside the guest house without notifying them and allowing them to provide whatever guard they thought necessary. I also agreed to do nothing contrary to their wishes. In former years, in this guest house I had a guard of four men, relieving one another whenever they saw fit, at the door. This time, at the door and in different parts of the house and in the street I had a guard of over a hundred men under arms, relieving one another at regular intervals.

The conduct of the General and the Prefect was in marked contrast to that of the Magistrate. I was a little unfortunate in regard to this Magistrate. A number of years before, in travelling through that section of the country, the then Magistrate had sent one of his subordinates with me as an extra *Wei Yuan*. The man was utterly useless, knew absolutely nothing of the country, smoked opium and was usually dead to the world the greater part of the day. He interfered amazingly in my work at that time, and at the end of some three days I told him what I thought of him, had him put in his official chair and carried back to the Magistrate at Hwai King Fu with my compliments.

This man was now the Magistrate. He expressed great joy at seeing me; that there was nothing in the world but what he would do for me or any of my party; that I must not believe the stories I heard as to any unpleasant feeling through the country; that the Chinese were most anxious to have the foreigners open up the mines and show them how to do the work; that he could guarantee my safety and the safety of all my people at all times and in all places; that in travelling through his district it would be much better for me to take his *Yamen* runners as guards, rather than regular troops, and that the General and Prefect were both busy with their own affairs, and that it would be much better if I allowed him to arrange everything for me rather than trouble the other officials. He also confided privately to my interpreter that he had been requested by both the General and the Prefect to say this to me, as they did not wish to be troubled by having to dry-nurse a body of foreigners, and that they were most anti-foreign men.

The trouble with the Magistrate was that he overdid his affection, and not only made me a little suspicious of him but made my servants exceedingly so.

My *Wei Yuan* became exceedingly friendly with this Magistrate and seemed willing to vouch for his entire good faith in all that he said. Of course, none of my servants or interpreters held sufficiently high rank to call upon the Magistrate by themselves, nor upon the General or Prefect. They could only go with me. The *Wei Yuan* could, of course, call on the Magistrate when he chose as an equal.

It was at this point that my Chinese Secretary, Mr Lo Hsi Luh, became of great use to me. His rank was really higher than that of any one else in my party, and nominally equal to that of a Governor of a Province. He could go where he chose and when he chose, and he also spoke English perfectly. Within the next few days he had gathered quite a great amount of information in regard to the situation. He was a man without any personal courage, and this led me to believe that a great many things he told me were exaggerated. I doubt very much now whether they were.

His review of the situation was that the people were ready to rise at any moment; that the Prefect and the General were perfectly honest in all they had said and proposed to prevent any trouble; that the Magistrate was a low-down scoundrel anyway; that he had not sufficient Christian charity to forgive the insult I had put upon him a few years previous, and that he wished very much for me to get out into the coal regions among the mountains where I would be more or less cut off from assistance, and that then he would take care that although possibly none of my party would be killed, we would have an exceedingly disagreeable quarter of an hour.

Mr Lo Hsi Luh disliked very much my *Wei Yuan*, as did also my interpreters and servants. My servants made no secret to me that they considered him a scoundrel and a traitor who hated all foreigners, and that he was only watching carefully to see what turn events would take in order to know what to do.

Anything was better than sitting still and listening to these conflicting stories and getting nervous over them. I found, after being two or three days shut up in this house, that unless something were done I was in the way of losing entire control of my party, so I ordered that ponies should be purchased and arrangements for a hundred-mile trip through the coal region be made.

There was no wild enthusiasm on the part of any of my people for this, but they did the best possible.

There was one noticeable thing occurred at this time. In the years gone by I had purchased ponies at Hwai King for my caravans, and had never had the slightest trouble in getting very fair ponies at a fair price. This time it seemed impossible to get a pony that was capable of making an ordinary day's march. Every difficulty was put in the way of my pony men, and the prices asked for the ponies offered for sale were sometimes ridiculous. The ordinary townspeople would not offer their ponies for sale; every pony that I bought had to be bought through some member of the city government, and a more sorry lot of arrangements you never saw. The price for the necessary carts had more than doubled, and the carts seemed to have shrunk in size.

At last, however, we got enough livestock together to make a start, leaving all unnecessary luggage with one or two servants in Hwai King. We set out for a week's trip in order that this coal mining engineer from England might examine some of the Chinese workings in the coal fields, where he would eventually start foreign works.

We were gone a week and examined three separate groups of mines. These mines were not new to me as I had stopped at all of them before. I had always found the miners a good-natured set of people who had shown much childish curiosity in my outfit, and I had always been treated well by them.

This time all was changed. As soon as we reached a mine or group of mines all work was stopped. If the mine had been working ten minutes before, the superintendent showed no hesitation in saying that it had been flooded for a year, and it would be impossible to make any examination. The miners came from all parts of the country in enormous crowds.

The best inns were always occupied, and at least for the first two nights we were obliged to take what we could get. After that, however, we took the best inns wherever we went, just as usual, and found that they were only occupied by official orders and not by people.

I soon found that it was an absolute waste of time trying to do anything, and I began to have a certain amount of fear for the safety of my party. We were threatened by mobs a number of times, treated with the greatest discourtesy, for which we could get no redress from our guard, and at the last mine, the *Lao Nieu*, we were hooted and jeered at and my servants more or less maltreated. Serious trouble was only averted by my interpreter and we started back at once for Hwai King.

It was now getting towards the last of June. On reaching Hwai King I found couriers from different mission stations waiting for me with letters. The news was most serious, and that received from the coast almost beyond belief, although, as was afterwards proven, a great deal was actually true.

All the foreign Legations were besieged in Peking and were to be killed. Tientsin had been taken by the Chinese, the foreign settlement burnt and the foreigners driven into the sea. Apparently the foreigners were doing nothing. Some of the mission stations had been burnt, etc.

In one letter the missionaries would ask me what they should do, where they should fly to; and in another letter, by the same courier, they would say that they would not under any circumstances leave their mission stations, they would stay there and die as martyrs, if necessary.

There was only one thing on which they all agreed, and that was that they had no money with which to hire carts or boats, or to pay for food necessary for a long trip to the coast.

Under the protection of the General in Hwai King I felt perfectly safe, and in consequence sent word to all these missionaries that when things reached such a stage that they deemed it necessary to escape, that they must arrange some concerted action amongst themselves, and that I would meet them on any day they said at the crossing of the Yellow River, forty miles south-east of Hwai King; that I could undoubtedly hold my position in Hwai King much longer than they could at their missionary stations, but as for staying there and being martyred it was blank nonsense, and they must remember that they had their women and children with them and their duty was to get them out of danger; that as far as I was concerned I was not there to be made a martyr of, it was not in my contract and I wanted nothing to do with it.

During the next four or five days couriers came in, two or three a day from all these stations, the danger growing apparently more and more serious every moment.

At last, on the 25th of June, the General came very quietly to see me in the afternoon. He came at a time when he knew my *Wei Yuan* would not be present. He told me he had received orders to march with all his soldiers to the north, possibly on his way to Peking, and that consequently he would be unable to afford me any protection after the first of July, when he must march, and that he would advise me to do either one of two things. Either to go with him with my whole party and be held prisoners of war, when he thought he could guarantee my safety, but at what time he could get me down to the coast was uncertain; and the other was to start south, at once, through a section of the country which I well knew, and take my chance of getting through to the head of the Han River.

{Note: Jameson's journey ended successfully in Shanghai with most of the 56 foreign and Chinese people then accompanying him in his party being in good health.}

Note

[1] [By the author] 'A foreigner new to China has much difficulty in remembering Chinese proper names, and servants are frequently called by numbers and occupation rather than by names. My No. 2 Boy, as he is always called, is my valet. His elder brother, who is my head servant and responsible for all my domestic affairs, being known as No. 1 Boy.'

Letter from Miss Ione Woodward, American Tourist

Ione Woodward was 17 years old when she arrived in Peking on 4 April 1900 with her mother and a friend, Cecile Payen. They were guests of the American Minister, Edwin H. Conger. This letter was sent to her father, Morgan S. Woodward.

United States Legation, Peking, China
May 28, 1900

We are approaching a serious crisis. The ministers met yesterday at the Spanish Legation, and after having consulted together (eleven being present), told the *Tsungli Yamen* that they must get the decree against the Boxers from the emperor, which the *Yamen* have at last consented to do. The emperor is to state the punishment and the penalties for the crimes of the leaders, and to have them enforced, unless the conditions are changed and the Boxers stop their lawlessness.

Today they burned a railroad bridge near Tientsin, and the foreigners have all left the city on the other side of the bridge. Mr Conger is very grave and says it is a serious time, and that a few days, perhaps to-morrow, will culminate either in the emperor quelling the forces or in the Boxers getting more power, and then heaven help us.

Admiral Kempff is expected tomorrow afternoon, but we are doubtful of his arrival, for the train of today from Tientsin has not yet come up, and they may be burning the lines below us to cut off all communication. Fortunately they have not as yet cut the telegraph wires and everyone is surprised that they have not.

Mr Conger says that if a person were not in Peking, but in some coast town near Shanghai, there would be comparative safety, and he told mamma at 'tiffin' that at the coast, they might stand some show of escaping, while we would have to go on horseback or in sedan chairs to get away, even if we were permitted to leave, which may be an impossibility in a short while. Mr Conger's family, of course, will not leave, as they are all together, but they strongly advise us to if things get more serious.

It seems terrible to think you will not get this for five or six weeks, and think how much can happen in that space of time. I know you will be worrying, and I do wish I could see ahead enough to tell what we will be doing, but until the crisis we can simply wait and hope for the best.

A week ago 500 Christian refugees came to the Catholic compound, from a village where the Boxers had killed, by throwing them into a fire, sixty men, women and children. The bishop is half-crazed with fear and the poor French minister is besieged with questions and prayers for help from thousands of Catholics all over the country. He is nearly overcome with the gravity of the situation. Mr Conger says that the only way we would be massacred would be that the Boxers would burn all the legations and the people in them. They have gone so far as to kill an officer of their own government.

We are in hopes that the admiral will stay long enough so that we can arrange to go as far as Tientsin with him, as it is very risky for two women alone on a Chinese train, but he is only going to stay long enough to talk over the matter with Mr Conger and then return to send us guards, probably a battalion of marines. By that time the railroad may be destroyed and the marines will have to march from Taku-Bar to Peking, a distance of about 100 miles. Even then the small number which of necessity can only be sent will be no guard against a mob of 1,000,000 Boxers.

Miss [Polly] Condit-Smith of Washington is here and there is no telling what she will do. She is a young lady of 22, and has been all around the world. She may go on, even in the face of this great danger. I tell you the question is very serious, and mother is already packing her trunks so as to be ready to leave at a moment's notice. Mr Conger would not hesitate to tell her to go at once, and he would expect us to leave whether we thought we ought to remain or not, for the fewer women he has on his hands, the better he will feel.

Well, do not worry until you have more occasion to, and if the worst comes and we are forced to leave, we will cable 'safe'.

Lovingly, I am your own daughter,

Ione

SECTION TWO

THE SEYMOUR EXPEDITION

Introduction

As the crisis in Peking deepened during the first week of June 1900, the various ministers at their desks in Peking began communicating a sense of urgency to their home offices. They also reached out to the commanders of the Allied fleet anchored in the Gulf of Pechihli.

A council of war was held on 9 June 1900 among senior naval officers from many nations, meeting on board the British flagship HMS *Centurion* under the leadership of Vice Admiral Sir Edward Seymour. They decided to send a naval brigade – later termed the International Relief Expedition or the Seymour Expedition – to Peking under Seymour's personal direction.

The Expedition, consisting of seamen and marines from all the nations represented, was assembled in a matter of hours. In the early hours of Sunday 10 June, men selected for the force were transferred from ships lying offshore in the Gulf to smaller ships that could cross the bar at the entrance to the Peiho River and land at Tongku. They were sent at once by train to Tientsin, the departure point for the Expedition.

Seymour assembled a force of 2072 men, of whom 116 were officers. The British contingent of 921 was by far the largest. Germany contributed 450; Russia 305; France, 158; United States, 112; Japan, 54; Italy, 40; and Austria, 25.[1] At Tientsin, five engines and more than 100 railroad cars were assembled to take them to Peking.

Seymour organised his force into five sections. Train no. 1 contained half the British force, all of the Austrians and Americans, plus coolies and supplies to repair the railroad. No. 2 took the remainder of the British, all the Japanese, and some French. No. 3 was composed entirely of Germans. No. 4 held the Russians, the balance of the French, and the Italians. No. 5 was a supply train, which was supposed to run back and forth from the furthest point to Tientsin.

The Expedition did not reach Peking. In fact, it was fortunate to extricate itself from its journey and return to Tientsin – as unfolded in the accounts that follow.

Note

[1] This count is drawn from *The Royal Navy: A History,* Vol. 7, p. 523.

Account of Captain Lieutenant Paul Schlieper, German Imperial Navy

Paul Schlieper was born in Germany in 1860 and joined the Germany Navy in 1880. By the end of the century he had risen to the rank of Captain Lieutenant – the German equivalent of First Officer. He arrived in the Far East in the spring of 1899 as First Officer aboard SMS Hansa, *one of the new generation of German warships sent to create a larger naval presence for Germany in the Far East. In 1899, the Germans had seven warships stationed at their newly-acquired Chinese naval base at Tsingtau; by the end of 1900 there were twenty-one.*

Schlieper was wounded while serving on the Seymour expedition and was evacuated at the end of June 1900 to the German Naval Hospital in Yokohama. He convalesced there from 8 July to 25 August, when he departed for a sanitarium in Germany.

Schlieper organised this translation of his account as a fit to Admiral Seymour.

{Saturday, 9 June}
Next morning's light showed us a striking spectacle. A crowd of ships of every nationality and the newest types of construction lay close around, our nearest neighbour being the Russian armoured cruiser the *Rossia,* certainly the most impressive example of her class in that mighty fleet.

As a result of very disturbing news from Peking, a meeting was held on board the flagship of the senior officer of the combined fleet, Vice-Admiral Seymour, on the morning of June 9. No general resolution was arrived at, but Vice-Admiral Bendemann on his own initiative ordered the reinforcement of the garrison at Tientsin by three hundred men for the following day. During the night however [9 June] we received an order to land the detachment *at once,* a manoeuvre that in an anchorage like Taku Roads is attended with considerable difficulty. It is a place where, in a dark night, lowering, manning and equipping boats entails an expenditure of great trouble and exertion.

The cause of this haste was bad news from the Legations at Peking, who besought instant help if it was not to be too late. This unexpected signal flashed from the flagship was the cause of no little confusion on board, in the height of which however an order to stand fast tended to tranquillise us – the supply of boats requisitioned from shore had proved insufficient. We turned in to sleep till dawn, but our rest was short, and I was awakened again to hear the welcome words, 'Signal from the flagship – The combined details for shore to land with a week's supplies – to leave at once in boats...'

{Sunday, 10 June}
A lively time followed on deck and every other part of the ship, and one constantly caught the exclamation, 'This means Peking and fighting the Boxers.' How everything was finally got through all right I cannot tell to this day; I only know that on the stroke of nine I sheered off from the *Hansa* with all the boats, in command of the landing party, carrying in my pocket an order to steam up to Tientsin with all possible speed and place myself under command of Post-Captain Von Usedom with the other shore detachments...

We headed for the coast and as we crossed the bar, came across our Commandant who ordered me to go on to Tongku. After a two-and-a-half hours' passage we ran into the mouth of the Peiho, which is defended on each side by the renowned and menacing Taku Forts; from this distance the ships of our squadron looked no bigger than specks to the naked eye. Chinese soldiers urged by curiosity came running down to the shore as our long train of boats passed. The same idea occurred to most of us, that some day we might possibly find ourselves fighting against these gentry and one lingered for a moment on the thought. On the whole, however, we pictured our march to Peking as a tolerably peaceful one, and only contemplated opposition from the Boxers...

It was midday when I and my detachment reached Tongku, where the gun boat *Iltis* was anchored. Here we at once set to work with high good will to transfer everything – stores, ammunition, water casks and baggage – from the boats to the train drawn up in readiness for us, little anticipating that its carriages were to serve us as our lodging for a long while. The respective squads were told off to their carriages, which by the way it may be mentioned were all open and on nearer inspection left no room for doubt that up to the present time they had done duty as cattle-trucks. However there was nothing extraordinary in this; in war one looks upon this sort of thing as a joke...

We had about two hours to wait before leaving. The two hours' journey was beguiled with lively singing, and we reached Tientsin about half past four in the afternoon. Our reception at the station was a hearty one; the German residents greeted us with cheers, and by way of refreshment, had brought hundreds of bottles of most excellent beer to distribute among the men. It was a most welcome draught for throats dry with the burning sun and the dust of the journey . . .

We left a detachment of sailors and mariners from the *Irene* at Tientsin to reinforce the guard that had arrived there a few days earlier, so that the German contingent under Commander Kuhne of HIMS *Iltis* now consisted of 120 of all ranks. At the station a reflection of the agitation in the town could be seen in every face. Neither German officers nor civilians made any secret of their apprehensions, and all were delighted at our bringing reinforcements. The station swarmed with Chinese who took careful note of our business and urgency generally, with a cynical smile or some contemptuous remark. We soon grasped the fact that our expedition did not evoke much sympathy on the part of the Chinese. The station-master, for instance, declined to let us proceed – and it was only by commandeering an engine, whose driver we bribed by the offer of high wages while we placed it under an armed guard of sailors, that we persuaded our gentleman we were in earnest about it. A little while previously, however – and this gives an idea of their insolence and fanaticism – an attempt had been made to tear up the rails in our immediate neighbourhood so as to hinder our advance. Some English sailors from the *Endymion* were promptly detached, who drove the Chinese off at the point of the bayonet and then cleared the station of spectators. After that we were not molested at our work any further.

About half past five we were able to make a start. We left the kit-bags with some of our own things behind at the station. As Admiral Seymour, the leader of the expedition, had already left for Tientsin with the English contingent, we were directed to join him as quickly as possible, and we hastened our departure all we knew. The three cheers we gave as we left the station were answered by a derisive shout from the Chinese, an immense crowd of whom had collected near it. It was one mass of pigtails as we looked down at it, and must have numbered thousands . . .

After this our train went rattling on past towns and villages, hurrying us on over the flat thickly populated country without meeting any hindrance. The engine drivers were under the immediate eyes of sailors seated on the tender, who let no movement escape them. We soon came across traces of the Boxers. The rebels had set fire to the wooden sleepers after drenching them with petroleum; many were charred, and several still smoking. The discovery warned us to be on our guard, but no further hindrance was met with. In different places we passed camps of Chinese regular troops. These were regiments of General Nieh's force, about 4000 men, who watched our progress with indifference. In explanation I may observe that they were supposed to be our very good friends, for nominally they had been called out to oppose the Boxer hordes. That we could see by the threatening looks of the field-guns drawn out on the flank of their positions ready to resist an attack. The impression however was modified by the fact that the gunners, rifle in hand, were all peacefully asleep at their posts and only casually aroused by the noise of the passing train. It did not look as if the camps feared the terrible Boxers much, and experience was to show us later pretty clearly that the regulars had secretly made common cause with them.

It was seven in the evening when a halt was made, necessitated by the fact of the English trains having stopped short near Lofa station. A broken railway bridge was the obvious cause of their delay. All the strength available had been utilised at once towards making it passable. Admiral Seymour had in the train with him about a hundred Chinese labourers and a large store of railway materials for the repair of the line; our train too carried several loads of sleepers.

Captain Von Usedom reported himself to the Admiral, who was obviously gratified by our prompt arrival. He immediately allotted us a covered carriage ranking as a first-class which our senior officers could make their sleeping quarters, for ours was crowded. An open carriage – I will not go the length of calling it a cattle-truck – in the rear of the engine served us as a club. It formed an interesting study in itself, for club life here was certainly most original. At first we observed the distinctions of rank and meaning as on board ship; but later on, when first the bread and then the preserved meat began to give out, everything was thrown into the common stock and we all messed together. The cellar was managed separately, and each man's account entered to him; but how this was done when, say, the alarm sounded and our good steward had to rush for his rifle, or when the order was given to fall in for the march, I will not venture precisely to say; it might have served as a problem in the examination paper of a candidate for one of the higher grades of finance.

We were now to make our first bivouac and experience our first taste of camp cookery, for the men had not yet had a hot meal ... A position was selected for our bivouac close to the line. We had no tents; the men lay on the water-proof sheets served out for the expedition and they rolled themselves in the woollen blankets, for the nights were perceptibly cold. The moon shone down on a curious and interesting scene – three long trains surrounded by the bivouacs of different nationalities ...

{*Monday, 11 June*}
Our night's rest was not a long one. By four o'clock next morning the coffee had been made, and at seven we proceeded on our way, stopping however, now and again, to repair the line. This was effected quickly by the Chinese coolies who accompanied us under the direction of civilian engineers, for the Boxers had mostly only destroyed one of the two lines of rail, and the

material of the other could be turned to the advantage of quicker repair. The journey so far had been uneventful, when all at once at a railway-crossing the Boxers' cruelty and their inhuman mode of warfare became apparent to us. Near the ruins of a burned down passenger shed, the bodies of four Chinese railway officials were lying, horribly mutilated. It was a sudden glimpse of war in her darkest colours, an unmistakable indication of the way in which our prospective enemies did their work. Men's faces grew pale and the blood froze in their veins, when this first example of it met their gaze. The bodies had been cut to pieces, the hands and feet hacked off, and in one case the heart had been torn out. Such would be our fate if we were found wounded, such the last tribute of respect paid when they came across us lying dead on the field!

Shortly after this we reached Lofa, where an English detachment from the cruiser *Endymion* was left to fortify the station as a defensive post, after which we named it 'Fort Endymion'. The destruction of the water tanks for the engine was a great hindrance to our progress. At Lofa the station buildings were destroyed, just as along part of the line we had passed over, every passenger shed had been burned down. In the afternoon we resumed our journey to Peking. The heat was tropical, and in the open carriages as time went on it was terrible, even after the men had rigged up awnings of plaited mats stretched over bamboo poles as a protection against the sun. When it is further considered how closely they were crowded in the trucks, which were packed in addition with stores, ammunition and baggage, it is obvious their position was far from an enviable one. In the course of the afternoon another train came up from Tientsin, with 200 Russians and 50 French on board, a welcome reinforcement to our corps, which now amounted to 2100 of all ranks.

About six o'clock the engines of the leading trains suddenly gave the whistle agreed on as the signal of alarm, and we saw the English jump down in great haste and run forward to an adjacent wood. We instantly repeated the signal, and our companies formed up together. That from the *Hansa* got an immediate order to rush forward and clear the wood of Boxers, who could be seen there in great numbers. The company was instantly drawn out and the advance guard thrown forward with a party in support – it was the first attack we had ever made and every heart beat a little faster. In a short time we got news from the right wing that there had already been a brush with the retreating Boxers ...

Just as we got into the open, clear of the wood, a couple of Boxers sprang out of hiding close in front of the firing line. I instantly opened fire on them from my left, by way of reminder. For a moment a strange feeling came over me that I had for the first time the disposition of life and death, but it was no use thinking about it, it had to be, and no one could doubt they were enemies that we were dealing with. A sharp fire followed, and in a few moments the first victim had fallen, the first of many who were to follow him. Then we pushed on across the open towards a group of houses where a strong force of Boxers had taken up a position. The sun was near its setting but the heat was still great. We rushed forward, eager to show the rebels we could stand no nonsense, and had no fancy to have our journey stopped. I may mention by the way that we were still ignorant what amount of opposition we were to meet from the Boxers, as well as how they were armed or what tactics they would employ.

In a long line, followed by the *Hertha* company in column as a reserve – a section of which I now sent forward to support the left wing – I flung my force against the enemy now acting on the defensive. We were all pretty well exhausted – the heat, the excitement of our first engagement, the unaccustomed situation, our hurried advance in heavy marching order, could not fail to tell upon us – but we forgot all as we waited to attack. In the nearer distance, as we advanced by successive rushes, the fire grew hotter again, we could now see the enemy coming at us with wild gestures swinging their spears, lances or swords about their heads, and a few bullets fell quite near us. We often saw Boxers spring up into the air, execute a sort of war dance and then drop to the ground, and naturally supposed they had been hit; but when we got nearer and could see them plainly, they proved only to have been shamming to make us believe they had been killed and so avert our fire...

This is the place to observe that the Boxers, by wearing a red turban, a scarf or sash, and gaiters of the same colour, formed a uniform of their own, and that these distinctions in a bad light and at a distance might easily be mistaken for that of the regular army. I was soon to be made quite easy in this case, for as we went on we found one of the fallen wearing all the above-mentioned badges, but more convincing still the Boxer amulet, concealed in a small breast pocket. This amulet consists of a yellow card on which a sentence written in Chinese characters runs something like this: 'Long live the Manchu dynasty; down with the foreign devils'. A badge stained with blood, though it is often only coloured with red paint, is particularly characteristic of them. This amulet is to render the wearer invulnerable. The common people believed in the charm, and hence their fear of these cruel bands...

When we had made a certainty of having organised Boxers to deal with, we fell back by our left towards the railway, from which meanwhile a signal of recall had been sounded. We then saw the rebels were gathering in the next village, but following them further would have detained us too long, and moreover the object of the attack had been gained. The sun had already set when, dead beat and raging with thirst, we regained the train after our first skirmish.

Experience had shown us that at such a temperature men loaded with heavy packs could only advance very slowly, and the exertion needed to come up with the enemy was frightful. The sailor's want of practice – for as a matter of fact he is rarely called upon to fight on shore, and his battle-field is the sea – had handicapped us heavily. In subsequent engagements, when possible, we therefore left our packs behind . . .

About eight in the evening we resumed our slow journey, but soon stopped again and bivouacked . . . The day just over, with our first action and unaccustomed exertions in the tremendous heat, followed by the now constantly recurring expectation of a night attack, kept my nerves pretty well on the stretch. Rest on the railway embankment was out of the question, every moment I seized my field glasses fancying I had seen a Boxer creeping steadily towards me. But the Chinese were afraid of evil spirits in the dark, and I may say we were never molested by our enemies at night. False alarms induced by single shots at the outposts often occurred, but we were spared real attacks or assaults when we bivouacked.

{Tuesday, 12 June}
Our progress towards Langfang was very slow. Here again we found great destruction both of the station and the line. We hoped to get through with the repairs quickly, but as time passed the mischief proved far greater than we had imagined. Watering the engines entailed very hard work, for the water-tower was completely wrecked, and we company officers went out in the afternoon to look for wells in the village which had been deserted by the inhabitants. We searched it thoroughly with our revolvers cocked, and in a small courtyard came upon a cripple crawling about on all fours, who began making signs to express his helplessness before we got near him. The poor creature, who could only go on his hands and knees like an animal, had been left behind at our mercy. On our assuring him that all we wanted was to be shown water, he crawled with a beaming face to a well, took a bucket and cord, and drank a first draught of water to prove we need have no fear of poison. This was a most acceptable discovery. In the dwelling house on the same premises we unearthed two old women of seventy whom the Boxers had equally left to their fate. The lot of the aged, the sick and cripples who were left to look after themselves was a hard one. I can still see the poor women shaking with fright as they assured us they knew nothing of the Boxers' movements. We found plenty of fowls, pigeons and eggs in the out-buildings, but could not find it in our hearts to take anything away with us, though our stomachs were beginning to develop quite a craving for fresh meat.

Our little reconnaissance had attained its object in the discovery of a good well. On our return to the trains, with the news of drinking water having been found, a great exodus towards the village took place! . . .

In the course of the afternoon, a messenger from the American Legation in Peking brought news that the advance of our expedition had produced a tumult in the city. He also gave information about the condition of the gates at Peking and the best way to attack them. The *Gefion* company under Lieutenant Weniger was detached here, as that of the English cruiser *Endymion* had been at Lofa, to put the railway buildings at Langfang in a defensive condition so as to form a strong post and also to ensure communication with our rear. This was done in the promptest and most workmanlike manner, which made it a pleasure to see the *Gefion's* men at their task. By way of a change the sailors were now promoted mastermasons; the machine guns were mounted on the water-tower and the roofs, whence they commanded the surrounding plain, while by means of a hastily constructed banquette the gunners were enabled to offer an effective fire to the approaching enemy. This block-house was at once named 'Fort Gefion'. To our extreme satisfaction a train conveying stores arrived today from Tientsin; it brought drinking water in big earthen jars, and also a large number of straw mats of the sort used for roofing the trucks as already described. The arrival of this consignment, especially of the drinking water, was hailed with great joy, for the need of it as well as of some little change of food had already become apparent.

For the first time in the night that followed there seemed a fair chance of rest. I slept magnificently on the hard carriage seat; I could not have done better in the train *de luxe* from Cologne to Berlin. And yet this was nothing in reality but an ill-formed goods train that could not move because the sinful Chinese had carried off the rails in front of it!

{Wednesday, 13 June}

The repairs of the line at Langfang were reckoned at about three days' work, which suggested to us to settle down comfortably. The inadequacy of the water supply, however, induced supreme authority to send one train back to Yangtsun and our own to Lofa, to fill the engines, boilers and water casks ...

When we had completed our water-supply at Lofa we steamed back to Langfang, but found plenty of work sprang up before us on the way. Six trucks of our apparently over-long train ran off the metals, and instead of getting in to camp we had to toil up to two o'clock in the morning getting them on the track again. At one time our men were working with Russian sailors and I feel bound to say what capital labourers they are, and how willing to tackle their work. When my men's task was finished they silently went off to another spot to help there, without waiting for orders — a fine example of zeal and devotion to duty. Of the Russian sailors on this expedition I have nothing but praise to offer. It was enormously tiring work getting the trucks on the rails again. A blue-jacket cannot be farther from anything in the way of training than railway work, though I venture to say with some pride that his business is to be able to do anything, and that he can do it too, when he comes across it . . .

{Thursday, 14 June}
As a longer stay in Langfang had now proved necessary, the order was given for washing clothes this forenoon at the village near by, in the wells spoken of above. As a precautionary measure I left the section of my company that was on guard on the embankment under arms, and went myself to the village to see that all was right. As I was returning, when I was a couple of hundred yards from the railway, I heard the sound of shots in front of me near Fort Gefion, which increased in numbers till they became a volley. It was plainly a sudden assault. I sounded the alarm, and sent messengers back into the village to call all the men in, then ordered the company to take up a position on the embankment while the rest of the men, part of them leaving their washing behind, hurried up and fell in as quickly as possible.

Several hundred Boxers had suddenly attacked Fort Gefion, but had been received with an energetic fire by the *Gefion's* men from the machine guns mounted on the station tank. A short but exceedingly sharp fight had ensued, in which the Boxers displayed wonderful courage and a fanatical contempt of death. They advanced at a slow pace under the murderous fire of our men, though they were only armed with swords, spears and knives. Eighteen Boxers were killed in this affair, the brunt of which fell on Lieutenant Von Krohn's section, and was victoriously repulsed.

Today, alas! we had to mourn our first dead. As the Boxers advanced to the attack they came across a picket of five Italians who had not time to run in to their train. I cannot undertake to say whether the outpost had been forgotten to be withdrawn, or whether the fault lay in the train not having been sufficiently closed up, but briefly these unfortunate Italians suddenly found themselves without support and surrounded by some hundreds of Boxers. They sold their lives dear, firing away their ammunition to the last cartridge, and then fell into the power of the cruel brutes who literally cut them to pieces.

In the afternoon news came that Lofa station, or to call it by its most recent name Fort Endymion, had been attacked by a large force of Boxers; Admiral Seymour at once proceeded to the threatened point with No. 4, the French and English train, and succeeded in arriving in time. Here again the strongest proofs of an almost incredible contempt of death, pluck and fanaticism were shown, for in this case also the enemy without firearms ventured to attack a strong position defended by machine guns and modern repeating rifles. The result was a complete victory over the enemy, who took to flight leaving 200 dead behind them . . . Several standards and two old guns were taken, and No. 4 train was received on its return towards evening with cheers. Its carriages were hung with trophies.

Sunset brought us a sad duty, the burial of our first dead, the Italians who had fallen at the outpost. The bodies had been laid in the engine shed at the station, and the graves dug in front of it. The whole force was paraded, and arms presented by a guard of honour composed of men of the different nationalities, after which the unfortunate victims were laid in the grave whilst prayers were offered by the English naval chaplain who accompanied the expedition. It was a very affecting scene – many must have asked themselves the question, Shall I too soon be laid to my last rest? Some men turned faint and had to be led away . . . Our Italian comrades had given their young lives for their country in the steadfast performance of their duty.

{Friday, 15 June}.

With the object of safeguarding the work on the line, and if possible procuring some cattle in the villages, the companies from the *Hertha* and *Kaiserin-Augusta* received orders to search those on the left of the railway. Both companies returned in the afternoon having prosecuted their search through seven villages in all, but without coming in touch with the enemy, who had withdrawn before them. They brought back five interesting specimens of flags and several weapons, as well as some cattle and two prisoners. Today my company was not employed, but I was told in the evening for certain that we should have similar work to do on the next [day].

At the council held this afternoon it was decided to apportion the trains among the nationalities. This had the result of linking Captain Chagin and his 300 Russians with the German detachments, as from the first a great sympathy had been established between us and the Russians. Captain Chagin, who spoke German fluently, was an especially congenial personality; his fine figure and his friendly manner will be remembered by everyone who took part in the expedition . . .

That evening I received the following order; to return with my company on a ballast train, and restore communication with Tientsin. Where the longer gaps occurred on the line we were to transfer stores, water and despatches from trains, presumably sent out from Tientsin, to my train No. 5, and thus to provide the expedition with the much needed supplies.

{Saturday, 16 June}

As early as three o'clock am, the *Hansa* company had been roused and entrained in No. 5, which was provisioned for a two day's trip and filled up with railway material and Chinese coolies. An English railway engineer also accompanied the train as superintendent of repairs . . . The engines and tenders carried marksmen prepared at any point to fire upon chance

Boxers found destroying the line, and off we went in the direction of Tientsin.

Lofa was soon reached and during a short halt employed in 'embarking' the wounded I was able to get a sight of the battle field of two days back. From the station roof a crowd of dead Boxers could be seen lying on the field in front, their scarlet badges shining in the glaring sunlight. There were from 150 to 200 of these who, with the courage of superstition and delusion, had ventured to advance under the direct fire of machine guns of the newest pattern. The sight will long remain in my memory. Proceeding hence towards Tientsin we came upon the first damaged bit of the line, which only delayed us a short time. Further on, however, we found such havoc in front of us that I judged it necessary to report to Admiral Seymour that it would undoubtedly require two days, with only the force at my disposal, to carry out the repairs. I therefore asked for a reinforcement to enable me to get through it quicker. Proceeding, or more correctly speaking retrograding, further, we found a partly decomposed body, already completely stripped of its clothes, which we presumed to be that of a Chinese messenger carrying despatches for Tientsin who had been captured and murdered at this point.

In Langfang meanwhile the apportionment of the separate nationalities among the trains had been proceeded with, and it had been resolved at a Council of War to abandon the march on Peking, and begin a retreat, as the line was out both before and behind. Confirmed in this decision by my message, Admiral Seymour ordered the evacuation of Langfang station, while he himself ran down to mine on his own train to assure himself personally of the condition of the railway and to encourage us at our work with his presence.

Before the English train arrived we had noticed Boxers collecting in the village nearest us on the left of the line in great numbers. With huge three-cornered banners in front, they marched into the village in single file, their spears, long knives, and other unsheathed weapons glittering in the sun. More and more followed, and soon the flags were floating over the roofs of the little mud houses. Our gentlemen, however, seemed to have no particular wish to come to blows, and did not disturb us in our toilsome labour.

Whilst I was keeping a look out on the movements of the enemy, prepared in a general way for a possible attack by a fanatical mob, the engine driver suddenly informed me he was running short of water and must return to Lofa for it, as there was none to be had in the immediate neighbourhood. Those thirsty locomotives again! What was to be done now? Should I withdraw with the train in the face of the enemy just established in the village hard by, leaving the whole day's work at the mercy of the Boxers; or should I send back the train – or the engine only – to Lofa, and with my company unprotected in the open, maintain the patch of ground we had occupied against a force in any case far exceeding mine in numbers? Whilst I was debating the matter, a train steaming in from Lofa helped me out of my difficulty. It was a French patrol engaged in keeping the line open between us and the other stations. On my proposition the French captain gave me a party of blue-jackets as a reinforcement, in consequence of which I decided to send the engine back to Lofa to take in water, whilst I remained on the scene of our work. With this addition to my strength I should be able to withstand an attack from the large body of Boxers, and on the other hand, need have no fear of the long day's work being destroyed. The French train and my engine then ran back to Lofa, while the French officer with military precision reported himself and his detachment under my orders.

We now watched closely for any further movement of the enemy, who was entering the village rapidly in large divisions. Meanwhile he seemed to have no disposition to attack us or our work; the fact of invulnerability appeared to have become less of a certainty as time went on. What good in fact is the strongest faith on the part of other people when one does not oneself come to life again after being shot? That is really the chief thing. Before sunset the engine came back from Lofa, and my train thus regained mobility. When it grew dusk the French train also took away its detachment, for whose support I expressed my best thanks to its captain. A few days later I met him again in melancholy circumstances on the hospital boat.

This evening another messenger reached Langfang from the Legations, with the report that matters were growing still worse and imploring instant aid. The situation was certainly no enviable one for Admiral Seymour. Influenced by the gallant determination to carry help to the sorely-pressed Legations with all possible expedition, he found obstacles increasing as he went on, and at the least, still more pressing difficulties were to be anticipated in the future. To this was now added the feeling of being cut off from Tientsin and of having to renounce any hope of support from it either in the form of troops or ammunition. The whole Boxer movement, as was soon to become clear to us, had suddenly acquired vast dimensions, and seemed to spread from place to place like wild fire.

On his arrival at the scene of my work Admiral Seymour judged this damage to the line not so great as he had supposed from my report and that of the engineers with me. He thought we should be able to reach Tientsin in three days. This supposition, combined with the repeated petitions for help from Peking, induced him to rescind the order for the retreat and once more to occupy the stations of Lofa and Langfang. Facts proved later that my pessimistic impressions on the condition of the wrecked line were unfortunately correct. Happily no further difficulty arose from this repeated alteration of plans, as the events of June 18 were later to show. As to the repairing work we went on doing our best to get through with it.

The night now approaching proved once more a quiet one; we were not attacked as we had imagined we should be from the large gathering of Boxers in the village; but naturally a very sharp watch was kept on it ...

{Sunday, 17 June}
Early in the morning our work of reparation was resumed with all the forces we could muster. Henceforward the commanding officer of the American detachment, Captain McCalla, assumed its direction. It would be wrong for me to omit the mention of this gentleman's name, for he won the highest credit throughout the difficulties in which the expedition was so constantly involved. Those who learned to know can never forget him, nor how always in advance of his men, his rifle on his shoulder, he gave his orders with a cheery face and that inestimable quality, humour, as quietly and deliberately as if he were on parade, superintending the repairs with singular judgment. He could always make sure of everyone, under the influence of his unvarying geniality, being ready to go with him through thick and thin.

As it was considered advisable to eject the Boxers from our immediate vicinity I received orders from Admiral Seymour, through his flag-captain Jellicoe, to dislodge those who had entered the neighbouring village the previous evening. The project gave general satisfaction; one could see in both officers and men what pleasure this 'morning parade' excited. I immediately formed the company in column for the attack, and ordered the leading section to assault the village in front; while I directed the rear one upon its right flank.

Before we started, Captain Jellicoe had three shots from the nine-pounder mounted on the front carriage of the English train thrown into the village. They were very well directed and fell crashing upon the roofs of the mud houses, throwing up a great cloud of dust and smoke. When the firing ceased the order to storm was given, and the attack began in the manner I had arranged. Fire was opened upon the Boxers as soon as they became visible, especially on the bolder ones who were engaged in setting fire to the houses. These good people might as well have left it to us, and we took the business off their hands very willingly, only we wanted just a word with them in addition. This they seemed less inclined for, and on our further advance many of them fled into the open country, and only a part took up a position on the right side of the village to oppose us. These, however, did not long resist the increasing fire of the flanking party, but slowly retired.

The two remaining sections now pressed into the village to search and clear it of Boxers. Their big banners still floated over several roofs, that is their long poles were still standing upright in the courtyards towering over the roofs of the low mud houses.

Most Chinese villages present some appearance of fortification, the houses being built to touch each other along the outer side of the circumference, or else the circle is completed by means of mud walls connecting them. One or two breaks in this form the only entrances to a village, and these too can be quickly closed in defence. Every house in such a place forms a small defensive post in itself, as each is surrounded by a wall of mats.

Experience has shown that in searching such a locality all supervision or direction of troops is lost; and this danger was especially encountered in these Chinese villages. Each house had to be taken separately and searched. The men naturally soon got to know the best way of breaking down fences and forcing doors. At first it was rather anxious work stepping into the darkness of the rooms after breaking down the entrance, but gradually they got to face the idea of a blow or a shot from hidden Boxers quite steadily. However we soon ascertained here that the entire hive had been deserted, unless we were to count the opposition of the feathered folk. These were left behind. Such consideration for our poor empty stomachs was a truly beautiful trait in the otherwise cruel character of the Chinese, for which we thanked him heartily when the time came for the consumption of our booty. Besides this they had left a young Chinese woman, who was temporarily placed under guard with the object of gaining information from her.

After we had searched the entire village, house by house, we turned for a while to the consideration of our own well being and 'swept up a trifle or two in various yards'. As a result, a tremendous cackling arose, and our gallant seamen were shortly to be seen marching gaily and grinning, as they carried one or more specimens of the fair feathered race under their arms. In one house that seemed to have been used as a store, we found a quantity of arms, and among them some very antiquated pieces, as well as a gun of ante-diluvian pattern and dignified age. In accordance with Admiral Seymour's orders every house in which arms or stolen railroad material was discovered was set on fire. The enemy had been steadily retreating, so fire was soon set to it, and now nothing more was to be done except to clear out the village and commandeer its supplies. Five Boxers altogether were killed in this affair, while we had not one wounded . . .

In the afternoon we went on with the trains as far as the railway bridge on this side of Yangtsun station. It was to be our last halt on the line, for a monstrous destruction not only of the bridge, which was hardly reparable, but of the permanent way beyond, pronounced the unwelcome decree, 'Thus far and no farther.' No more rapid work in the direction of Tientsin was to be thought of now. Admiral Seymour was able to convince himself of this when he had gone down the line accompanied by a detachment of fifty men. The havoc was so complete that the co-operation of regular troops, already suspected, had to be accepted as a certainty . . .

At nine o'clock in the evening the senior officers of the different nationalities and also my juniorship of the German contingent present were bidden to a Council of War. I assisted at it in the dimly lighted railway carriage with the representatives of the various nations, and had to record my vote on the question, What next? I thought Admiral Seymour very nervous and unstrung; it was only too obvious he must be carrying a load of care, for his optimistic opinion on the question of repairing the line had disappeared with the day's events.

Admiral Seymour pointed out to us the general situation – naturally far from favourable – showed from it that we could neither advance nor retire, and that obviously if we were again to abandon Langfang and the reoccupied stations in advance of where we stood, in a very brief time everything there would be destroyed also, and then all that had been gained in the seven days would be completely lost. He asked the opinion of each officer of the different nationalities. Good advice was scarce. We all entirely agreed about dispatching a messenger to Captain Von Usedom with discretionary powers to hold Langfang station if his supplies allowed him to do so. An endeavour would be made to send him further provisions from this Yangtsun district. Immediately after the council, at which it was decided to requisition supplies next day in the said district, an English officer was sent on a trolley to Langfang to carry the order to Captain Von Usedom. Meanwhile in Langfang the station had been reoccupied, and further reconnaissances made in the direction of Peking, which established the facts of the prosecution of extensive damage and the presence of strong patrols of Chinese cavalry.

{Monday 18 June}.
I received orders for my company to patrol the line in the direction of Tientsin, and with this object sent Lieutenant Rohr there with a party, while the rest of my men were ordered to work at the repairs. From the railway bridge this officer noticed a junk employed in embarking railway sleepers. When he got near and shouted to them to stop she slipped hastily away, upon which he opened fire upon the Chinese, Lieutenant Rohr very rightly considering that the possession of transport for our expedition would be of great value. He knew quite well that the idea of abandoning the railway and recovering touch with Tientsin by way of the river had already been favourably entertained. As the expedition was unprovided with vehicles, and had simply been cut off on a railway journey, boats would eventually remain its only means of transport. How useful the acquisition of these junks became we were to experience later. Farther up, on some boats anchored halfway under the bridge, Lieutenant Rohr observed several Boxers all apparently engaged in hauling railway material. After a short opposition four junks were taken, on board which were found divers weapons, a standard and the well-known red badges of the Boxers. Altogether fourteen

of these lost their lives during the capture of the junks, all of whom apparently were intending to escape in them. The boats were then brought under the bridge and a guard placed over them.

About half-past nine in the evening the other trains ran up to ours at the bridge of Yangtsun. A very important event had happened ... [Captain Von Usedom, while executing orders to retreat from Langfang, was attacked by Boxers and Chinese regular troops. The enemy was repulsed and fled. Captain Von Usedom abandoned Langfang and Lofa and retreated to Yangtsun.]

Thus, that evening all the trains were united again at Yangtsun, and all the long days of hard labour spent in turning the stations into fortified posts were wasted by the destructive fury of an enemy now consisting no longer – the bitter truth had been forced upon us by this single stroke – of bands of Chinese robbers only, but of Imperial troops also, drilled by European methods to the use of modern firearms.

It was by extraordinary good fortune that after the attack of today all the trains were enabled to join the main body in the evening. How easily damage might have been done to the line at any point between Langfang and Yangtsun; it would inevitably have occasioned a dangerous check to their return and the different divisions would have found themselves in a very difficult situation if the attack had been renewed. However, all the nationalities joined forces in a comparatively short time at Yangtsun, where the whole force – numbering altogether about 2100 – were assembled on the evening of June 18. It was the first wet day the expedition had encountered, and the most unpleasant circumstances accompanied it. How were we to protect ourselves from the rain? The carriages of the German troops were almost all open, so the men crept underneath them, but that did not answer long, for soon a very perceptible drip came through the seams of the flooring of the trucks.

We had no tents and it proved a most unenviable night. The *Hansa* company in particular got little sleep, for we had the watch at the Tientsin end of the train. An especially sharp look-out had to be kept on both sides, for here the embankment was bordered by a swamp. Hence it was not possible to throw out vedettes in advance of the outposts, and every moment we had to be ready for an attack by the Imperial troops who might have reassembled and, possibly strengthened by a further contingent, have followed us up. Now and again a shot in the direction of the outlying pickets bore witness to the existence of great nervous excitement; even the calmest nerves would become suddenly conscious of Chinese hiding in the hedges with the object of wading in through the swamp. Shots too in the direction of Yangtsun did not tend to soothe our tempers.

But tonight again passed without an attack, the evil spirits apparently scaring the regulars also; or perhaps today's reminder at Langfang had served temporarily to keep the Chinese out of our way. This night a vast glow was visible in the direction of Tientsin, where without our knowledge hard fighting had been proceeding since the previous day. How should we know it? We were entirely cut off from news or even rumour; we were, as they say, like rats in a trap, and one that could not have been better set.

{Tuesday, 19 June}
The nineteenth of June broke gloomily on a situation alike gloomy. In addition, deprivation of all kinds – bad food, bad water, and wretched quarters – had by this time joined the wet weather in our despite. At first our many discomforts had been laughingly met, but after a full ten days passed in the country in the midst of unexpected hardships – we had expected to have been in Peking three days ago – by this time, men gradually grew sick of it. Anyone in command thinks less constantly about his sufferings and privations as he is continually asking himself how he can do the best for his men, so that many a renunciation has left only a slight impression on my mind, and I should not find it easy to say what we all had to go without. But I do know one thing and I will state it plainly here; we suffered much, we endured incredible privations, we were tormented by hunger and thirst in a way I never can forget. How could one restrain men when at last, raging with thirst, they plunged into the foul stream of the Peiho and drank its water, muddy and impure as it was from the bodies of men and animals purposely thrown into it by our enemies? It is true every third man carried a small charcoal filter, but who was to ensure the water being always filtered properly? It cannot be denied that we were exposed to frightful hardships and unexpected suffering of all kinds which we certainly had never imagined we should have to face when we set out...

A council of the united commanding officers under the presidency of Admiral Seymour decided on quitting the trains and retreating with the force along the Peiho, on which, in the four captured junks, the sick and wounded, some guns, ammunition, provisions, and baggage were to be transported downstream. Only absolute necessities were to be taken with us, no useless ballast.

Before the council sat, our comrades who had fallen in the engagement of the previous day were carried to their last resting place. It was a mournful funeral, with no mound or cross to mark the spot where a faithful soldier who had died for his country had been laid in the cold earth. We dared not do anything, for even the dead were not suffered to rest by the terrible hordes surrounding us. They would have ruthlessly dug up the graves and mutilated the bodies – we had already heard of such cases. So we could only carefully note the place where a comrade was laid to rest so that later, after the war was over, a better tomb might be arranged.

After the holding of the council we at once began to unpack the trains and load up the four *praams*. An idea of the condition of things in such a boat may be conceived when it is considered that one small vessel had to serve for the supply, catalogued above, of 500 men. That the vessels were small is obvious, as the Peiho at this point is about the size and volume of the Ruhr. Each boat was under the command of a lieutenant, whose appointment was not an enviable one.

The work of unloading was concluded about four o'clock, and we took a sad leave of our carriages which, however little of the poetry of life they might have afforded, had provided us with a shelter for ten days beneath which we had led a highly original life. It was with sad hearts that we threw all our trophies of war into the stream – the large standards, the curious weapons, all the plunder with which our carriages had been hung, all had to be sacrificed. Most of them were thrown into the river that they might not fall a second time into the hands of the enemy. The ground near the trains looked really charming; everywhere lay chests and cases, articles of clothing, travelling trunks, strewn promiscuously around. How could it be helped? The men had already enough to carry with their arms and ammunition; everything else was left behind, without – *horribile dictu* – a single schedule of the lost property being issued. By half past four we were ready to march, that is to sail, away. The order for today's march was: English in front, then French, Americans, and Russians, with us Germans as rearguard . . .

It was an interesting night when the motley column, united for the first time as a single corps, moved off. The advance was slow, for the boats, *praams* as the sailors call them, grounded every now and again owing to their heavy lading, and could only be got off with great exertion. Unfortunately, this always caused an involuntary delay, and we wanted to reach Tientsin as quickly as possible. Now for the first time too, the column was in the open country; no defensive post was left us, whether in the shape of a fortified station or a train. Weapon[s] in hand but shelterless, we had a hostile land around us.

We had not proceeded far when the Boxers poured in from all sides to the deserted trains and began plundering them. We could see them with the naked eye searching one carriage after another, no doubt shouting with delight; then in a moment the whole brotherhood was out again on the plain. The Chinese have a wonderful faculty for concealing themselves. The total want of cavalry in our force was naturally very obvious on this occasion . . .

After our simple supper was eaten and all the missing courses had been imagined we flung ourselves on our couches, which I on this occasion did in our commandant's tent as it was not possible to get my baggage out of the *praam*. I was well frozen too in the tent, for beyond a handkerchief and the list of my company I had nothing to serve as a counterpane. However, I slept very well, only the next morning my limbs pained me a good deal at the delightful moment of being called, on account of the hardness of my bed. There had been a heavy dew in the night, and a frightful coughing all round accompanied the unwelcome notes of the bugle.

{Wednesday, 20 June}

The twentieth of June was ushered in by a sad duty. Two Englishmen severely wounded had succumbed during the night, and before the march was resumed we had to bury them on the river bank. It was a sad scene – no music, no pageant, only a short prayer by the English naval chaplain and then the poor sufferers were laid in their early grave whilst a guard of honour provided by the different nationalities presented arms. Two more gone from among us; how many might there not be to follow? But in time of war it does not do to be too much affected by such sad events; we are in God's hands – where or when the bullet awaits a man, must not trouble him. He cannot escape it, so forward with courage to meet the foe!

Still breakfast had no flavour, a funeral so soon after rising does not induce the right frame of mind for it. About seven we moved on down stream keeping the four *praams* always close to us. The Boxer gentry arranged a pretty spectacle for us as a send-off, by setting the collected railway trains on fire, as a sequel to their previous thorough ransack of their contents. It was a strikingly fine, though at the same time distressing, sight to watch from a distance; the four long trains, out here in this country so valuable a munition, a prey to the devouring flames . . .

After a few hours the whole force was suddenly halted; the head of the column had been fired on from a village. The English and Americans went forward to attack, and hot rifle fire was soon audible, alternating with shots from our guns which fell upon the roofs of the houses with a loud crash. The standards of a body of regular Chinese troops could now be recognised. Then suddenly some Chinese bullets whizzed over our heads, who were not engaged in the affair, and wounded a man . . .

Our advance now proceeded very slowly. The enemy showed wonderful tenacity and had to be pushed back step by step. When one village was cleared a still hotter fire was sure to be opened on us from the next. It was a tough bit of work, and the sun made himself uncommonly obliging – we had to fight our way forward in tropical heat. As an example of the sufferings we had to endure I might adduce the following. As has been already said, the nights were cold so that the men slept in woollen blankets; on the other hand in the daytime during our march (which included one rainy day), we had such intense heat as to make sun helmets a necessity. Owing to the exigencies of our transport, as already described, it had not however been feasible to get out the white clothing from our *praam* – there was not time for it. So there was nothing left but to let the men go on wearing their thick blue clothing – in which, for example, they do their work in the North Sea in winter. The sun-helmets presented an odd contrast to this singular kit. Thus it fell out that at the close of the expedition our men had to march in their winter clothing. It was one more hardship, occasioned by the unfortunate disposition of the baggage and the other entirely unexpected events that had taken place. One is not surprised that the poor fellows looked on the point of fainting. They had not been able to wash for days either, on account of hasty calls to arms or sudden orders to march...

About three o'clock it was at length possible to think about the midday halt, as the sharp fire of the enemy was in some measure silenced. The German contingent camped in a little village close to the river, where mercifully we again found a good well. On the way there we passed several recently killed Boxers. The sight of distorted features, the sign of the last death struggle, makes a strong impression on men who see it for the first time. We were now able to find shelter from the frightful glare of the sun under the shade of leafy trees, to our great delight, for the dust and the endless heat had told upon us. On this occasion I indulged in a great delicacy at 'dinner', consisting of preserved pineapples, a box of which valuable acquisition had been sent me by our ship's steward with the last consignment from Tientsin...

I thought to indulge myself with a special treat after the meal when I pulled off my shoes and socks and cooled my burning feet with water. It is comical what presentiments one has in life! Hardly were my preparations completed when the thought flashed through my mind, 'There! now the alarm ought to sound instantly, that would be grand.' At the selfsame moment that sinful enemy really did begin to fire from the next village. One shot, two, three, then a volley. Thus was my presumption punished. It was all up with the siesta too, to which we had been looking forward. It had to be 'marked off' as so often before. Never yet in my life have I made so quick a toilette as on that occasion. My sword in my right hand, revolver in my left, one stocking and my sword-knot left behind, I rushed out; and shouting '*Hansa* company forward!' led my brave lads for the first time into action. For today the *Hansa* company got its baptism of fire. I had begged our commandant to give us the next chance of an engagement, for so far it had not had the privilege of fighting against regular troops, and my officers had been just as keen. Now the wish was fulfilled...

We approached the village in front of us by rushes, the Chinese firing at us smartly from strong cover. It was only now and then that the head of a Boxer peeped out from behind the corner of a wall, to disappear again the moment he had delivered his shot. We quickly reached the containing wall of the village without actual loss – only two men wounded. Then we went on into it between the other German companies, supported by the fire of the Americans. We searched the place thoroughly, but the enemy had deserted it. We captured one flag; the English, who had had no share in the fight, later found an old gun. Passing through the village we followed the enemy who showed himself here and there, to the other end of a wood beyond, and then halted. We had no packs, having rushed out of camp with nothing but our arms in our hands.

After repulsing the enemy and clearing the village, we were naturally obliged to think of getting our packs again. With this object a French company was detached, whilst we went back to the *praams* to resume our old formation. Pushing on further was not to be thought of, for by advancing beyond the head of the column we should have struck the enemy again, who had rallied in the next village and now saluted us for the first time with shots from his guns. These were light pieces, mostly drawn by one or two horses, modern 5 centimetre Krupp field-guns. He directed his artillery fire not only on the attacking companies nearest him; but also paid some attention to us in the rear...

We made all our men lie down behind the shelter of the river bank. The shells crashed on to the houses with a loud report, making matchwood of them, and here and there one was set on fire. For the rest no damage was done to us; we found later that we had profited by their having forgotten to screw the fuse into the shell, without which the best shells fail to explode.

Presently our shore guns were able to answer with shells. They accurately struck a house from which a heavy rifle fire had been opened on our column. At this point I may mention that our shore guns had always to be dragged at the cost of great labour by the men themselves, since horses do not exist on battleships...

The enemy's resistance was again gradually broken, and he fled further down stream, so that at last we were able to march on again. It was a real boon that he had been driven back by nightfall, for at this halting-place where groups of buildings and copses obscured our view we should have spent a very disturbed night in the event of an attack. From this point, after passing the ruined village our way lay over an open plain where we were to bivouac. We once more observed how quickly the enemy was on our heels, for the column was hardly in motion again before a Chinese force was descried behind the houses by the rearguard. When fire was open on them they instantly disappeared...

Clear of the village a halt was made, and we bivouacked at last after a day fraught with toil and fighting. Before reaching our camping place we met with a few Boxers hiding in the high grass outside the last village. One of the company officers walked close past without any suspicion, but fortunately was just in time to see one of the Boxers as he struck at him with a long cavalry sabre. He was just in time, however. The incident was another proof of the incredible fearlessness, *ie* fanaticism, of the Boxers. It was sheer madness to let the column approach in the long grass when it would have been so easy to get clean away. Apparently these men were lurking there either to obtain the information necessary for a night attack, or with the object of falling upon our outposts insidiously.

We were heartily glad tonight when we could lie down in the open. Three villages in flames illuminated the motley camp where an exhausted and unenviable force bivouacked in the face of an uncertain fate. During the evening I, with the other captains of companies, stood for a while with our eyes turned to that wide glow in the south west where the sound of heavy firing indicated severe fighting at Tientsin, that closely-pressed Tientsin whose situation was only in a slight degree better than our own. None of us could have failed to feel acutely the uncertainty of our fate as we stood there in silent reflection . . .

{Thursday, 21 June}
Early in the morning we proceeded, this time on both sides of the river, as the enemy now offered resistance on both banks. The German contingent, combined with two Russian companies, a detachment of Japanese and some English Nordenfeld Gunners, crossed the river and marched off under the chief command of Captain Von Usedom at the same time as the combatant force on the other side, which at first passed safely through some completely deserted villages. Presently in the far distance we could see great masses of fugitives leaving the villages in hundreds, with their goods and gear carried on two-wheeled carts which at first we took for guns. This led us to conclude that further down stream Chinese troops were awaiting us, and that the inhabitants had determined on a general flight in anticipation of an approaching engagement.

It was not long before this supposition was proved to be correct. At half-past eight the first rifle fire opened on us from the left side of the river, followed shortly afterwards by shells from a Chinese battery posted on the opposite bank. A shell struck the ground close to where our commandant was standing with his senior officers in a little temple, but did no damage. Captain Von Usedom now threw the *Hansa* and *Hertha* companies forward, giving them provisional shelter in a depression of the ground behind a group of houses. Meanwhile our machine guns opened a lively fire on the enemy on the left bank. As his fire slackened somewhat our whole column moved forward to a general attack, the *Hansa* company this time in front.

The leading section under Lieutenant Schulz had at first to go along the fully exposed embankment of the river under an increasingly brisk fire from the enemy's rifles, whilst I sent the other two on through the village lying close to the bank. The situation of the first section was far from an enviable one, owing to the impossibility of taking cover; the bullets whizzed in a very suggestive way over our heads, while hardly any of ours reached the wicked enemy who fired valiantly at us from excellent shelter behind the last houses on the opposite side. Everywhere, needless to say, we replied with the greatest spirit to their warm welcome, with the result that they soon disappeared.

After passing the village we got a more extended view of the field of battle. We now observed that a heavy column of Chinese infantry, with two triangular standards on their right wing, had taken up a position behind a mound on the opposite bank of the river. Behind them was a body of cavalry, according to our calculations about three squadrons strong. At the same time, straight in front of a large village on our own side, we observed a long line of hostile marksmen pouring out of it, while the Chinese field-guns had taken up ground on the left wing of their position. These, together with the infantry, now opened a murderous fire on the international force as it advanced. We were fired on with the newest pattern of arms, smokeless powder, small bore rifles, quick firing guns, everything one could desire. The advantage of smokeless powder was so evident here as to make it, for example, very difficult to locate the position of the enemy's infantry, who besides had entrenched themselves admirably. Our blue-jackets, on the contrary, still carried repeating rifles of the 71/84 pattern. Small-arms practice on board ship is a matter of minor importance, but here on land, on this occasion, we heartily cursed the old powder and longed as we did so for the newly-invented naval arm[s] just being introduced.

The spectacle of a murderous engagement now lay unrolled before us. We were in the thick of the bullets, shells were falling right and left with a loud report, striking on the roofs of the houses and the little temple with a crashing sound. Here and there one of ours was knocked over by a vicious bullet, the ambulance bearers hurried hither and thither to carry off the wounded, loud words of command, the shrill pipe of the petty officers, then again the cheery 'Forward, march!' a command that inspires the laziest limbs — so went matters in the face of a foe who was pressing us hard with four times our strength. Meanwhile the sun glared down hotly again on the fierce strife, and did anything but alleviate our lot. After several forward movements I allowed the company to continue their fire from behind a little mound. A quantity of graves, which the Chinese construct above ground, also provided us with tolerable shelter.

Fighting our way through the village had involved us, as is generally the case, in some confusion, in consequence of which I suddenly found Russian sailors in front of me in my line of fire. Now we could give orders to fire or cease fire easily enough, but no other orders. Our Russian went no further than that. They were very jolly over it however, shared our fighting pluckily and listened attentively when the petty officers shouted at them, 'Russians, attention – fire!' or 'Russians, hold hard!'

After continuing the rifle-fire from this position for some time, which enabled the men to catch their wind somewhat, I went to the front with the object of leading the men in the next rush. Hardly had I reached it and given some orders than I was wounded by a rifle shot, apparently from the enemy behind the little hill. If I am to say more about myself I may explain that the ball penetrated the shin-bone of my left leg through the centre and broke it. My first sensation was that of a blow from a stick, then I felt my leg grow heavy as lead and next a burning pain in the wound that prevented my standing, and I fell to the ground. Those nearest me ran hastily to my help, removed my gaiters and bound up the wound from which a stream of blood was pouring. My servant, Lampke, who was acting as my orderly, then stumbled upon the not unreasonable idea that the prospect of saving my life, or at any rate healing my wound, was not a favourable one under the very considerable hail of bullets concentrated upon the spot where I was lying. I was therefore hurriedly carried into a hollow behind a little hillock where by good luck there was a beaker of water.

As a consequence of the loss of blood my senses took it upon themselves to leave me for a time ... When I recovered from my swoon after an interval, I heard the rifle fire already at a distance. On my urgent question as to the state of the battle I was told of the enemy's repulse, an announcement that, needless to say, delighted and calmed me. I developed a ravenous appetite and unquenchable thirst. I drained two service-bottles of the precious Peiho water – we nicknamed it later Château Peiho – while my companion sprinkled me affectionately with the muddy water from the beaker to prevent my going off again. I gratefully recall the charitable devotion of my men at this time, especially of my servant and the chief boatswain's mate, Mengalla, who bestowed much tender care upon me. It would probably have been much worse if those near me had not bound up the bleeding wound so skilfully.

My fighting was now at an end, and the command of the company devolved upon the lieutenant next in seniority, as my successor, Lieutenant Von Zerssen, had also been wounded, though only slightly, by a shot that grazed his head. What now fell to my share in common with the rest of the wounded was a long succession of manifold sufferings and endurance, the bodily and mental tortures of a most wretched sick-bed, that despite the self-devoted care and nursing of our surgeons, tried both health and temper severely. Whilst the fighting was proceeding my men cut branches into lengths, laid me on them and carried me slowly back to hand me over to the ambulance bearers who remained further in [the] rear. When our singular procession got into motion, true to my old sense of the ludicrous I could not help laughing. As my bearers put on such deplorable faces I challenged them with a sort of condemned criminal's hilarity to make some poor jest about it. But they opposed me with incredulous faces, and would not take it as I intended.

By good luck a Russian surgeon shortly came up, who applied a tourniquet, had me packed onto a Russian litter and sent [me] to the *praams* which were awaiting the issue of the battle in a bend of the river guarded by the *Gefion* company. I was then taken in a little boat to the German vessel where our surgeon with the expedition, the untiring Dr Schlick, at once applied a temporary bandage. Then I had to disembark again for want of room, to be conveyed to the French *praam*. It was a journey of many stages, not exactly the right thing for a broken limb. Here I was laid down in the hold of the junk next to a dangerously wounded seaman of the *d'Entrecasteaux* with whom I struck up a friendship, and in whose company I was to wear away many hours, as well as some moments of anxiety.

Behold me then lying on a roll of French hammocks with a broken leg, a groaning companion in misfortune close by, in a wretched camp hospital of the strangest kind. But I must not forget with what extraordinary sympathy and tenderness I was nursed by the French, as well in the matter of surgical treatment as, and this especially, of diet. With gratitude do I recall Fourier and his constant enquiries as to my wants, which he even indulged in the form of a bottle of good German beer, a long-foregone enjoyment. In this one way there was an advantage in being wounded; I was also able to revive my acquaintance with French in conversation with my neighbour. Fellow suffering, trouble borne in common will bring the greatest strangers together quickly. I often handed my canteen bottle filled with water made somewhat more palatable by the addition of crystallised citric acid, to my suffering neighbour on the left with an 'à votre santé', for which he has often thanked me with good wishes for my country and a chunk of French ships' tobacco. The commander of the French boat was the naval officer who had been under my orders with his section when we were repairing the railway. It was a melancholy meeting, and for a long time his orders for the management of the *praam* rang in my ears as an echo of weary hours of misery.

Now things were going on outside with the engagement I could no longer see for myself. At twelve o'clock midday the enemy had been repulsed, but he made a fresh stand in the next village from which he was once again dislodged by a general advance in the afternoon. He fled in great confusion. In the evening the troops on the right bank were brought back to the other side so as to be more easily available in case of an attack, and also because the main body of the enemy and his artillery were established on the right bank. It was obvious that to advance by daylight against an enemy always increasing in numbers as this one was, was only to induce fresh sacrifices, and it was decided in future to march by night.

The German losses for the day amounted to fourteen wounded, among whom were two officers from the *Hansa*. It had brought the combined force together for the first time in a fight with regular troops whose numbers were increased by Boxers carrying firearms. It was, one might say, the first real battle, in which six to seven thousand men had fought in hot blood. The next day was to be sorerer still. I may conclude by adding how that evening the bodies of women and children were carried down by the stream. Many Chinese had killed their own families, as they were unable to hide them for lack of time. They no doubt had no idea but that we should butcher them all after their fashion.

{Friday, 22 June}

We broke camp at one o'clock in the morning. After proceeding a short distance shots suddenly fell among us. Admiral Seymour, seeing that an exceptional contest was impending, sent for Captain Von Usedom, so as to have his potential successor near him.

At once the eloquent order rang out; 'Germans to the front!' which, given as it was in anticipation of urgent danger, made every honest German heart beat higher, an order that bore undesigned testimony to the conduct, the readiness and courage of our men, an utterance that, spoken by a foreigner, showed as clear as day the universal feeling that people were reassured when they saw us Germans fighting in the hottest place . . .

I would however [like to] draw attention once for all to what is perhaps too lightly noticed in all the reports, that is, the fact that the Seymour expedition was composed of seamen only. It was a corps in which there was only one small detachment of English marines, perhaps more accustomed to infantry work than the rest. That a war against trained soldiers is somewhat unusual work for sailors, that sailors as a rule are seldom called upon to capture fortresses and sustain long infantry engagements in an enemy's country, everyone knows. But the harder the position was the grander is the acknowledged fact that the foe was continually repulsed . . .

Advancing still, we finally reached the arsenal of Hsiku . . . The Chinese could be seen lying ready for an attack with their guns pointed towards us. When our column had got to within about 150 yards of it, Admiral Seymour sent the interpreter Campbell forward as a pursuant to explain to the Chinese that we had no desire for hostilities and only wished to return to Tientsin unmolested; as a matter of fact we were not at war with China as every one knew. The emissaries were however instantly fired upon in Chinese fashion before they could even take cover, and fighting immediately began again in earnest. A desperately savage fight followed. The English marines attacked the arsenal in [the] rear, and a disorderly flight of an opponent who far out-numbered us was the result of the hard-fought engagement. The severely wounded, of whom I was one, heard something of the fight, for many a bullet whistled over our heads . . .

The arsenal was now taken. For us it meant salvation from most serious danger, for in a continued march across the open country the destruction of our expedition must have been decreed. By the capture of the arsenal however we acquired a strong defensive position in which we could halt for a while in order, we ventured to hope, to receive someday the long-desired reinforcement from Tientsin. We were not without suspicion that between us and that city the Chinese held some fortified posts which we should also have had to capture in the open. So it was decided to make a halt at Hsiku, an arrangement General Nieh and his force did not approve of, for in the afternoon he tried by every means in his power to retake the arsenal. He attacked it systematically from every side and opened a murderous fire with small arms and artillery that placed the hospital boats in great danger . . .

As a naval officer of twenty years standing I have not escaped the dangers of a sailor's life. Many perilous situations, many catastrophes have I experienced, but never did I feel as on the afternoon of this day, I felt in the boat. It was a madly torturing position to be in; an actual rain of bullets poured over us, making the water spurt high close to us; presently a shell fell near the boat, then one on the bank, and again a house close by was struck with a crash. Shrapnel burst over our heads – and then, suddenly a shell struck the leading boat on which some guns had been mounted, and sank it. Mercifully no one was killed. The shot might just as easily have struck our boat and then all would have been over with us. If not actually hit we must have been drowned, for we lay there helpless on our backs unable to move, and could only see a patch of sky and had calmly to let everything go on around us . . . The thought that as wounded men we might eventually have to surrender at the discretion of a cruel enemy was torture. The hours of that afternoon in the boat were truly the worst of the whole expedition; they can never be forgotten.

But the day was not yet at an end. As the *praams* gradually worked down under the walls of the arsenal men hurried down to us and began to get us on shore. Orders had been given to get all the wounded out of the boats as quickly as possible and into the arsenal, as the danger of our being struck by the enemy's shot would not allow of our remaining there longer. Now we were again picked up for transfer, not the best thing in the world for broken limbs – anyway it was always a very painful one. The operation of disembarking us was done so quickly that I had hardly time to press my French fellow sufferer's hand as a farewell, then up the sloping bank we went as quickly as possible with the 'blue beans' piping gaily around us again.

Arriving in the courtyard of the magazine I was laid in a corner by the door, for the sheds selected as the hospital for the wounded still had to be cleared. I well remember the kindness of Captain McCalla and the English interpreter Campbell, who brought me hot cocoa and cakes. These usually cheerful gentlemen were looking thoughtful, and the humour of Captain McCalla, who had himself been wounded, did not seem to me quite of its earlier quality. My servant who stayed with me first endeavoured to get me into better shelter, for the enemy's shot still whistled uncomfortably in my vicinity . . .

At length they had got on so far with the clearing out of the sheds that the wounded could be carried in. An idea of the extent and high quality of the comfort provided will be obvious to all when I explain that they had made beds for us out of the wooden boards of the window shutters, on which they spread woollen rugs. Our heads lay on our tightly packed knapsacks, and a second rug served as a counterpane, but as that was not quite enough, a Chinese dust storm obligingly broke in upon us and spread the loveliest desert sand over our soft couches. We could not have been tucked up more charmingly.

{Saturday, 23 June}

The day after the assault, from eight to ten thousand Männlicher rifles; stores of cartridges filled and empty; swords, cannon and machine guns of German construction; and also, thank God, bandages and medicaments all from the Kiel chemist Rüdel; Esmarch belts with directions for use in German; and finally several hundred sacks of rice as well as good drinking water, were found in the arsenal. It gave us all fresh courage. The wall was at once armed with the discovered guns; the Russians and Japanese, who had exhausted their ammunition, were supplied with the new rifles and the doctor was able at once to apply fresh bandages to his wounded.

Our poor dead were buried within the arsenal, the enemy taking part in the ceremony, for he fired briskly on the crowd of men gathered to pay them the last honours, and it was to the music of their salvoes that the dead were laid to rest.

That night a futile attempt was made by a scouting party of English marines to establish a communication with Tientsin. The force returned leaving five dead behind them – afterwards found in a mutilated condition – with the information that the district was strongly occupied by Chinese troops . . .

{Sunday, 24 June}
Another day of torture, amidst the groans of wounded and the cries of dying men. During these hours of tedious 'lingering and longing' for relief we registered a solemn vow never to the end of our lives to complain again without good cause.

{Monday, 25 June}
The day of release came at last ... a messenger from us had been fortunate enough to repeat the news of our situation in Tientsin. The answer came in the form of white capped and coated men a thousand strong, carrying Russian, German and Japanese flags. It was the force for our relief and was greeted with cheers as it came up, that seemed as if they would never end. I cannot describe that time, one must have experienced it oneself after such a long suffering that preceded it. Not one of us will forget this happy day which can best be compared to one of Jubilee.

In the afternoon all the wounded were carried out into the open, litters contrived for them, and the next morning at three o'clock the march to Tientsin by land was commenced, as the river route would have been exposed to the fire of the Chinese forts. Shortly after we broke camp we were aware of a dull roar that shook the ground proceeding from the arsenal at Hsiku. By Seymour's orders, the magazine had been fired by an English party to prevent its valuable store of arms falling again into Chinese hands. A heavy cloud of smoke hung for a long time over the spot where the Seymour expedition had stood face to face with their fate for three days and nights and, exhausted to the last degree, had longed and lingered for relief.

It was a singular train with its 320 wounded, the greater number of whom had to be carried. Staff surgeon Schlick in his report, says among other things, 'It took us six hours to reach Tientsin. The road led through stubble fields and ravines, along railway embankments and across bridges; the wounded had a great deal to suffer between jolts and shaking. It was a great mercy the enemy left us unmolested.'

{Tuesday, 26 June}
At ten o'clock in the morning of June 26, we re-entered the heavily can-nonaded Tientsin, among smoking heaps of ruins and charred corpses. The company marched past my litter once more, their faces covered with dust and burned by the sun, their clothes torn, but still upright in bearing and firm of step...

In Tientsin our wounded were provided for in the German Club where German ladies played the part of good Samaritans, endeavouring to supply the place of those who would have tended us still more devotedly had not hemispheres and oceans lain between. It is unnecessary to state how extremely fortunate we wounded considered ourselves, to be in such a hospital after all the hardships we had gone through. People came from all quarters with the object of alleviating our situation; our sympathetic countrymen brought us mattresses, coverlets, cushions, everything that can contribute to furnish a hospital. On the faces of these poor things, the traces of terror and anguish were still apparent. Owing to the severity of the fire they had taken refuge in the cellars of the German consulate, where the miserable hours had been passed in ceaseless anxiety and agitation over the issue of the fighting. The men had fully made up their minds to shoot their wives and children if the Boxers had got the upper hand and were turned loose among them. From the description given us it must have been a terrible time.

Account of
Commander Gitaro Mori,
Japanese Naval Officer

Commander Gitaro Mori achieved worldwide recognition in 1904 when, disguised as the valet of the Japanese Consul in Port Arthur, he prepared an assessment for Admiral Togo of the strength of the Russian fleet at anchor. His report of 8 February precipitated the Japanese attack on 9 February, which set off the Russo–Japan War.

{9 June 1900}

On my way back to Peking I was compelled to stop at Tientsin owing to the railway being interrupted. On the 9th of June at 9 pm the British Consul invited all the Consuls and all the naval officers in Tientsin to a Council. Commander Yamashita of the *Kasagi* being absent, I proceeded to the conference in company with Mr Consul Tei and Captain Nomura. The British Consul addressing the conference said that, according to a telegram just received from the British and American Representatives in Peking, the condition of that city was becoming hourly more critical. They therefore desired that the naval commanders at Taku should be requested to despatch a further force of men with all speed. Judging from this telegram things seemed to be in a dangerous state and, in conjunction with his American colleague, he, the British Consul, had invited the attendence of the other Consuls and officers to the end that they might unite in applying to the Viceroy of Chihli for materials and workmen to repair the railway, so that the work might be commenced and a special train despatched on the following morning.

{10 June}

The Consuls and others then prepared a joint memorial in the proposed sense, and received a favourable answer ... Orders were at once issued for an immediate start, and ... 50 men of the *Kasagi* were marched to the railway station. Admiral Seymour was already there with his command. He informed me that he had received a communication from the British Consul that the French, the Germans, and the Russians reported that their troops would take

73

part in the movement; that he was now getting the necessary carriages ready; that he had come that morning from Tong-ku, and that as the Japanese were first on the field, he wished them to follow by the next train. The first train set out at 10 am. The second followed at 10.30, carrying our party of 50, together with 250 English, 100 Russians and 100 French. At Peitsan we saw 1000 of General Nieh's troops, and at Yang-tsung 5000, encamped in the open and prepared to repel any attack by the Boxers. At 12.30 pm we found that the progress of the first train had been arrested at a point one mile beyond Yang-tsung, in consequence of a large bridge having been partially burned and repairs being required. At 2.35 pm the repairs were finished and we advanced 3 miles when another broken place several yards long was found. Thenceforth such places were found at intervals of 2 or 3 miles, so that we did not reach more than 25 miles beyond Tientsin that day. Guards were posted for the night at a distance of 1000 yards all round the train.

{11 June}
On the morning of the 11th a party of 50 English marines advanced to examine the state of the line. They reported that its condition was very bad in the neighbourhood of Lo-fah. The whole of this day was devoted to repairs, the men working with the engineers, and by 6.25 pm we reached a point 3 miles south of Lo-fah. There we saw a number of Boxers on the right of the line, and we received the order to dismount and form [a] line on the plain. They fled without fighting, pursued for 3 miles by a company of British marines. According to the report of the marines, they overtook the Boxers and killed 30 of them, but the rest escaped under cover of darkness and the marines returned. On that evening the third train arrived from Tientsin, carrying 200 Russian troops, 50 French, and 250 English.

{12 and 13 June}
The 12th and 13th were devoted to repairing the line; nothing unusual happened. On the 13th, a fourth train arrived with 450 Germans and a further force of English. We halted that night near Lang-fang station. Our force then consisted of 915 English, 100 Americans, 315 Russians, 51 Japanese, 40 Italians, 25 Austrians, 450 Germans, and 158 French, a total of 2054.

{14 June}
At dawn on the 14th, the first train went ahead alone and reached a point 3 miles north of Lang-fang. The second train, carrying our detachment, was taking in water at Lang-fang station at 9.50 am when about 300 Boxers carrying flags with '*Iho*' inscribed on them, and brandishing swords and spears, advanced to within short range of the train. The English, French,

Russians and our own troops, who were inside and outside the train, charged them and gave them several volleys, when they fled, pursued for 2 miles by 100 English and 200 Germans. On examination I found that 80 of the Boxers were killed on the spot or died almost immediately. There were young and old among them, their costumes were various, and they had red bands tied round their heads and hanging down behind, as well as red aprons on their bosoms. Their shoes also were tied with red. From the number of the bodies thus attired, I judged this to be the uniform of the Boxers. Unfortunately, inferior as were their weapons, they killed 4 of the Italian marines who had been on the guard about 1000 yards away from the train. We had no other casualties.

At 4.20 pm a message arrived from Admiral Seymour saying that the detachment left behind at Lo-fah was surrounded by several hundred Boxers and in some peril. The Admiral desired us to move back to the rescue, which we gladly did. Almost immediately Admiral Seymour entered our train, and we proceeded to Lo-fah at our best speed, our force being 150 English, 100 French, 100 Russians and 51 Japanese. At 5.15 pm we drew near to Lo-fah. The fight was raging furiously and the English were evidently hard pressed. We began firing from the windows, and at 5.20, on arriving at the station, we left the train, and forming line, advanced into the fight. The English were on the right, the Japanese on the left, and the Russians and French in the centre. We advanced keeping up a hot fire, and the enemy throwing away their swords, fled in disorder. At 6 pm, we received orders to desist from attacking, and we returned to our train. About 200 of the enemy were on the ground. Our casualties were only 2 wounded among the English. We took a flag and over 20 swords and spears. At 7.37 pm we left Lo-fah and advanced again to Lang-fang, reaching it at 8 pm.

{15 June}
It was proposed to send a train back to Tientsin for provisions and ammunition, but there being no water for the engine we had to spend the night carrying water, and the train could not start until 6 am on the 15th. I took the opportunity to send to the Consul in Tientsin a written statement of what had occurred. This train, however, returned to us at 4 pm on the same day, reporting that the railway south of Yang-tsung was again injured and that communication with Tientsin was impossible; also that General Nieh, who had been guarding the station up to the 14th, had retired to the neighbourhood of Tientsin. Thus the column was cut off from its base.

{16, 17 June}
On the 16th instant Admiral Seymour held a council of officers in the morning. He said that 5 days had passed since the column left Tientsin, and

they had not made even half of the journey to Peking. It appeared, also, that the line northward was in a very bad condition, both rails and sleepers being deficient, so that no hope could be entertained of reaching Peking in a reasonable time. Moreover the state of Peking was unknown, but it was impossible not to fear that a very critical situation existed, therefore it seemed better in the first place to effect the repair of the line in the rear and then, having obtained supplies of ammunition and provisions, to set out again for Peking via Tung-chow, moving independently of the railway. All agreed to this proposal. Accordingly trains No. 1 and No. 4, which carried rails and sleepers, were sent back to Yang-tsung to commence repairs, while trains No. 2 and No. 3 moved between Lang-fang and Yang-tsung for purposes of protection. The 16th and 17th passed without incident.

{18 June}

At noon on the 18th, the commanding officer, who was in No. 1 train, sent word that the injury done to the railway to the south of Yang-tsung seemed to be the work of the imperial troops, not of the Boxers. He therefore desired us to return for purposes of consultation. We thus understood that the situation had undergone a complete change, and we would have returned immediately, but the engine of No. 2 train was without water, and while this deficiency was being remedied, our patrols brought news, at 2.20 pm, that a body of cavalry numbering 100 were advancing against us.

Acting, then, under the orders of the officer commanding the German detachment, who was the senior present, the English troops formed up on the right of the line and the Russians and Japanese on the left, the two companies of Germans being in front on the right. In that order we advanced. But when the Russians had reached a wood 400 metres distant, they observed a force of cavalry some 500 metres in front. They opened fire at once, and the enemy retired. At the same time, a body of infantry emerged from a wood in front and another body from a wood in the left-rear of the latter. Thereupon the English troops deployed in front with the Russians and Japanese on the left and the Germans on the right. Advancing to the attack, they came into contact with the enemy, the British and Germans at a range of from 300 to 400 metres, the Russians and Japanese at a range of 300 metres.

The troops facing the British were General Tung's main body. They carried flags with the ideagraph *'Tung'* blazoned in gold on a red field, and in the intervals of these flags were banners with green borders surrounding a red field. These standards showed that we were confronted by a mixed army of regulars and Boxers. The troops on the enemy's left were General Tung's rear-guard, and the whole numbered about 2000. Our force at the time mustered about 1100. After 30 minutes' fighting, the enemy's van took fresh ground on a small hill to the north, and the English and Germans advancing to attack them, the Germans charged, driving them in confusion from the position.

The fight on the left had meanwhile lasted for 27 minutes, and the enemy, retreating, made a long countermarch and advanced again at a point further to the west where, being attacked by the Russians, they retired to the cover of a grove. The Russians and Japanese then advanced, but the main body of the enemy now appeared again on the field, when a company of the English, making a detour to the left, attacked them suddenly and drove them back. It was then half-past five. About 140 or 150 of the enemy had fallen, and our casualties were 7 English and Germans killed, and 2 German officers, 1 Russian officer, and over 40 English, German and Russian soldiers wounded. The Japanese had no casualties.

The flags captured by us had the ideographs 'Imperial Command' inscribed on the right corner, whereas all the Boxer flags previously taken bore merely the name '*Iho*' and a place-name. They had also 7 ideographs signifying 'The *Iho* save the empire and destroy foreigners'. Such a legend was now seen for the first time. It showed that the Boxers and the imperial troops were acting in combination.

At 6 pm we left Lang-fang, and at 6.30 pm we reached the rendez-vous at La-fah, where we found Admiral Seymour. At 7 o'clock there was a council of officers. Admiral Seymour said that examination showed that the whole railway on the south had been destroyed and that no hope of repairing it could be entertained; that Tung was holding the region south of Peking and that Nieh's men were between the allies and Tientsin, the two Generals cooperating to cut off the allies.

The situation having undergone such a complete change, the Admiral thought that the best plan would be to retire to Tientsin, and having formed a junction with the troops there, to resume the advance. When, however, they lost the use of the railway, the transport of their wounded would become a matter demanding serious thought. He had therefore sent scouts that afternoon to the river, and they had found 4 large junks and 5 small boats. He proposed to put the wounded in these, and make the return journey via the Peiho, the troops marching on the eastern bank so as to be in a position to deal with Nieh's forces. All agreed to this course. The order and hours of advance were then fixed: the Americans with one gun to march in the van; the English to follow, with one field piece and four machine guns; then the Austrians; then the Japanese; then the Russians; then the Germans; then the French; and finally the Italians, all on the east bank of river, the rear being brought up by one field piece and 4 Maxims. That night – 18th – no incident occurred, but during the night the sound of cannon was heard from time to time in the direction of Tientsin.

{19 June}

On the 19th, having buried our dead, and placed over 47 wounded in the boats, we left the railway in the afternoon, and commenced our return journey. At 7.30 pm we halted at Peh-shin-chang on a moor and the night passed quietly.

{20 June}

At 6 am on the 20th we set out again, the Japanese troops having been transferred to the western bank by order of Admiral Seymour. At 8.10 am the enemy showed to the north of a village, and the Japanese troops received an order to recross the river. The enemy were then about 3000 metres distant, and our artillery opened fire. At 9.05 am fighting commenced. The enemy, composed of imperial troops and Boxers, did not exceed some hundreds. At 10.20 am they fled to the north-west, and we halted for a time at the evacuated village. At 10.55 am the enemy again appeared at a distance of from 3000 to 4000 metres and opened fire. We at once replied, and by 12.40 pm they were driven back. We then marched to another village and halted. Before we had resumed our march the enemy, at 2.30 pm, re-opened the attack from two directions, using rifles and artillery. The Americans and Germans attacked and drove them back, capturing their position. Our left also attacked. The Japanese occupied the ground taken by the Germans and advanced thence in company with the Americans and the English . . .

Our attack lasted for a considerable time, but the enemy did not retreat. Therefore at 6.08 pm, 200 English, 90 Americans and the Japanese received orders to advance and charge a village where the enemy had their chief position. The enemy were driven out of this village and from two other villages, and at 7 pm the firing ceased. The English and Japanese burned the three villages and we all bivouacked for the night, which passed without incident.

{21 June}

At 6.30 pm on the 21st we resumed our journey. The disposition of forces was different – the Japanese, the Russians, the Germans, and the Austrians being on the west bank, and the British, the French, the Americans, and the Italians on the east bank. The Japanese formed the van on their side. At 8.20 am, as the Japanese were about to pass Wang Village, the enemy appeared in fighting order, with artillery, at a wood near Peh-tsang, and the Japanese, Russians, and Germans deploying, advanced to the attack. At 11 am we drove the enemy from Peh-tsang, and took possession of the place at 11.30, whence advancing at 12.49 pm, we passed Wan-kia. At about 300 metres from that place, the enemy opened fire from Nan-tsang, and we replied, firing across the river. After three hours they broke and fled. They numbered about 2000, and had artillery, cavalry, and infantry. We pursued them vehemently, and they rallied in the neighbourhood of the Chintsu temple.

We abandoned the pursuit at 6.30 pm, and crossed from the west to the east bank to hold counsel with the commanding officer. In the meanwhile, the force on the east bank had encountered the enemy at a point 2 miles from the river near the railway, and had not succeeded in silencing their artillery until evening, when the force returned to the river and joined us. Altogether the fighting had lasted 6 hours, and there had been many casualties. The enemy were Nieh's troops, infantry, artillery, and cavalry, aggregating about 5000 of all arms. That night we camped at Lian-tsang, and the commanding officers, after consultation, decided that we should set out at midnight, and, marching quietly along the River, endeavour to reach Tientsin without further fighting.

{22 June}
Accordingly, at 1 am on the 22nd we left Lian-tsang and marched down stream for about a mile, when, on approaching Mu-rei-cha, we were fired on from the western bank. A reconnaissance under cover of the bank discovered the enemy in small force near Chintsu. We therefore showed ourselves at once, and at the sound of our shouting the enemy dispersed. After half an hour, the advance was resumed, and at 4.25 am we reached the military stores at Si-ku. They are surrounded on the east, the south, and the north by a mud wall, the river being on the west. The wall is embrasured at intervals, and guns are mounted there, so that the place forms a fort. It is known among foreigners as the 'Arsenal'. None of the allied officers were well acquainted with this locality, and we had been advancing by the aid of map No. 314, which was in my possession.

Now for the first time we discovered that there was a fort at this spot. No sooner did we appear in front of the fort than the enemy opened on us with rifles and guns. We were taken unawares, and, seeking cover under the river banks, we returned the fire. The river at this point is not more than 30 yards wide. The enemy's shots fell like hail about the boats containing the wounded, and, as their peril was imminent, we had to remove them up stream. We then opened fire with the whole of our artillery, but the distance being only 200 metres and the enemy having the advantage of a parapet, it was an extremely difficult matter to silence their fire. Fortunately 2 companies of Germans and 1 of Americans, returning up stream, crossed to the other side, and, creeping along the bank, escaladed the fort, the garrison flying in confusion. The English quickly followed into the fort and by 5.30 am it was in our possession.

But at 6 am the enemy advanced, to the number of about 5000, from the directions of Tientsin and the railway. We fought desperately, and in 30 minutes the enemy on the Tientsin side were beaten back. Those on the railway, however, placed a number of guns in position and held their ground stubbornly. We therefore used the guns found in the fort, and by 10 o'clock succeeded in partially silencing their artillery. At 2 o'clock in the afternoon the attack was renewed from the same directions, and not until we had fought for two hours did the enemy retire. By 4.30 pm the whole of the allied forces had entered the fort. At 11.50 pm the enemy sent several shells in our direction, but we did not reply. In this fight we had over 60 killed and wounded, 3 of the wounded being Japanese.

{23 June}

At 4.20 am on the 23rd, the enemy renewed the attack from the east and the south, and kept it up for hours, not retiring until 11 am. During this combat the Japanese worked some field guns and had 2 men killed. A short rest was then taken, and, on examining our reserve ammunition, the Japanese found that they had only 20 rounds per rifle, the Russians being in the same condition. We therefore opened the arsenal and took out some new-pattern German magazine rifles, 25 of which were given to the Japanese. The enemy's attack became weaker in the afternoon. That night (23rd) a hundred English marines were sent out on patrol duty in the direction of the railway. After advancing a mile and a half, they were suddenly discovered by the enemy, and retreated, having had a Captain and 4 men killed. Evidently the enemy had surrounded the fort and were lying in wait for us to advance.

{24 June}

During the 24th the enemy made several attacks from the east and the west, but were quickly driven back. The Arsenal was about 240 yards square and there were over 30 storehouses, containing hundreds of various kinds of field-guns, machine-guns, and tens of thousands of German and American rifles, with an ample supply of ammunition. As the allies were short of ammunition, the capture of this place was an immense advantage. Moreover, there were about 5 tons of hulled rice, which was equally necessary to us. But, on the other hand, we had lost over 200 of our people – or fully one-tenth of our total force – in killed and wounded . . .

At a council held that night, it was decided that although, judging from what had passed, the allies could doubtless force their way to Tientsin, yet the care of the wounded would hamper them greatly. Fully 800 men would have to be told off for transporting the wounded, which would reduce the allies' fighting force to about one thousand, whereas Nieh had some 15,000 under his command. Therefore the commanders resolved to remain at the Arsenal as long as possible, and if possible to devise some means of communicating with Tientsin. Arrangements were made in that sense, and the same night two Chinese servants were sent secretly to Tientsin.

{25 June}

At 7 am on the 25th we observed a force of foreign troops advancing northwards along the railway. We displayed all our flags and signalled to them. After a time they wheeled to the left, and at 8.10 am reached the Arsenal, a Russian officer riding in front and calling out that they had come to our succour. The troops raised shout of joy, and joined hands in congratulation. At 8.40 am the enemy opened fire from the west and south, but were immediately driven back by the Russian detachment of the relieving force. In the afternoon, the wounded, the provisions, the ammunition, etc. were passed over the river, and at dusk the troops all bivouacked on the opposite bank.

{26 June}

At 3.40 am the allies set out from the Arsenal, the relieving troops acting as escort. We advanced by the railway. A hundred English marines remained behind in the Arsenal, under command of the gunnery captain of the Centurion, and set fire to all the stores, so that by 5 am the conflagration had assumed large dimensions. The allies reached Tientsin at 10.20 am without further mishap.

Letter from Flag Lieutenant Frederick A. Powlett, Royal Navy

Frederick Armand Powlett (1873–1963) was the son of Admiral Armand Temple Powlett. He followed his father into the Royal Navy and rose quickly, becoming Flag Lieutenant to Vice Admiral Sir Edward Seymour, attached to HMS Centurion *at the time of the Boxer Rebellion. He retired in 1919 with the rank of Vice Admiral.*

This letter was written to Miss Beatrice Jackson, one of four daughters of Sir Thomas Jackson (1841–1915), Chief Manager of the Hong Kong and Shanghai Bank. The Jacksons were a prominent family in the Far East, due largely to the importance of his bank. In 1906 Miss Jackson married Major Raymond John Marker, a distinguished veteran of the Boer War, who died on the Western Front in November 1914. This letter, like that from Roger Keyes to Miss Jackson in Chapter Five, descended in the family of the Markers' son.

27 June 1900

Dear Miss Bee,

I wonder if it will amuse you to hear the 'Adventures and Wanderings of 200 sailors of 8 nations.' Anyhow I am going to risk boring you and give you an account. To begin with you must understand it is the history of a failure, but a failure I think from reasons impossible to foresee. They tell us we are not at war with China but this very day we have been fighting for seven hours against 3000 Imperial troops in an Imperial arsenal. The Russians, Germans and ourselves took it with comparatively small loss, about 18 killed and 60 wounded.

This is a curious country. You once said men were queer creatures to fight, and now (I didn't before) I agree with you. There is a very nasty brutal reverse to the medal.

Now for my story! We had been off Taku bar for some time when late one night (June 9th) a wire from Sir Claude[1] arrived saying that unless we came to relieve Peking very soon we should be too late. All our men were told off and we bundled ashore 500 men in the next two hours. We were ashore by 3.30 am at Tongku and at Tientsin by 8 am from which we pushed on up the

82

line at 9.30 am. You probably won't remember the railway stations on the Peking line so I have put a small plan with this to make my meaning clearer.

The first night we got to four miles below Lofa, having had to repair several small breaks in the line. We moved slightly on the 11th and in the evening were attacked by the Boxers. We had an advanced guard of marines about a mile ahead who we saw retiring and firing, and when they got within a few hundred yards of the train the Boxers appeared amongst the trees and made their attack. My impression is that the Boxers didn't really realise the trains were so close, but were so mad keen to cut off and cut up the marines that they overshot; but when they saw the train thought they might as well have a smack. They are marvellously brave; armed as they were then with swords, spears, and banners, they came on against a withering fire, stopping only when downed. The proportion that seems to stop them is about one-tenth left dead. Our proportion of wounded to dead has been 4 or 5 to 1, so we may assume theirs is much the same, which means that it takes 50 to 60% of casualties to stop these extraordinary Chinamen. Our losses were nil. The Boxers left 35 dead behind. I know of one man (to show the pertinacity of the beggars) who took four revolver bullets, all of which got him fairly in the body, to stop him and still was quite unfriendly.

The Boxers wear red turbans and sashes and tie their sleeves and ankles with red and have red on their weapons. They make good targets. When we first made their acquaintance they were armed only with swords and such like, but now a beneficent Chinese government with whom we are not at war has supplied them with the best modern rifles.

The next day the Boxers made three separate attacks but with little success. Our force by this time was 2000 – roughly 1000 British, 450 Germans, 150 French, 200 Russians, 40 Japs, 40 Italians, 30 Austrians, 120 Americans in four trains, two British, one other commanded by the German captain and one by the Frenchman. There never was such a mixture.

On 13th June the Boxers made a large attack; I think 2000 must have come on. They came at noon with beat of drum and by about 12.30 were on the run leaving about 150 dead. We lost 5, an Italian picket which was cut up.

In the next two days, during which we lay at Langfang repairing the line and filling up with water, there was only one attack which was made on a small garrison left at Lofa station, a lieutenant and 60 men. Roughly 1500 attacked but didn't get within 200 yards of the station and left 150 dead. So far it had been mere slaughter, sitting behind a trench and bowling these real brave men over. We kept on moving slowly forward, repairing as we went, finding the line worse and worse till the 16th we found ourselves cut off from Tientsin so we decided to fall back on Yangtsun to endeavour to re-establish our communications. We went back with the first British train, leaving the second British and German trains at Langfang and the French at Lofa. We had a small engagement on the 17th and took and burnt three villages. They had the impertinence to show Boxer flags. On the 18th the French train went to Langfang and came back to us to report that the German and Second British had been engaged for some hours with 5 to 6000 troops and Boxers, about two-thirds of them troops, and all armed with rifles. They came on twice with great determination and left four to five hundred dead behind when beaten off. Our losses – 15 dead and over 40 wounded, marvellously light.

This of course showed us we had Imperial troops to deal with and we were in possession of the rather disquieting knowledge that there were at least 7000 of General Nieh's, reputed to be some of the best in China, between us and Tientsin. A retreat by water was our only chance. We couldn't go by rail because our enemies had taken jolly good care that by this time there was no rail below Yangtsun; and our wounded made it impossible to march except by river. We seized four junks and prepared them for the wounded and on the afternoon began our retreat. Only made 3 miles and bivouacked by the bank, starting again early in the morning; all our clothes and all stores not necessities had to be left behind (I burnt my garments which I have now begun to regard as their natural death).

At 9 am on the 20th we were obstructed by Nieh's troops who held village after village and they are pretty thick; it got quite monotonous. They had two guns, one of which we captured in the evening. They began by shelling us, then we shelled and advanced and rushed them out. The Chinese apparently have no use for the cheer that is always given with the last rush, they always legged it. Bivouacked for the night; of course more killed and wounded. The 21st was worse, we fought literally the whole day, pushing the Chinese before us till at last we were brought up at about 5.30 by guns and troops in a position which at the time we couldn't get at. They were most annoying, kept up a heavy shell fire. Shell fire is a disagreeable thing, the shells are so noisy and abrupt in their movements; rifle bullets unless very close are quite apologetic, they phew rather quickly, when very close pssttt – A shell comes with a howl and explodes in a most disconcerting manner. We lost a great many on this day, in one charge the leading company had the lieutenant and midshipman and 14 out of 50 of the rank and file hit, Capt. Jellicoe[2] was wounded and the admiral's coxswain mortally wounded. Edward [Seymour] has behaved absolutely disgracefully, exposed himself recklessly, led most of the charges and generally been most naughty. The men are awfully pleased, naturally, but it is not right, his life is too valuable.

That night it was decided that the only thing to be done was to make a night march and turn this position; in fact it was our only chance of getting through; our wounded had increased to over 100, we were short of ammunition and food. The only thing we really had in abundance was water of the best Peiho brand which has plenty of body in it if nothing else. At 1 am we started and by dawn found ourselves opposite an earthwork on the right bank (we being on the left). Two sentries hailed us what we wanted. We said we were friends. They said 'Can do, pass on'; about 1000 were perched on top of the bank (which there is banked up considerably) like crows on a twig when they fired a volley and opened with guns on us. I've never seen such a dive for shelter. We got all our men beneath the bank and steadied them and started replying. The guns didn't give us much trouble, we shot the gunners . . . It became apparent that the place must be taken at all costs so we pushed 120 marines and Luttrell's[3] company across half a mile further up. They got within a hundred yards under cover of a village and rushed it in great style, clearing the garrison of 500 out in one rush. The Germans crossed lower down and we quickly had all our force over and found ourselves in possession (rather to our surprise) of one of the biggest armouries in Pechihli. When I tell you one item of the stores was 38,000 rifles and 38 million rounds of ammunition, you will understand we rather fell on our feet. We also found guns and Maxims and ammunition, all of which we rapidly availed ourselves of, and mounted and prepared for an attack which was of course certain to be made.

Sure enough, at about noon we were attacked by General Nieh with 25 battalions. Each is supposed to be 500 strong and is probably 300 so we calculate rather over 7000 troops attacked us. It lasted about four hours. Incessant shelling and rifle fire on three sides like the rolling of drums, and the air raked in all directions by bullets. We lost heavily in spite of our good cover, our casualties nearly doubled themselves. The Chinese are such rotten bad shots that really the safest place is the forefront of the battle. At about 4 pm they were choked off attacking and retired, their guns went on for a bit but we silenced them with two of their own guns taken from their own arsenal which was most gratifying. The next morning they attacked in a very half-hearted way at daybreak and were cleared out without much difficulty. But we lost men; our captain of marines and five men were cut off and of course killed.

For two days we had rest and quiet and dust storms and on the morning of the 25th we were relieved by the force which had relieved Tientsin. We went to Tientsin next day, our total losses being 60 killed and 230 wounded out of the 2000 we started with. The marvel is they were so few. It takes many bullets to kill or even touch a man.

Roger Keyes will have to be careful or he will go and get promoted; he has been capturing destroyers and destroying forts and generally distinguishing himself. Murray Stewart is here as special to the *Times*. I wish all the specials were like he, the others are pigs. They are fairly meek because they have been informed that all their messages must be read and if they are naughty they'll be trod on. They come and prowl round all day and ask questions.

Please give my respects to your family and please forgive me for the extent of my babbling. Hope to see yourself, Sir Thomas and Miss Jackson in the autumn but goodness knows when this will stop. I hope to be in the big adventure on Peking before then.

Yours sincerely
F. A. Powlett

Notes

[1] Sir Claude Maxwell MacDonald (1852–1915), head of the British Legation in Peking, who organised the defence of that place during the siege.

[2] Captain John R. Jellicoe (1859–1935) of HMS *Centurion* and flag captain with Sir Edward Seymour on the China Station, 1898–1901. He was later to achieve fame at the Battle of Jutland during World War I. For his services he received an earldom in 1925. He was buried in St Paul's Cathedral.

[3] Lieutenant John L.F. Luttrell, RN, of the *Centurion*.

THE TAKU FORTS

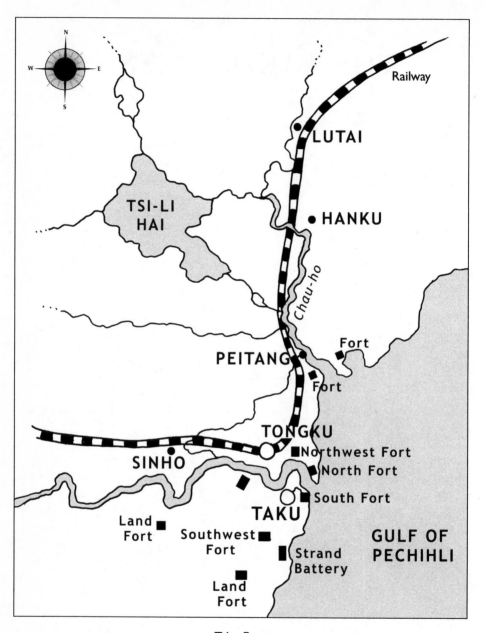

Taku Forts

Introduction

The mouth of the Peiho River at the Gulf of Pechihli was defended by five Chinese forts: the No. 1 Fort or North Fort and No. 4 Fort or North West Fort, on the north bank; and on the south bank the No. 2, No. 3, and No. 5 Forts, known collectively as the South Forts.

By mid-June 1900 the Allied commanders – based on ships located ten miles off shore in the Gulf of Pechihli – became concerned that Chinese control of these forts constituted a menace to the safety of Allied troops in Tientsin, as well as those *en route* to Peking with Admiral Seymour. They met on 16 June and agreed to notify the Viceroy of Chihli that Allied occupation of the forts was now deemed necessary, and that if the Chinese did not peacefully surrender control on or before 2 am on 17 June, the Allies would occupy the forts by force.

Only the smaller ships could enter the mouth of the Peiho because of the sand bar. The Allies positioned ten naval vessels inside the bar – three Russian, three British, and one each from America, France, Germany, and Japan. The main part of their battle fleet had to remain in the Gulf.

The Chinese initiated the confrontation, opening fire at 12:50 am on 17 June. During the early morning hours there was continuous bombardment from both sides. At 4:30 am the Allied troops advanced on the North West Fort, with British and Japanese troops scaling the parapet; by 5 am the Chinese had fled. The Allies occupied both forts on the north bank. At 6 am there was a huge explosion at the South Forts, after which the Chinese abandoned all three. All action had ceased by 7:10 am, with the Allies in full control.

A total of 904 Allied soldiers and sailors participated: 321 were British, 133 Germans, 244 Japanese, 159 Russians, 25 Italians and 22 Austrians. (The American commander did not allow Americans to participate.)

Within the bar, at the mouth of the Peiho, the most memorable event was engineered by Commander Roger Keyes, who with a small contingent was able to seize four Chinese torpedo boat destroyers at anchor between Taku and Tongku. These were recent additions to the Chinese navy, and were distributed to the Allied navy as prizes of war.

Account of Mrs James Jones, American Visitor

{On 16 June 1900, women and children resident or visiting in Tientsin were urged to travel at once by train to Tongku in order to be out of harm's way in the event of a Boxer attack on the Tientsin Foreign Concession. Mrs Jones and the other refugees were met by Captain Wise of USS Monocacy. *Crew members gave up their cabins to accommodate Mrs Jones and her companions. Her story of what happened is as follows.}*

Even here our troubles were not at an end. We seemed to have fallen 'out of the frying pan into the fire', for soon after getting on board we heard there was a probability of the Taku Forts being taken that night. It appears that the naval captains had called on the General of the forts, taking Mr Johnstone, a good Chinese scholar, as interpreter, and informed him that unless they surrendered by 12 o'clock that night, they intended to bombard the forts at 2 am, it having transpired that thousands of soldiers were entering them and also laying mines across the channel during the day . . .

About 1 am the Chinese opened fire . . . From this time till about 6.30 am was an increasing bombardment, the roar of the cannon being almost deafening. The first fort taken was the North, by, we presume, the Japanese, as that was the first flag we saw hoisted, followed shortly after by the British on the outer North fort.

After taking these Forts the men-of-war steamed towards the mouth of the river and soon after the German and Russian flags went up on the South Forts. Shortly after daylight we saw four torpedo boats being towed in stern first by the *Whiting* and *Fame,* flying the British flags. During the time of bombardment we and the ships at Tongku were right in the line of fire and had anything but a pleasant time, the shells whistling above and around us in all directions, and the marvel is that the *Monocacy* was the only one struck; she received a shot right through her bows. The *Lienshing,* lying at Jardine's, besides running the risk of shells from the forts, was attacked by a party of Chinese who were looting the cargo, but the return fire from the *Lienshing* eventually drove them away. A shell falling into one of the Tongku hotels near the railway station killed three Chinese, the only ones that were in the house at the time.

About 10 am when all was quiet some of the officers of our ship went off to explore, Mr Conley going to the North Fort, Mr Burgess to the South, and Mr Miller to Taku, to see how the foreign residences had fared. On their return they had most ghastly tales to relate. The forts were a mass of ruins, rivers of blood, with headless and armless bodies everywhere, which the blue-jackets were gathering together and cremating in heaps.

Several of the houses at Taku were complete wrecks and nearly all had suffered in some way. As soon as it was daylight we saw in the distance a black mass of Chinese hurrying from the forts and the villages round about. It is feared they will make for Tientsin and join the Boxers.

Account of Chief Officer
J. Gordon, Steamship Officer

{Since the hostilities at Taku erupted without advance notice, numerous coastal vessels – involved in carrying either local passengers or merchandise – were caught at the wharves of Tongku and Taku. One such boat was the China Steam Navigation Company's SS Hsin-Fung, *whose Chief Officer, Mr Gordon, reported as follows:}*

We were right in the thick of the fight, the shot and shell just clearing our awning boom. There were no big ships in the action, only gunboats or small craft, comprising three Russians, one English, one French, and one German.

One of the Russians got a shot in her bow and is now aground in shallow water. She was hit five times in all and another of the Russians was hit three times. The *Algerine,* the British vessel, sustained no serious damage and only took two shots through her stoke-hold ventilators. The heavy loss of the Russians is accounted for by the fact that a shot or shell fell in the magazine, causing an explosion of ammunition.

An ultimatum had been sent ashore to the effect that if the Boxers were not checked other steps would have to be taken. Then some of the naval officers went to see the General at 12 o'clock on Saturday night, to ask what he intended doing. The General replied that he meant to fight, and a bombardment by the fleet was arranged for 2 o'clock that morning. The Chinese, however, began firing a little before 1 am, using the searchlight. The USS *Monocacy* had been up river on patrol work, and as she came down men on shore near the wharves opened fire on her with rifles but they were soon silenced.

It was one of the Russian torpedo boats that silenced the fire of the riflemen along the creeks near the river, the work being done in very short time.

On the inner side of the forts the British and Japanese flags are flying, on the outer side the British and Russian flags, and on the south side the German and Russian colours fly. The Russian flag flies at the Navy yard and the docks. The four captured torpedo destroyers are all under the British flag . . .

The forts do not show much damage from the outside, but on entering

93

them a very vivid idea is gained as to the effect of modern shell fire. The place was wrecked and mutilated men and horses were thickly strewn over the blood-stained ground. The visitors, after the fight, made quite a harvest of mementoes, and we were shewn yesterday a drum, a sword bayonet, and packets of gun fittings, portions of shell and other grim relics of the affray. These were taken from the fort, including also a crystal cap button and red tassel that were lying near one of the dead.

Report of Captain
M. Nagamine,
Japanese Naval Officer

{Captain Nagamine commanded the Japanese cruiser Naniwa.}

... On the 15th instant a military council was convened by the senior naval officer, Vice-Admiral [Hiltebrandt], on board the first-class cruiser *Rossia*. The facts which the council had to consider were that the insurgents, numbering about 2000, showed a disposition to attack the Taku Forts, to destroy the railway, and to lay torpedoes in the Peiho. In view of these dangers, it was resolved that steps must be taken to guard the railway station, and to preserve communications with Tientsin. In carrying out this resolution, the allies determined to adopt a defensive attitude, and to refrain from assuming the offensive unless they were attacked, in which event they were to assault the forts and render them incapable of doing any mischief. It was further decided that a force of 300 Japanese marines should be landed and posted at the Tong-ku station, with orders to guard it until relieved.

On the 16th instant at 11 am another council was held on board the *Rossia*. The facts before this second council were that although the Chinese Government had raised no objection to the Foreign Powers cooperating to preserve good order and secure life and property, and had undertaken to discharge its own duties in those respects, there was now every appearance that the Chinese troops were laying torpedoes to block the river and were advancing to destroy the railway in conjunction with the Boxers. The naval commanders found themselves obliged in consequence to adopt measures for preserving communications with the men already landed from the ships and to prevent Tientsin from being isolated. Therefore, they determined that the Governor of Chihli must be called on to hand over the Taku Forts, and, if he declined to do so, they must be assaulted.

An intimation in that sense was forwarded to the Governor, as well as to the officer in command of the Chinese troops; 2 o'clock am on the 17th being named as the hour by which hostilities would commence in the event of the Forts not being handed over. At 3.15 on the afternoon of that day (16th) a force of 180 Russians was landed; and at 4 pm they were followed

95

by 250 British and 130 Germans. By 8 pm the situation had become very critical, and it was evident that hostilities might commence at any moment.

At 12.50 am the Forts opened fire on the *Atago, Iltis, Algerine, Monocacy, Koreets, Bobr, Silatch* and other foreign craft lying inside the bar, and a fierce cannonade at once commenced, lasting without intermission until 4.35 am, when a terrible explosion occurred, one of the Chinese magazines having been blown up. The Japanese torpedo-destroyer *Kagero* had meanwhile been steaming round and round the Chinese cruiser *Hai-yuen,* but, as the latter showed no sign of taking part in the hostilities, the *Kagero* was despatched at 5.20 am to ascertain how matters were proceeding on shore. Owing, however, to the low state of the tide, she could not cross the bar. Fifteen minutes later, namely at 5.45 am, the Japanese flag was seen waving over one of the Forts on the northern bank of the River.

The report of operations on shore shows that at daybreak the forces for the assault of the Forts were marshalled, 200 Russians forming the van, 380 British and Germans the main body, and 300 Japanese the reserve force in the rear.

The advance was commenced in echelon of columns, but, owing to the hot fire opened by the Chinese, a command was issued to take skirmishing order. Captain Hattori then perceived that the Russians in the van were making little progress owing to the heavy fire kept up by the Chinese, and that the advance of the British and the Germans was impeded by heavy ground. He himself was marching with two field-pieces at the head of his men, but, observing a short road of access to the Fort, he doubled his marines at each side of the guns and pushed on rapidly, leaving the rest of the allies behind. The Chinese troops still kept up a brisk fire, and Captain Hattori, seeing that a bayonet charge was the only resource, gave the necessary orders. He fell dead himself just as he reached the parapet, but Lieutenant Shiraishi led the men. Their charge was successful, and the rest of the troops followed immediately.

THE SIEGE OF TIENTSIN

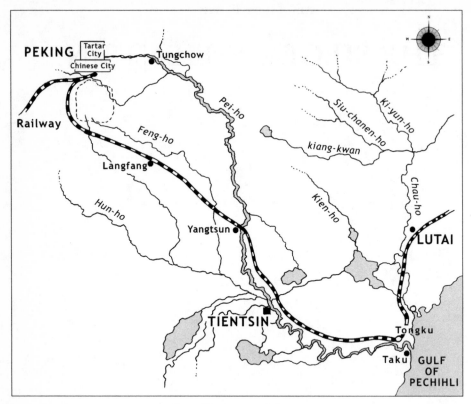

From Tientsin to Peking

Introduction

The city of Tientsin had both a strategic location and a large concentration of western residents, mostly businessmen and missionaries. It was, therefore, an obvious target for Boxer aggression and of equally clear importance to the Allies. When the Allies decided to mount a military campaign against the Boxers, Tientsin was a pivotal factor as a base for supplies and troops. No sooner had the Seymour Expedition departed on 10 June than troops and equipment started moving in; by 13 June, 1700 Russian troops, with cavalry and field guns, reached Tientsin.

The Boxers (who by this time were cooperating with the Chinese Imperial soldiers under General Nieh) cut the telegraph wire between Tientsin and Taku on 15 June, and on 17 June started to bombard the Foreign Concession. The 27-day siege of Tientsin, starting on 17 June and ending on 14 July, is an often-overlooked part of the events of this period. The citizens were not totally cut off from the outside world, as were their counterparts in Peking, but their hardships were substantial.

A relief force of Allied sailors, marines and soldiers arrived on 23 June and removed much of the immediate danger; 24 June brought General Stoessel and his Russian troops, and also the First Chinese Regiment (known as the Weihawei Regiment) serving under British officers. On 25 June the Seymour Expedition returned. The Allies captured a large arsenal, two miles from the British Concession, on 27 June; on 4 July the Chinese made an unsuccessful attack on the railroad station; on 9 July the Allies captured another arsenal; on 11 July there was a three-hour battle at the railroad station, resulting in many Allied casualties. All during this time the citizen population of the foreign area of Tientsin endured bombardment, rifle fire, and Chinese attacks.

On 13 July the Allies gathered their strength and initiated an attack on the Chinese Walled City, which was taken on the morning of 14 July. This ended the Siege of Tientsin.

Journal of
Captain Edward H. Bayly,
Royal Navy

Captain Edward Henry Bayly (1849–1904), was born in Trim, Ireland. He signed on as a Naval Cadet on 9 June 1863. His father had served with the British Army in India, but died while Edward was still a Cadet.

Bayly's service with the Royal Navy took him to Africa, South America, and ultimately to China. He served as Captain of the British ship Aurora *during this period but played a major role among the Allies, especially after Seymour put him in charge of British civilian and military personnel, with authority also over residents of the British Concession (the largest and most important component of the foreign settlement).*

Bayly distinguished himself in three minor colonial campaigns; he was awarded the order of Commander of the Bath for his service during the Boxer rebellion.

June 10, 1900–Sunday

The Admiral [Seymour] and nearly all the landing party from [the] fleet proceeded to Tongku and entrained there, leaving after some delay in getting trains made up, for Tientsin, where they arrived between 7 and 7.30 am on 10th June. A second train followed with guns and guns' crews, and the Marines under Captain Lloyd . . .[1]

On arrival at Tientsin, no consular official of any kind was at [the] station, and the few railway officials could not tell us much. Apparently the Tientsin authorities had not contemplated any early arrival though they must (should?) have known that Captain Jellicoe's visit would produce speedy results. (They are so slow they cannot understand the Navy's ways.)

The Admiral and staff went off to the British Consulate to gather commanding officers of different nationalities together for a consultation, and gradually the station became filled with various detachments, hurriedly got together to join Admiral Seymour's force, about to march to the relief of Legations, or to endeavour to relieve them.

On the return of the C. in C. to the station, he placed me in command of the British forces in Tientsin, leaving the *Aurora*'s small arms companies, those of *Orlando* under Lieutenant Wright, who had been for some days in Tientsin, [and] some signalmen.

The Admiral proceeded after leaving final orders with me, and was accompanied and followed by such of the Allies as were ready to start, about 110 being Americans under Captain [Bowman H.] McCalla of the United States Flagship *Newark*. The officers commanding small detachments of Austrians and Italians had most courteously reported to me as wishing to place themselves under the Admiral's orders (to attach themselves to the British) and room was made for them in the Admiral's train by his orders, some British detraining and following in the second train, which followed soon after the first, with Commander Boothby of *Endymion* in charge. This train contained, besides British, a few French, Japanese, and Russians. (There was, or had been, some slight hitch about the going on of the British and French forces, perhaps political, but a few started, representing the nations, and more followed next day.) A third train arrived from Tongku with the remainder of British, mostly guns' crews, who had been detained at Tongku, and about 450 Germans, under Captain Von Usedom of the flag ship *Hertha*. A couple of guns, an officer (Sublieutenant Ballard) and a few men were taken from these gun parties and kept at Tientsin.

What has been called the 'train incident' arose over the third train, owing to the growing obstruction of the Chinese railway authorities, the attitude of the mob, and the orders of the Viceroy of Tientsin. The European officials at the station informed me at last that their director, acting presumably on the Viceroy's orders that no more trains were to be sent on to Peking, refused to allow an engine to be taken out of the shed. Said director, whom I did not know by sight, spoke to me on the subject – it appears; and as it appeared to me that the most important matter just then on hand was the despatch of nearly 600 men and some guns to join the Admiral's force, I expressed my opinion and intentions to him plainly, and sent a guard to seize the engine. (The 'audience' concurred in the opinion that I threatened to hang [the] director, so it seems likely I did. I think so myself! At any rate the effect produced was all that could be desired.)

Then a mob obstructed the entrance to shed, and also commenced to 'rock' the line, to destroy its accuracy anyway, if not to tear it up. I accordingly had twenty men sent round, and gave orders that if any more attempts to injure the line were made, the wreckers were to be fired on. The director vanished, and the train after much delay, was got together. The mob by this time filled and overflowed the station limits, and large crowds were on the plain round, impeding the work etc. Some, doubtless many, only impelled or drawn by curiosity; some mischievous, as when the train finally started, a good many stones were thrown. The crowd collected in front of the engine, apparently to intimidate the driver, a Chinese (who had to be bribed to drive) who started very slowly, but I ordered him to go fast, and scatter the mob. The latter scattered.

It was then about 5.30 pm. As I had been at the station all day, deeming the trains just then the most important matter, Lieutenant Wright of *Orlando* had seen to the accommodation of all who had come up that day to form the defence force. In this, as in all other matters under his care, he had been most painstaking and careful. He had also stationed the newcomers in their posts, either new ones, or those lately held by *Centurion* and others gone on with [the] Admiral. After a visit to [the] Consulate, where I was kindly given a room, I went round the lines, accompanied by Lieutenant Perfect of *Orlando*, having ordered Lieutenant Wright to rest till morning, as I found him absolutely done up when we were starting, fairly tired out from fatigue and want of sleep. He was a most indefatigable and zealous worker. The visits to the quarters of the defence force, and to the lines of posts, took well into the night, and so ended up the 10th. As far as could be ascertained, there were about 700 (or maybe a few more) of Allies present then in Tientsin.

June 11, 1900 – Monday
The principal work this day, and for some days afterwards, lay at the railway station. More and more difficulty – and consequent irregularity – in despatch of trains occurred, and any regular traffic may be said to have ceased on [the] 14th, even between Tientsin and Tongku. It had ceased with Peking when the Admiral started. The remainder of Russians and French[2] going on to join the force advancing towards Peking went on after much difficulty in securing a train and driver. They copied my proceedings of [the] night before, but quarrelled with the European railway employees, a matter which caused them extra delay and trouble, as they had lent me all the aid they could, though ostensibly carrying out orders from their director and the Viceroy. I succeeded in pacifying the insulted ones, and outward calm reigned.

The *Barfleur* arrived off Taku in afternoon, and immediately sent up 160 officers and men under Commander Beatty, accompanied by Major [Edward V.] Luke, RMLI – this addition to our force was very welcome, as half Lieutenant Roper's Company had gone to Tongshan, the other half went next day (12th). The purchase and despatch of fresh provisions, stores etc. to the Admiral's force began. Chinese began to leave in large numbers. Eight trains left for Taku. A Chinese General and about 800 men and 4 guns went in a special train, said to be for Sinho, but they detrained at Chun Liang Cheng[3] and proceeded across country, stated to Shan Hai Kwan. An engine and brake ram arrived from front, a Corporal (Appleton) US Marines and 6 men as a guard, at 5.30 pm returning later. Shops closing, ready money only taken.

June 12, 1900 – Tuesday

Sent remainder of Lieutenant Roper's Company to Tong Shan under Mr Clark-Hall, Midshipman. Train arrived from front at 11 am bringing despatches and several passengers. Left again at 3.45 with several tons of stores, and rifle ammunition for Admiral's force. Shops closing and Chinese leaving. (A special train brought a Chinese General, prisoner, who was at once conveyed to the Native City in a covered cart, said to be a prisoner of war on account of not suppressing Boxers!?)

June 13, 1900 – Wednesday

Engine and brake ram arrived from front under American guard, bringing some wounded Boxers (four) – (The mob believed Boxers to be invulnerable) – A Russian force under Lieutenant Colonel Anisimoff arrived. Stated numbers varying from 1500 to 1800, including 4 field guns and about 150 mounted Cossacks. Also a little temporary friction was caused by the action of some French, who, under orders from their Consul General,[4] seized an engine, placing a guard on it, and were stated to have threatened (him) the locomotive overseer with bayonets. Both parties very excited, but settled affair amicably. Consul General is now most friendly whenever we meet. (Says I spoke French like an angel! Truth is economically used by the French, and I don't think their knowledge of angels is great. Are there any French angels?)

June 14, 1900 – Thursday

No train arrived from front, but a courier from Peking came in, who reported the burning of all Mission houses in the Western Hills, and the Summer Legation.

Captain Burke of *Orlando* arrived from Taku, having left the ship the night before in obedience to Admiral Seymour's order, transmitted by me the day before (13th) – After some hours' delay, owing to the running away of Chinese drivers and firemen, he started for the front, but returned later owing to obstructions (the tearing up and burning of line) beyond Yangtsen.

The Russians sent a force (stated at different times to have been from 200 to 600 strong) to Chun Liang Cheng to hold the station.

The Viceroy's secretary came to me at station, and backed up by our Consul [W.R. Carles] (!) urged me to send an escort of 50 men to protect Viceroy!!! This I did not do, having a suspicion that said Viceroy was trying to play double, and that escort would have been murdered in Native City, diminishing our small force considerably. I referred Secretary elsewhere.

June 15, 1900 – Friday

Three French mission houses were burned by Boxers, and many fires lighted amongst the native houses near French Concession (between Native City and

Foreign Concessions) – Telegraphic communication with Tongku was interrupted. Captain Burke again attempted to proceed to the front, but had to return later owing to the destruction of line, two bridges being impassable, one on fire. He reported having had a brush with Boxers, or Chinese endeavouring to destroy the line.

A patrol train went down the line to Chun Liang Cheng and Tongku. Brought back some 30 stoker and mechanic ratings. This train carried search lights. Major Luke in charge.

A large quantity of stores, provisions, aerated waters etc. for Admiral Seymour's party (also ice) also failed to get through, and most of these articles subsequently fell into the Cossacks' hands at Station, or went down their throats. Some ammunition in the train subsequently proved useful. (Not being eatable or drinkable, it survived.) The train was not a reconnoitering one as stated by a writer at Tientsin, nor had it a Maxim gun.

Lieutenant Irwin, USN, of *Monocacy*, arrived with 22 men to reinforce American guard, bringing it up to 50 (about).

The Roman Catholic Cathedral in the Native City was burnt during night of 15th.

June 16, 1900 – Saturday

The Boxers made an attack on [the] settlement early in morning, and set fire to houses (Chinese) nearest the Wool Mill and Recreation Ground, but were soon driven out. They had cover from Native City from native houses until close to Concession. (First report made to me by a volunteer, who clattered into the Consulate shouting for me and proclaiming his news at top of his voice, effectually rousing out the whole family.) The Boxers also attacked the Railway Station, but were driven off by the Russian guard.

Mr Hancock[5] reported all employees left or run away. Everything at a standstill. Telegraph operators from *Aurora*'s Chief Yeomans of Signals and Yeomen worked instruments till the people at other end bolted.

A train (patrol train) with mixed force went down line towards Tongku. Lieutenant [Herbert M.] Perfect of *Orlando* accompanied, but a German officer was in command. This train, on nearing Tongku, came under some shell fire, probably stray shell from one of Taku Forts, at the commencement of the action which ended in their capture, and returned, calling at Chun Liang Cheng and informing Russian guard.

Final disappearance of Chinese servants, employees of all kinds, except some Cantonese, occurred.

A repairing train was got together, taking all night to prepare, as 5000 railway sleepers and a large amount of tools, pins etc. had to be found and placed in trucks.

June 17, 1900 – Sunday

At about 8 am on 17th a start was made. The train contained 26 British under Lieutenant [Frederick L.] Field, *Barfleur* (who was in charge), to work a 6-pounder QF gun on front truck, ahead of search light, the light, the engine, and some to repair line. There were also 150 Russian troops, 12 French, 15 Germans, 9 Japanese.

The progress of this train was soon interrupted, and it only got 5 miles out, in the end. At half a mile from the station the line needed repair, and frequent stoppages were necessary. Also after passing first bridge, skirmishes with line destroyers and Boxers became frequent. By 3.45 pm a large body of Chinese had assembled between the train and Tientsin. Train was backed towards them, and the troops and train engaged them, covered by 6-pounder gun. Repairing train was shelled from direction of Native City.

At 5.00 a train came into sight from the Tientsin direction. This was one containing a large force of Russians (accompanied by Lieutenant G.B. Powell of *Aurora*) which had gone out from Tientsin in consequence of a report brought in about midday by Midshipman [Henry C.] Halahan of *Aurora*, whom I had sent out with an engine and one truck containing a 6-pounder gun and about 20 seamen (British, American, and two French sentries who had been placed on engine previously) to drive away a crowd of Chinese observed wrecking the line at less than a mile from station. Mr Halahan had gone on to the first bend, just out of sight, and became engaged with a party of Imperial troops, in uniform and well armed. Having killed several, and driven the rest towards Native City, he returned and reported.

I informed the Russians, who shortly afterwards asked for a train with the gun and some trucks to contain soldiers. They had gone out along line, and Lieutenant Powell accompanied them. I have reason to believe that they detached a small party to proceed under a bridge and cut off some Chinese, and that this party was completely cut off and destroyed. All Chinese near line were dispersed. The repairing train was joined up to this train of Russians, and both returned to Tientsin.

It was resolved by some of the commanding officers to capture the Chinese Military College which stood on the left bank of the river, opposite the Concessions, at about 200 or less than 300 yards from the bank. An enclosure or compound with a mud wall about nine feet high, with small trees and shrubs, stood between it and the river bank. The force of about 200 strong who were to attack, consisted of British Marines, about 50, under Major Luke, Senior Officer of the whole; Austrians, French, Germans, and Italians.

The attack began at about 3.00 pm. Shortly after the first shells of the bombardment of the Settlements burst overhead. The shell fire from the City was not at first accurate as regards elevation (I thought this, some thought differently), but speedily improved. Several shells burst down river, a hundred yards or so below the attack, probably intended to reach it.

The College was successfully carried and the guns found rendered useless. Most of the attacking force soon returned to the Tientsin side of river, but Major Luke's Marines remained for some time, fighting from room to room with the bayonet. A Marine hauled down the large yellow dragon flag from the roof, which he climbed. The building was then set on fire, and the force retired. One company of seamen had by this time crossed the river, in case of any further aid being necessary to cover our Marines. British casualties: 1 killed, 4 wounded, German 1 killed, Italians 2 wounded (4 per cent of force). This was a very busy day, the first of the siege and bombardment.

A patrol train, to hold a large force, was prepared to endeavour to communicate with Chun Liang Cheng. Owing to the displacement of parts of line, engine etc. it took all night to get it ready. Lieutenant Field of *Barfleur* had nearly 48 hours of uninterrupted work over this and the repairing train of day before.

June 18, 1900 – Monday
Train was got ready by 6.00 am, and went out at 6.15 with 750 Russian troops and 15 officers, having the search light and a 6-pounder truck in front. Train, light, and gun worked by British. Lieutenant Field in charge. In half an hour this train became engaged with the enemy. From 8.15 to 10.0 am it was repairing line, and occasionally using 6-pounder QF gun, while Russians were skirmishing. It continued fighting and repairing until after 2.0 pm when material gave out, and a return was decided on. The train arrived most opportunely to complete the defeat of the Chinese, who had for some time kept up a very heavy attack on the Railway Station. The Russians had found themselves pressed, and requested our support. Two Companies and a field gun were sent, and did good service. Commander Beatty was in command, and [the] gun was worked by Lieutenant Wright. The Russians cheered the gun, which took up a position one of their own had been withdrawn from. The Russians from the train were able to somewhat outflank the attacking Chinese, and Lieutenant Field used the 6-pounder QF with effect as long as possible. The attack was defeated and enemy fled into Native City.

The SS *Pei Ping*, a very large one for the river, arrived. She was owned by the Mining and Engineering Co. and was supposed to have come up to take away Mr Chang Yeh Mao,[6] the director, and friends. There was a deal of trouble over this steamer (which I detained then). First with Tientsin Volunteers,[7] and then with the ship herself. Her officers gave much trouble, some being usually drunk, and quarreling with each other. In various ways she was a perfect nuisance...

The Customs launch *Spray* was sent down, with British working her,[8] and took letters to Taku. The Captains [were] Cox of *Orlando*, an AB of *Aurora*, ERA *Barfleur* stokers, a French engineer officer [Seeberg] (good man), an official or other person from US Consulate [R.S. Maclay, Interpreter], and a pilot[9] (an ass).

The British ran this boat; the pilot was an ass, and got her aground several times. Finally the bluejackets carried the letters overland the last few miles.

The Volunteers, like many people in Tientsin, were affected by the wild rumours and beliefs flying about the Settlement. Suspicions, resting on the vaguest foundations – if any – were rife. Accusations were made by all sorts of people, and under cover of searching for concealed arms, a good many people were said to have broken open desks, safes etc. and searched for 'trade secrets' or pried into other people's business.

The lives of a certain few were hardly safe. Indeed accusations of treachery, double dealing, relations with the enemy etc. were common, and, in one case, the Consul was asked to get me to execute one person! The charge was absurd on the face of it, and a most natural and reasonable explanation was ready. Indeed, the accused has always rendered service and given useful information, I have reason to know, and was far less likely than some others to have held any communication with the enemy. Too much 'touch' with the Chinese was undoubtedly kept up, and too great faith in them held to, for too long a time, by certain people in Tientsin, who had been mixed up with them for years, in business or in various schemes and projects. Apparently most serious accusations were believed in, on suspicion principally, and there was intense dislike, amounting to hatred, felt towards a few, by many. Indeed, threats were openly made use of, and the most terrible charges talked of. There were many bright exceptions to this sort of thing, and though the first shelling cleared the streets of many, the few remained, doing such service as they could.

The 18th swelled the casualty list greatly, and there were many kind helpers to look after the wounded, who were at first brought to the Tientsin Club, which had been turned into a hospital.

June 19, 1900 – Tuesday
Proposal to leave Tientsin, and 'seek a better military base' nearer Taku, was made to me, and distinctly declined. (Letter from M. subsequently called this matter up) – It was never reported 'officially', but was known to a very few, and letter proves it, if proof should ever be wanted. Letter is in my possession. Nice kettle of fish would have resulted if Tientsin had been abandoned. Legations could have fallen, and Admiral's force been cut off, as Chinese could have turned full attention to these objects.

In addition to guns in [the] City, the enemy early placed two small guns (field guns) to the eastward of British Concession, close to railway embankment, between the compounds of two buildings formerly occupied by some railway officials, which opened fire on the Concession, causing much annoyance. An attempt to surprise these was made by a party under Commander Beatty, the Russians promising to make a flank attack from [the] railway station. The attacking party crossed the river and under cover of the houses reached a space under fair cover by a few houses and trees, not much exposed to the guns, if at all. Here they halted, waiting for the flank attack to develop.

The Russians took some time working out from Station, under cover of lines of carriages and trucks, and while the front attack was waiting, a large force of Chinese had worked round under cover of the railway embankment and a mud wall, and taken up a position on right flank of attack, completely enfilading them, on opening fire. This they did with the effect of causing serious casualties. Commander Beatty and two Lieutenants, A. Sterling of the *Barfleur* and G.B. Powell of *Aurora*, being severely wounded, and Mr [A.P.] Donaldson, midshipman of *Barfleur*, dangerously wounded (Mr Donaldson subsequently died of pneumonia supervening [3 July]), and several men wounded, more or less severely. A 9-pounder field gun had been brought into position on the Bund outside Consulate by this time, and was making fair practice after obtaining the range – which had to be done over the tops of intervening houses on the opposite bank of river.

The surprise having failed, and any chance of success having disappeared, the attacking force withdrew, and the Chinese finding the position of guns untenable in face of increasing accuracy of fire from 9-pounders on Bund, withdrew them, having brought up horses or ponies from under cover, but not before dangerously wounding Lieutenant Wright of *Orlando* who was on the Consulate roof, directing the gun, reporting each round. A shell exploded alongside gun, pieces flying up over Consulate, and a portion of Lieutenant Wright's skull was carried away. The services of a most valuable officer were thus lost to the defence, and since, most unfortunately, to the Navy, as after undergoing two operations and apparently making a mar-vellous recovery, he was invalided home, but succumbed months later under another operation. Wright and I had only changed places a few minutes when he was hit by shell which shook us up at gun.

There was promiscuous fighting in many places this day. Supports were sent as required. German steam pinnace fired on from disused mud fort below Military College grounds and run ashore by crew owing to damage to pipes or boiler. She was run ashore on Allied side of river.

Barricades were put up in various places, at a few street ends, along part of Bund, and round hospital. Few of any real service, but it kept some people employed and out of mischief. Mr James Watts of the Volunteers rode out about 9.30 pm accompanied by three Cossacks, to communicate with Taku. He carried no despatches for British. The ride was accomplished. It was a gallant piece of work, but as a matter of fact, did not hasten the reinforcements one minute, nor save one life in Tientsin. Much exaggeration as regards this ride has been shown. I, personally, never spoke to, or to my knowledge, saw Mr J. Watts until after Admiral Seymour's return (this by the way). The letter I sent by *Spray* on 18th was given by the blue jackets who went. *Spray* had been grounded by [the] pilot before reaching her destination, and the party proceeded overland. Some Chinese were arrested in the Settlements.

Skirmishes, exchange of artillery fire, and false reports and alarms continue.

June 20, 1900 – Wednesday
A search for arms produced some results. Cossacks went out south and had a brush with enemy.

Bombardment heavier in afternoon, more Chinese guns in position. Usual small attacks, and also the usual false alarms.

Two Chinese found with Boxer proclamations were shot. Much misrepresentation about this later, owing to a correspondent's bad or careless writing, apparently. The Shanghai papers published, and others followed suit, that 'Two women, found with Boxer documents, were shot by the British', or 'The women etc.' – probably careless writing on the part of the correspondent, and 'Two men' may have been misread and turned into 'The women' etc. I have reason to believe the correspondent is the same who wrote a pamphlet, 'Tientsin Besieged and After the Siege'[10], which is crammed with inaccuracies and idle rumours from cover to cover! The report annoyed me as I was the 'British Authority' alluded to.

A San Francisco paper subsequently published an 'interview' with one of the 'Besieged' in Tientsin, in which the besieged one states that he 'shot 56 or 57 Boxers from the roof of the Wool Mills[11] during a fortnight.' The mills were burnt out and no roof left – 4 days after bombardment commenced.

June 21, 1900 – Thursday
A heavy bombardment. Having only the abominable 9-pounder ML field gun and 16-pounder QF available, can do little to annoy or silence guns in Native City. The black powder smoke gives away the 9-pounder, and its range is poor. The 6-pounder QF is useful in scattering parties of Chinese to the westward. The Wool Mills were set on fire by shell, and burnt out. This deprived us of an excellent signal station, as only the walls of the tower were left, all stairs and inside destroyed. One Chinese, identified by Belgians from Paoting Fu, shot.

Distant puffs of smoke observed to the southeastward. Also firing to northwest. Shelling all day with an interval of quiet in afternoon.

June 22, 1900 – Friday
Mr Chang Yeh Mao and director Tong arrested (?) (their lives were not safe in Settlements).

A large body of troops, apparently all armed, observed to be advancing from Tongku direction. They were distant, and were seen from Gordon Tower. Heavy firing again heard in northwest. A courier, sent out by Russians, returned stating that Admiral Seymour's column was at Peitsang, with many sick and wounded, surrounded by Chinese.

A shell entered the hospital, luckily without exploding. It struck the wall behind Lieutenant Stirling and covered several patients with debris, mortar etc. from wall. More shelling, and apparently more guns mounted. Probably Imperial troops becoming available to man them. We subsequently learned that on this day the Admiral's column captured Hsi-ku arsenal or armoury, occupying it with main body in afternoon.

In evening (dark) 100 Marines under Captains Doig and H. Lloyd made an attempt to get to Tientsin, but soon got into conflict with Chinese, lost several, and were forced to return. Courier from Peking arrived, having started on 19th, bringing news that all Europeans had been ordered to leave within 24 hours. Observed puffs of smoke and signs of an engagement going on some miles away in Taku direction. Too far off to allow of sounds being heard. This was evidently the engagement in which the US Marines and Russians coming from Taku were repulsed and checked.

Knowing the position of the Admiral and party, [I] made arrangements to despatch a column to his relief, as soon as possible.

Search light observed to southeast during night (around 9 pm).

June 23, 1900 – Saturday
Captain Beyts RMA, HMS *Centurion*, in Admiral Seymour's force, was killed at Shiku [Hsi-ku Armoury] in early morning. In afternoon, the force mounted some guns and retaliated on Chinese by firing on them with good effect.

Some shelling and sniping early, also a fight near railway station. A runner got through from Admiral Seymour's column. Preparations made for the dispatch after dark of a column to join Admiral's force. As many as possible were to be sent, leaving Tientsin rather shorthanded, but it was imperative to help the detached column and risks must be taken at times. Rules won't always do. However, the arrival of the looked-for reinforcements from Taku changed the aspect of affairs. The British and Americans came into the Settlements and settled into quarters at once. Plenty of offers of godowns and various accommodation. The day of 'Claims' and Compensations had not yet set in. It was a case of 'placed at your disposal'.

A small force of Germans from Kiaotchao[12] specially sent to serve there. The Russians and Germans camped out north of Pei Yang Arsenal, between it and Military College compound.

General Stessel (or Stössel)[13] was in command of Russians. I received news from Colonel de Wozack[14] that the General would not hear of a column being sent out that night. I presume he and his force were pretty tired from their march and fighting. Endeavoured to get our original plan carried out, and column already told off, started, but was told (with, I believe, the sincere regret of Colonel de Wozack) that the General was in command, and no Russian troops could now move without his orders. This effectively stopped any move that day or night, and I determined to move over to see the Russian General myself, early next morning. Evening spent shaking down newcomers, more of whom kept dropping in. Much of their gear had been left at [the] railhead, the line being usable for a certain distance this side of Tongku.

June 24, 1900 – Sunday
Rode to Russian Camp and had a very satisfactory interview with the Russian General. (He had evidently rested, and was most courteous, as he continued to be to me personally, all the subsequent time while in company.) Made satisfactory plans, the General promising 1000 men and two guns, also if necessary or advisable, a demonstration of his force in support of relief column. As Russians were supplying by far the largest force, nearly one half of whole column, I agreed that no officer senior to Col. Shirinsky should be sent by us from settlements. Sorry, but it seemed only fair and courteous. Arranged for rendezvous, and for starting our force at about midnight. Details of reinforcements from Taku kept arriving, including one 12-pounder gun from *Terrible*, about the most welcome addition we could have had, as our abominable 9-pounder ML field pieces 'gave away' their position every round, with the thick smoke from the black powder, had very poor range, and were just as heavy as the new 12-pounder field guns. The ship's 12-pounder a most effective weapon, and the crew, from South African experience, [were] thoroughly acquainted with its capabilities. The dragging of the gun during the last part of its progress had been very trying, but its safe arrival was well worth the work.

The Settlement part of [the] Admiral's relief column was made up to about 900 strong, all nations. Commanders Cradock and Beatty went with it, the latter suffering from two severe bullet wounds, through left arm and wrist, received on the 18th. They started before midnight, and fell in on opposite bank of river, just alongside wall of the Military College compound.

The bridge of sampans and planks was not very stable, and two or three ponies slipped and fell into the river, or into the sampans or small junks.

The guide, the Consular Constable, named Brown (who turned out a regular bad lot subsequently, a looter, thief, and suspected murderer) led the column astray in two minutes. He soon after returned, and found his way to me full of complaints about his having been abused! He got no comfort.

Having seen column off, I returned with Captain Shimamura, the Japanese CO. An excellent man, always cool, perfectly calm and collected, and apparently without a care, and quite happy. He also was unable to accompany [his] column. Rank again. Sometimes it has drawbacks.

June 25, 1900 – Monday
At daylight a party with water, carts etc. and gear for the wounded was started from settlements to join up with relief column. Led by guides!! 'Who knew every foot of the country', of course. As usual, they failed to connect; so we had the mortification of seeing them all back shortly. They had met 'hundreds of Boxers' of course! And failed to hit off a column of men nearly 2000 strong, passing within 5 miles! Such are guides who know every foot of the country, shot over it, etc., etc!!

The City indulged in some shelling, directed both on relief column and on settlements. Having heard that the Hai Kwan Su or Western Arsenal was full of small arms ammunition, and probably other munitions of war, determined to shell the place with the *Terrible's* 12-pounder. (In fact, being debarred from Relief Column, [I] wanted a job and temper not pleasant till one was got.) Might as well blow up or burn the ammunition where it was, as let the Chinese have it to annoy us. They had a deal too much ammunition as it was, apparently. And any occupation of their attention would ease the trouble in Admiral's direction. Took 12-pounder out by Wool Mills – and before long had the Hai Kwan Su in a blaze. Mr [George] Gipps, midshipman, [15] with a 6-pounder gun on mud wall assisted, and planted several shells through the roof most effectively. As 12-pounder ammunition was not unlimited, having thoroughly set fire to Arsenal, retired the gun into Settlement, ready for another move in a couple of hours, against the City itself, or its guns, if able to locate them.

NB. Various merchants solemnly protested to the British Consul, urging him to represent to me that any bombardment of City would do an immense injury to their trade, as numerous undelivered cargoes of goods (paid for, I understand) were in canal and river, alongside banks. As if considerations of trade should be allowed to weigh against the urgent state of things then prevailing and the safe return of Admiral's Column. Such is dollar-grinding, and its effect on the 'business mind'.

The 12-pounder was placed on bank of river at end of Taku Road (about) in the French Concession. The adjacent houses had been deserted and were shelled and much injured. On opposite bank of river were huge heaps, mounds, of merchandise, salt etc., quite hiding the Native City from any one on the ground; but by getting on the roof of a house, a good view was obtainable, and the ingenuity of Mr Wright (gunner, *Terrible*) and his crew soon fixed up guides for aiming, instructions and directions, also reports of result of each shot being given from house roofs. After a few rounds, at Viceroy's *yamen* etc. had been fired, by great good fortune I happened to see the flash of a gun in City, which gun had just opened on our position. The state of the atmosphere suddenly changed, and became dark, just permitting the flash to show. We had tried for three days to locate these guns. The gun was brought to bear in their direction, and through the skillful adjustment of the guiding bamboo and attached mark (a white bag!) in about 20 minutes the two guns and the wall (battlement) on which they stood were in a heap of rubbish.

Some Chinese Regiment officers who were on the roof of house from which I spotted the Chinese guns, and directed ours, remarked that they had growled enough at the 12-pounder gun, in dragging it up, but they were well repaid for the trouble. Note: Some fires were started in the City by the 12-pounder also.

The settlements had a quiet night, and the columns coming in next morning were not shelled. A very satisfactory day's work, due to the *Terrible's* 12-pounder; Arsenal and its contents destroyed and the guns dismounted, giving rest to the Settlement and a quiet march in to the Admiral's column.

Mr Detring,[16] afterwards Acting Commissioner of Customs, has put on record in his official report, that the Admiral's column was not fired on, owing to the action of certain 'humane' Chinese, who besought the Viceroy not to fire on it! Well, that is his idea, or it suits him to say so, as he always has intrigued all his life with the Chinese, but I think the above account supplies the more probable reason for the silence of the guns! Take your choice.

In 48 hours or so the shelling began from them again, they having been dug out of the debris and remounted.

June 26, 1900 – Tuesday

After a night free from shelling, thanks to the damage done to the heavy guns of the enemy the evening before, we had the satisfaction of receiving Admiral Seymour's column, with its many wounded. I met [the] Admiral at [the] Railway Station. All stretchers and rickshaws we could muster were brought to help wounded in, and the whole force was shaken down, housed, etc. as quickly as possible. The Admiral first went to [the] Consulate, and was glad to get himself a bit more comfortable in my room. I hunted up a house for him. As usual, it was most kindly 'placed at his disposal' by the then tenant, but nevertheless the owner subsequently sent in a heavy bill for rent! Also claimed it for several weeks, but the Admiral only used it up to 11th July, on which date he returned to the *Centurion* at Taku Bar.

Col. A.R.F. Dorward, RE,[17] having been appointed Brigadier General to command the troops then in North China, arrived. The troops consisted of some RA (HK and Singapore battery), part of RW Fusiliers, part of 1st Chinese Regiment (Wei Hai Wei), part of Hong Kong Regiment. The Navy then present were about 1400 strong, but soon began to diminish, as many men were sent back to ships, and [the] sick, such wounded as could be moved, etc. were gradually sent down river.

Admiral appointed me (Capt. Bayly) Chief of Staff to himself, as of his staff, and to command specially all the Tientsin Defence force, retaining the officers who had been serving with me. Captain Burke directed to command 'Field Force' consisting of the rest, which Admiral told me I was to draw on to an extent I might require. 12-pounder gun was lent across river to pitch some shell into Pei Yang Arsenal from a spot just clear of Russian Camp, close by railway line.

June 27, 1900 – Wednesday
Admiral inspected hospitals, 'barracks', etc., Admiral Alexeieff[18] expected. Russians and Germans from Camp across river attacked Pei Yang Arsenal. Apparently found job rather harder than they expected. Sent over to us for reinforcements, 'supports'. Brigadier did not send any troops. Admiral said I was to send what force I could. Sent about 700 bluejackets and Marines, the whole under Captain Burke. They took position to north of Arsenal.

I saw the Chinese Regiment drawn up; waiting for orders, they said. Finding they were only too willing to take mine, I sent them out after the others. Our force soon changed their 'support' into an attack, carrying the side of Arsenal opposed to them, when the Chinese made a bolt. The Russian and German attack carried their side or angle, and the Chinese made off over the opposite side into the country. Three or four of the stores of powder and munitions were set fire to and destroyed by shelling. The Arsenal was a very large place, and contained many buildings, stores, factories, proof ground, etc. It was the great Arsenal of North China. It had a Mint, amongst other factories. There was an immense amount of valuable property in it, most of which found its way into the hands of the Russians.

The City batteries started again, and it may be said that more and more guns were gradually mounted from this time out, and were brought into action against us. Nothing much was done in the way of bombarding us for a couple of days, and luckily, as we were able to send for more guns – useful ones, not those wretched 9-pounder ML field pieces. It is disgraceful that in 1900 such things should form the field batteries of nearly every ship on the station.

Lieutenant Carlotte, Italian, died in hospital (Tientsin Chief) shot through chest. Had hoped he would pull through all right. He was most courteous and polite – till he lost consciousness. Sent a company to attend his funeral, the last one that had any attention from a force other than his own until after capture of Native City.

General Note

From the 28th June to 11th July there were almost daily small skirmishes and artillery duels. Thanks to the arrival of more 12-pounder QF guns from the *Terrible* (12-pounder 12 ... guns) and two 4-inch from *Algerine* and *Phoenix* at Taku, the allies were able to effectually reply to the enemy, and to annoy them in return. I insert only bare notice of this period, on loose sheets, as time will not allow more.

The British casualties in Naval Forces (varying in strength) between 26th June and 11th July were 14 killed, 53 wounded, 67 total. These included casualties at taking of Pei Yang Arsenal.

There was a reconnaissance in force on the 9th July, when the villages were swept of Boxers to the southwest.

Admiral Seymour and staff returned to *Centurion* at Taku on 11th. *Alacrity* and *Endymion* had gone after Pei Tang. *Centurion* went on 11th am. Sick, wounded fit to be moved, and weakly had been going for some time. Nearly all women and children had gone in first week in July, and some (civilians) with sick or wounded. Parties of *Barfleur*s, *Terrible*s, *Aurora*s, and *Orlando*s were left. Captain Bayly of *Aurora* remained as Senior Naval Officer, Tientsin. Captain Burke, *Orlando*, and Command. Beatty, *Barfleur*, remained until after capture of Tientsin Native City.

Capture of Native City

Assault or Attack, on 13th July; capture on 14th July at daylight or soon after.

The attack was made from two directions. The Russians and Germans (not many of the latter) and a few French (with small guns) formed the right attack, moving out from the Russian camp on north side of river, and working around to the east and north, the left attack consisting of Japanese, British, Americans and the other Allies, and remainder of French, moving out from Settlements, and working around to the southwest and up to the South Gate of City. The right attack was aided by one 4 inch gun, and the 12-pounder (British naval guns) close to Russian camp, and the left attack was covered by the remainder of the naval guns mounted on the mud wall, and western end of Meadows Road, clear of all houses in Settlement. One 4.7 recently received was not mounted, but the 4 inch [guns], three 12-pounders, and a half a dozen 6-pounders were in position.

As some of these guns could not see all the positions which were to be shelled, the batteries were joined up by telephone to the Gordon Tower (the western one), from which a clear view all round could be obtained. I attended to this spot from 3.45 am to about 3.0 pm and had a fine view of nearly all that occurred. Though it was intended to open fire at 4 am I waited till 4.20, on account of the mist and darkness, wishing to see as clearly as possible, consistent with covering the attacks and distracting enemy's attention. At first, and for some couple of hours, the enemy's return fire was directed mostly at the Settlements, which were heavily shelled. One shell wrecked part of the hospital in Tientsin Club, but luckily, all wounded but one had been moved, and he was not hurt by that shell. The Tower was struck, and one shell smashed up the best bedroom in tower, just below us on the top. The roof of German Club, about 80 or 100 yards away from our tower, was at first covered with sightseers, ink slingers etc., but the first shell which found its way near it (it was rather sheltered) cleared them out, and a good job too, as they asked silly questions.

As the attacking columns closed and were seen from the City, the fire on them from the walls was very heavy.

Very early, a magazine to the northeast on the Lutai Canal bank was blown up, said to have been by a French field gun. It was on the flank of the Russian attack. Several Cossacks were unhorsed, and the Russian General Stessel was injured by falling debris. His arm was damaged. The sight from the summit of [the] Tower was very fine. The column of smoke must have been quite 600 feet high, and was partly seen from Taku, I heard afterwards. The Tower rocked severely several times, when the earth waves reached it, and the sensation was not altogether pleasant up there. I need not go into details, as so many know the circumstances, but I may say the fire of the naval batteries was highly spoken of. I have received a letter from the CO of one body of foreign troops, in which he says that 'the capture was due to the Naval guns'! Even allowing for compliments, it is more the truth than such statements usually are. Nothing but accurate and sustained fire of guns capable of smashing the upper part of the wall, and blowing it and its defenders away, could have effected the stoppage of their rifle and – fire, which was very heavy. And they stuck very pluckily to their posts. The Americans lost heavily, through moving across fire in fours. In afternoon, things did not look quite rosy, and the ground gained was only just held, though firing ceased. Enough to add that it was held, and the Chinese, finding allies still there at daybreak, practically abandoned the position, and the peace was won.

Author's note: The casualties at the capture of Native City were far heavier in proportion to numbers engaged than in any South African 'battle'. The percentage in fact [at] Spion Kop alone (for which no clasp was given) approached, in percentage of losses, those at Tientsin in June and July 1900.

Notes

[1] Captain Henry T.R. Lloyd, Royal Marines.

[2] 200 Russians, 58 French.

[3] Also referred to as Chun Hiang Cheng and Chun Ling Cheng on various contemporary maps.

[4] Count G. du Chaylard, French Consul General at Tientsin.

[5] G.W. Hancock, Traffic Inspector at Tientsin for Imperial Railways of North China.

[6] Director General, Chinese Engineering and Mining Company; of the Bund, German Concession, Tientsin.

[7] A militia composed of male residents.

[8] The *Spray* was manned by British sailors, not officers.

[9] Captain J.W. Stavers, Taku Tug and Lighter Company.

[10] Tientsin Besieged and After the Siege: by The Correspondent of The North China Daily News'. Published in Shanghai by North China Herald, 1900. Second edition, 1901.

[11] The new Wool Mill, owned by Wu Jim-pa, was the first example of Western-style manufacturing in North China. It was also an excellent vantage point for the defenders of Tientsin. It was destroyed completely.

[12] Third Seebatalion, based at Tsingtau.

[13] General Anatole Mikailovitch Stoessel (1848–1915) was replaced as commander of the Russian army in China late in July by General Nikolai Petrovich Linievitch, who actually led the Russian soldiers in the march to Peking. Stoessel later achieved international recognition as the commander of Port Arthur during the Russo–Japan War. He surrendered this important Russian base to the Japanese in January 1905. He returned to Russia, where he was sentenced to death; this sentence was not carried out, and he was pardoned in 1909.

[14] Usually referred to as Colonel Wogack (also Vogak). By 1903 he was a Major-General in the Russian Army, serving as military attaché to Peking and Tokyo.

[15] Orlando.

[16] Gustav Detring was a German who had joined the Chinese Maritime Customs Service in 1865, was promoted to Commissioner in 1872, and was posted to Tientsin from 1877 until 1904.

[17] Brigadier General Arthur R.F. Dorward was 52 years old when he arrived in Tientsin from India. He had fought in campaigns along the Northwest Frontier (Afghanistan) and in Burma.

[18] Admiral Eugene Ivanovich Alexeieff (often spelled as Alexeiev) was born in 1843 in Armenia. He rose through the ranks of the Russian Navy and by 1900 he was in command of all Russian interests in the Far East, both civil and military. He was based at Port Arthur. He actually reached Tientsin on 30 June, and stayed at the home of the Russian merchant M.D. Batouieff. (The Russian Consulate, which was located in the French Concession, had been destroyed earlier in the siege.)

General Notes
by Captain Edward H. Bayly

The behaviour of the residents, or of many of them, on first arrival of naval forces (including Marines) was very hospitable. Club was open to us all, many had quarters in private houses, and godowns and other shelters were 'placed at our disposal'. While the place was under fire, offers of quarters for the reinforcements expected were common.

The Volunteers also, at first, rendered service, and some of the mounted ones patrolled efficiently. The 'Home Guard', as a body of residents called themselves, were not of any use; and indeed, it was said that one of them raised the first false alarm, and sent the women and children, many half dressed, to the Gordon Hall to seek shelter. I found numbers of them in Victoria Road or coming in from going around the Lines on [the] night in question and expressed my surprise. Of course, as usual, the real culprit could not be traced. The real commencement of the siege soon weeded out the numbers of people who had been so 'eager' to display their martial ardour. I may here say that as far as I was able to observe, the women behaved far better than a great many men. Many [men] even took refuge in the cellars of the Gordon Hall, occupying space intended for the women and children. This I discovered too late.

The wildest rumours originated amongst a lot of people who used to collect under the archway leading into the courtyard of the Gordon Hall. Many of these have been given to the world in print as facts. The writer of a pamphlet called 'Tientsin Besieged and After the Siege' is responsible for thus disseminating many false, exaggerated, and distorted statements.

The Volunteers gradually got tired, and the numbers fell off. There were only about 19 left some time before the Native City was taken, and only 3 were still doing duty on that day. In fact, as a corps, they had ceased to exist. General Dorward said that the fact of their declining to undertake certain duty, sentries etc., when required by Captain Burke, *de facto* broke them up. Nevertheless, their original list was submitted to me by their Captain, with a view to their 'obtaining medals'! I remarked at the time that I had not yet heard of any medal. This was in 1900 (July or August).

A few men did excellent work, and a few fair work. Many did nothing. They lived out of sight when any shelling was going on. A former Chief

119

Engineer RN, Mr Walker, did steady, good, and unremitting work throughout, and, aided by Engineers and Stokers from [the] naval force, kept the waterworks and gas works going. The men from the Navy mended and worked the boilers and engines, under fire frequently. After war was over, the local inkslingers spattered local men with praise, and ignored the Navy. They also bestowed indiscriminate praise on another foreign power, giving nearly the whole credit of the defence to them. Well, they were all friendly with us, and there was really no time for politics or squabbles at first, nor were either indulged in till the many generals arrived; but had the British not refused to entertain the idea, Tientsin would have been left 'in search of a better military base'!!

Some ladies were extremely kind and attentive to the wounded and, later, the sick. The ladies have since taken over care of the Cemetery, and had it tidied and kept decent. The Navy owes them thanks for this.

The wounded set an example to all. The sick, naturally enough, were more depressed. Enteric dysentery, and the usual illnesses of a campaign do not render the patients lively. The wounded were most cheerful, at any rate in the British hospitals.

Doubtless much good work has been done by many missionaries, but undoubtedly many highly exaggerated, even totally imaginative, stories were circulated in European and American papers by small numbers of various missions. All people in any profession or calling are not good. Some of the stories appearing in print were hardly reconcilable with facts as they occurred.

And when the danger was over, the rush to send in claims for compensation was absolutely ludicrous. The first great sum was on the Navy, who were asked to pay the most absurd and iniquitous claims. Huge amounts were claimed as 'rent' for godowns, originally 'placed at the disposal' of the Navy. In fact, at the beginning, it was a case of 'take what you like', 'please occupy my godown', etc. etc., and afterwards, it was a case of 'pay,' 'pay'.

As before stated, there were many good, kindhearted, and pleasant people, and there were also lazy, idle barloafers, who never helped, but hindered or did nothing. The usual crowd of hangers-on of armies soon gathered, directly after the Capture of Native City, indeed, more than enough seemed to be in hiding before, and to crop up out of the ground directly the prospect of loot appeared. The desire for loot even seized the diplomatic representatives of certain powers, two certainly (neither British), and they were busy amongst the busiest.

The irresponsible and untrained or inexperienced so-called 'Correspondents' [or] 'war correspondents' were, with few exceptions, very casual, and apparently any story was good enough. Either the correspondent blindly took what the 'staff' told him, or he launched out with 'high falutin'' and his own untrammelled imagination. The 'locals' subsequently showered praise on any local man who did anything, magnifying very ordinary discharge of duty into heroism, writing up local mediocrity if in the case of a local 'somebody'. First arrivals either stated Tientsin to be uninjured, or running gore, with corpses in heaps. Both statements gross exaggerations. If a man first came across a shelled and burnt-out quarter, he said all was in ruins; if Meadows Road, or parts of Victoria Roads and crossing it, parts, I say, he said, 'Oh, no great harm done, all the yarns we heard were false!'

Neither of these statements was correct. The 'claim'-making, and money-hunting, craze was in such full swing by end of August, that when the Naval Brigade (including Marines) left Tientsin for Taku and their ships, after Capture of Peking, only one man (Mr Moffat,[1] one of the locomotive Superintendents who had been with Admiral Seymour's March) went to the Bund to bid farewell to the men whose early arrival in June had saved their lives and property! Private friends, made there by a few officers and men who left later, did say goodbye to, and see them off; but it was as I state when the large body of the Brigade left finally.

And moreover, a bill for a man's grave was sent in through the military to the Navy; the said man, an AB, having been too ill to leave with the rest when the last of the Naval Forces left, and had died a few days later. As this man had served and fought for Tientsin for three months, he might, one would think, have had free burial. Such was the difference between the beginning and the end of the troubles at Tientsin. The municipal exchequer was hardly much swelled by the cost of one mud grave, nor would it have been revived by the loss of the amount.

The Taku Tug and Lighter Company charged extortionately for the use of their tugs and lighters, conveniently ignoring the fact that they were derelict up and down the river, that anyone might have looted or destroyed them. They also, in making out their first bill or claim, quite omitted to mention the fact that $5000 had been advanced them by the Admiral to enable them to pay coolies, etc. They grumbled and growled, and others did so for them, protesting that they could work the lighters and tugs better than the Navy. By the bye, the Navy kept them in repair for weeks, besides manning them. Ultimately, when the tugs and lighters were handed back, they could not run them and had to request the British authorities to keep them on. Though the Company's officials said they were being ruined, the Company paid a very large dividend indeed to the shareholders, and said officials took prolonged leave! This hardly looked like ruin. The writer of 'Tientsin Besieged' of course praised up the Company, being a locally worked affair; and said that many had wondered why the superior knowledge of the Company had not been made use of, as they could do things much better than the Navy! This gentleman calmly ignored the fact that when the tugs and lighters were handed over, the Company could not run them at all, for many a day.

The transport arrangements seemed to have been very irregular, and even at times chaotic, at Taku, Tongku and Sinho. As far as Tientsin is concerned, I can state from personal observation that lighters were cleared in from 8 to 10 hours by the Naval forces at first, and on the Secretary's (Company Secretary's) own showing, this was the best time the Company's own regularly trained gangs took. When the Navy handed over to the Military, lighters occupied in clearing 2 to 8 days. Not under 2. The waste of time was sinful. Coolie Corps were timed on one occasion (and they were at least 800 strong), when they left off work at 10 am for a meal, or meal and prayers, or at any rate they knocked off. They were to turn to at noon, or a quarter past. The Commissariat Sergeants (Very important gentlemen) did not trouble between 10.0 and noon, there being no coolies at work; and at noon the Sergeants went to dinner. Coolies, finding no sergeants, did not turn to till Sergeants came back, at 2.0 pm. Thus 4 hours were lost. And this in wartime on service. The Military Signallers, when they took on, also required 2 hours for dinner, and ensured getting it by the simple expedient of going away from the signal station for the time required.

After all naval explosion parties and their stores had returned to the ships, a junk and Japanese steamer sank and blocked the river about two or three miles down. The Military were impressed early in the day, but it was past 11 am on the next day before they sent any of the RE part down to see about it, though a tug had been kept ready from the first, by the Navy, to go with them.

The 8 hours working day does not suit in war but apparently some of the military get as near it as they can.

The system of the two services is as different as can be, apparently, and there must be changes in the military one, if disasters are to be prevented.

As far as North China went, the hard fighting finished with the fall of the Native City on July 14th. As that event was not followed up promptly, chiefly owing to scares down south, the Chinese collected at Peitsang and Yangtsun, at which places there was a little fighting, but not much. The Russians and Japanese had some at Peking. Much of this was due to the Russians moving off for the final march before the agreed-upon time. As they arrived at Peking long before the others, the Chinese withdrew from other posts to meet their attack, and consequently the British got into Peking first with scarcely any opposition. That was chance, but it was largely, if not entirely, brought about by the action of the Russians in marching before the time agreed upon by the allied leaders.

The German troops did not leave Tientsin till days after the others, and had no fighting at all *en route* to Peking. This must have been very annoying to them, as it was not their fault that they did not arrive earlier.

Their sailors, under Captain Von Usedom, had done capital work with the first expedition under Admiral Seymour. Great cordiality prevailed between the British and German sailors and naval officers, who were always friendly.

Note

[1] J. Moffat, Locomotive Inspector, Fengtai.

Account of
Sydney Adamson, American
War Correspondent

Sydney Adamson was born in Dundee, Scotland, and trained in London art schools. He began to earn his living as an artist in 1892 as an illustrator for various English periodicals. By the end of the 1890s he was working for American magazines such as The Century, Harper's Monthly *and* Scribner's, *largely illustrating and writing about his own travel adventures.*

In 1899, Leslie's Weekly *sent Adamson to the Phillipines, and in June of 1900 they sent him to from the Phillipines to China with the 9th US Infantry. They reached Tientsin on 11 July and went into battle on 13 July.*

I was roused in the early morning of the 13th of July by the quiet voice of General Liscum calling my name. I jumped to my feet and saluted him as he stood in the Chinese court-yard, the moonlight falling on his gray hair. We had talked together, before retiring on the 12th, for nearly an hour. I had asked for an orderly to waken me, Captain Noyes said he would see to it; but the kind general, who had been a friend to me from the first hour we met, months ago in Tarlac, came and awakened me himself. One remembers many little things about a man which happen on the day that he is killed. General Liscum, Captain Noyes, and myself were all that sat down to breakfast of the headquarters mess. The room has bare brick walls, and at one end is a pile of Chinese benches. Up among the beams is suspended a sedan chair. The headquarters mess still sits down in that room, but it is different now, for the table is turned across the room and a Chinese coolie swings a crazy *punkah* to fan us and keep away the flies. The general and Captain Noyes are not among the number of the mess, but Captain Noyes will come back some day. The barracks are low Chinese buildings including two court-yards, with many lamps hanging from the roof of the inclosure. Straggling, wall lined alleyways run along and across the outer parts and connect with the great godowns where the tribute rice for Peking is stored.

No bugles were sounded. Quietly, save for the murmur of voices and the moving of feet, the Ninth had its early breakfast, then filled its haversacks and canteens for a day in the field, and the two battalions present, the first

124

and second, formed up on the common outside in the moonlight. The roll was called, the report given to the general and duly noted by the adjutant. Then everybody's attention was turned to finding the road on which the other troops of the column were to advance. Two roads were discovered, and as it might be either one, General Liscum had his troops drawn up on the space between.

We had not waited many minutes when the Japanese cavalry began to file past on the farther road. Then came the Austrian blue-jackets, only forty men, and after them more Japanese. Troops now began to come up the other road – Welsh Fusiliers, the Wei-Hai-Wei regiment, American marines, and some gun detachments. General Dorward, with his arm in a sling (injured by a fall from his horse), directed the formation of the column near the Taku gate. The position designated for the Ninth was the rear of the column, just after the British naval brigade. The naval brigade was late in getting up, so the Ninth fell in ahead of it. Just as we approached the Taku gate General Liscum ordered a rear guard thrown out. Captain Noyes went down the line with this order. It was then that the general turned to me and expressed certain misgivings about the day's work. It seemed to him that our column was very deficient in numbers, and he had the uncomfortable feeling of a man who goes into a fight without knowing just what is expected of him. However, he said that there was to be a meeting of officers on the field before the fight, and then the plan was to be revealed. This did not take place.

As we turned from our southerly march to the right, and in a westerly direction, the gray light of morning began to show us the way. We were halted just around the turn. Evidently something had delayed the head of the column. During this halt we were overtaken by the British naval brigade. When the column resumed its march the Ninth waited till the naval brigade had assumed its proper position and then fell in behind it. It was then daylight. The column moved due west along a narrow country road. The fields that bordered the road were richly cultivated, showing abundance of market-garden produce. Soon we left the road and, crossing a ridge of earth, we saw the whole line of our column stretching across the fields, turning more and more to the north to face the arsenal. The steady rattle of infantry fire came across the field to us, and then the serious artillery duel was fairly started. As we marched I counted the shots from our position, and at that time they averaged fourteen a minute. The British 4.7 and four-inch naval guns were mingling their heavy boom with the sharper reports of the other pieces. Soon the Chinese gunners in the walled city turned their attention to our advancing column and ugly shells came ripping through the air, sometimes ursting uncomfortably near to us and sending clouds of brown sand flying into the air.

We doubled to close up the column, all the time swinging more to the

north. Ahead of us, and right across our front, stretched a great mud wall
with a canal skirting its base on our side. This wall lay between us and the
city wall, a mile away. Facing our centre was a large brick gateway in the
wall, with studded iron gates. At first the Chinese were in force on the mud
wall and in the arsenal, which is just within the gate, but they gradually gave
way before our galling infantry fire and the steady rat-tat-tat of the machine
guns. Then the field guns swung into position, and before the triple fire the
Chinese abandoned the arsenal and the allied forces rushed over the narrow
bridge that crossed the canal to the gateway. Some of the field-pieces and
machine guns were run through the gate, and they, with some infantry,
began to clear the broad plain dotted with mud houses that lies between this
outer mud wall and the high brick battlements of the Chinese city of
Tientsin, more than a mile beyond.

When the Ninth arrived at its position abreast of the gateway and in the
rear of the British naval brigade, the sharp 'ss' 'ss' of the bullets came as
regularly as the tick of a watch. We were preparing to lie down when I heard
a 'plunk' and a grinding sound, followed by a moan. I turned my head, to
find a poor fellow gripping his gun, every nerve strained to keep his balance.
He seemed dazed. I told him to drop his gun, and held him while he loo-
sened his belt. Then a hospital-corps man came, and together we dragged
him over a ditch to the partial cover of a low mud-heap, where Dr Morrow
dressed him. I lay here for a while, watching the fight and admiring the cool
behavior of British and Americans, who remained in this position under a
galling fire – a man was hit every few minutes – with cool unconcern. A
British soldier sat on the wrong side – that is, the side nearest the enemy – of
a mud-heap, holding a pony, which quietly flicked the flies with its tail and
tried for the stalks of grass within reach. The horse realized nothing, but the
man sat watching the bullets kicking up the sand at his feet, and seemed
more unconcerned than the animal.

A terrific explosion shook the whole earth. Away over to the east of north
a huge column of smoke rose. From the base spars of ragged smoke radiated
like the spokes of a wheel. Slowly the column ascended perpendicularly in
the still air, each moment assuming grander proportions, until the tiny spires
and houses of the foreign settlement were but the speck-like houses of a
distant village at the foot of a colossal mountain. On the top of this pillar a
great cloud-shaped ball of smoke bent over a little to the west. For a few
intense moments bullets and shells were forgotten and the forces in reserve
were lost in wonder at this unexpected sight. It was the explosion of a
Chinese magazine over on the plain beyond the city, that had furnished the
spectacle. I went over to where General Liscum was standing, watching the
artillery. Captain Noyes was near him. We talked a few moments, and I
asked his permission to go ahead to the wall. He gave it. I started alone

across the plain, the air filled with the soft 'ss' of the bullets. All around the earth sent up tiny puffs of dust where they struck. As I neared the gate I saw a rectangular mud wall with a sheet of water at its base on the side from which I approached. By the water-edge were some British blue-jackets, with ammunition piled in a rickshaw. I imagined there would be some protection from the wall in front, and sat down beside them to rest from the heat and the bullets. Two Japanese soldiers sat down beside me. In a few seconds one of them was tugging at my sleeve. I turned and saw a hole in his companion's leg. He handed me his first-aid bandage and I dressed the wound.

The Ninth had now been ordered to advance, and they were crossing the field in open skirmish order. I joined them, and soon we were massed among troops of all nations in the shelter of the great wall, while the shells ripped the air overhead with a sound like the tearing of cloth, and the bullets hissed on their way to the field that we had just left. Through the gateway, the ruined Chinese buildings were dimmed by artillery smoke, and the figures of the men could be seen moving quickly as they served the guns. On each side of the gate stood rows of Japanese ponies. Between them the neatly-capped heads of the Japs could be seen. Heads of tall Mohammedans and Sikhs, with their huge turbans, towered above the small Japanese; masses of blue-shirted Americans rubbed shoulders with the khaki-covered Welsh fusilliers; British middies in khaki rode about on Chinese ponies. It was a jumble of races from lands that touch around the earth. A mile away, over the wall and across the plain, the Chinese hordes on the ramparts of their great walls were hurling shells and bullets defiantly at the combined great nations of the world, for from the other side the Russians and Germans were attacking.

Through the great gateway the tide of human beings surged back and forth. With hoarse cries the Japs rushed their guns through. Then the pack-animals with ammunition followed. They ran forward amid the ruins of buildings into a mist of blue smoke where dim figures were moving, and the unceasing rat-tat-tat of the machine-guns was pointed by the heavy crashes from the field-pieces. Some infantry was sent through and the fire of the small arms sounded like the crackling of tiny twigs in a great blaze. Overhead the Chinese shells tore the air. One struck the wall of the gate and covered our clothes with dry earth. Soon the Sikh artillery mounted the wall overhead and the concussion from their guns shook us as we stood.

Now the tide of men had stopped rushing through the gate and a bloody stream of wounded began to flow back. Twisted, dirty heaps that a few minutes before were bright, tidy Japanese soldiers were brought out and laid in rows. On their clothes were great Venetian-red patches, grayed with mud and covered with swarms of ravenous flies. A few writhed and groaned; others lay still. One seldom looks twice to tell the dead; there is a color, a something indescribable, that tells when life is gone. Often the living were more awful to look at than the dead. I had seen men shot with bullets, but this was the first time that I had seen bodies mangled by shells.

We had left the barracks and formed in the column at three o'clock am. By 7.30 am we had lost one man killed and seven men wounded. General Liscum was grieved at these losses, occurring while the Ninth was still inactive. I talked with him for a while on a sand-heap beside the gate, just before the Ninth went over the wall to take up the terrible position which it held all day. Every one was interested at this juncture in a body of troops moving out by the west and south which had the appearance of Chinese cavalry, and whose object seemed to be to flank our left and drive us from our sheltered base behind the wall. All day long this body caused some anxiety, but General Dorward drew off some of the marines and sent them up the wall to its western end to watch their movements and check any attempt to gain the wall at that point.

At five minutes to eight General Liscum led his men over the mud wall and started up the road among the smoking ruins of the Chinese houses, across the little bridge over the canal and around by the arsenal to the open plain, then down the road to a point where they deployed. The Ninth met a sharp fire on its right flank from a dense group of Chinese mud houses over a bend in the canal. This caused General Liscum not to interpret his orders to support the Japanese too literally. With true military judgment he considered it his duty to face and silence, if possible, this destructive fire. General Dorward, in his letter to the Ninth Infantry after the event, appreciates the value of this work and acknowledges that by drawing the fire on itself and vigorously attempting to silence it, the Ninth performed a signal service in the fight, and prevented a heavier loss among the other troops, at the same time allowing them freer play in the centre.

I followed the Ninth over the wall and down among the Chinese grave mounds and ruined houses beside the canal. Our regiment dashed up the road past the Japanese pack horses, and over the wooden bridge, then swung to the right round by the arsenal. I lay down on one of the graves and watched the fight. On the right the field-pieces were firing from the arsenal. Overhead the Sikh artillery was adding to the din. Shells were screaming through the air and sometimes striking the dry sand into clouds among the houses and the graves; and a perfect hail of bullets chipped the walls or buried themselves in the dry mud. I watched a little body of French soldiers coming down toward the gate. A shell struck among the foremost group and toppled them over like ninepins.

There was nothing lacking, in this arena of fire and death, of those elements of spectacular and dramatic interest which the world associates with war – the dead horses and human corpses; the ruined, smoking buildings; the roar of guns and the rattle of infantry; the long train of wounded and the

Admiral Seymour and Staff, photographed on board HMS *Centurion*.
Left to right: Flag Lieutenant F.A. Powlett, Flag Captain J.R. Jellicoe, Admiral Sir E.H. Seymour and Secretary F.C. Alton.

Chinese soldiers of Wei-hai-wei Regiment in ceremonial dress. This regiment was trained and staffed by British officers. The Chinese troops of this regiment served with distinction during the Boxer campaign.

Horsemen on the road from Tientsin to Peking. *Photograph: Sanshichiro Yamamoto.*

Representatives of the Allied Army and Navy. *Photograph: Sanshichiro Yamamoto.*

The Taku forts. *Photograph: Nathan J. Sargent.*

The Tientsin volunteer militia, mainly composed of Tientsin residents, primarily businessmen, whose services were important during the siege of Tientsin. *Photograph: Nathan J. Sargent.*

Allied soldiers and sailors on the Peiho River at Tientsin. *Photograph: Nathan J. Sargent.*

Barricade of sacks of rice near the Emens residence, Tientsin, June 1900. Emens, an American merchant and local judge, was Nathan Sargent's employer at the trading company. *Photograph: Nathan J. Sargent. Courtesy, Peabody Essex Museum, Salem, MA.*

Russian Marines in Tientsin, 1900. *Photograph: Nathan J. Sargent. Courtesy, Peabody Essex Museum, Salem, MA.*

The arsenal at Tientsin in July 1900 after the siege. *Photograph: C.F. O'Keefe.*

Battery 'F' 5th U.S. Artillery, commanded by Captain Henry J. Reilly, in action at Peitsang, 5 August 1900. *Photograph: C.F. O'Keefe.*

Funeral service for Captain Henry J. Reilly, 5th U.S. Artillery. Reilly was killed in action on 15 August 1900 and buried at the U.S. Legation the next day. *Photograph: C.F. O'Keefe.*

A pavilion occupied by Hotel De Pekin within the British Legation compound during the siege. *Photograph: C.A. Killie.*

A Boxer is about to be beheaded. *Photograph: Sanshichiro Yamamoto.*

Above: The elegant house of Henry Cockburn, Secretary of the British Legation, barricaded during the siege. *Photograph: C.A. Killie.*

Left: The British Legation compound with the entrance to a bomb-proof cellar in the foreground and the Legation Chancery in the background. Matron Lambert and two nursing assistants sit at the entrance to the Chancery, which was used as a hospital during the siege. *Photograph: C.A. Killie.*

The six 'fighting parsons' at Fort Cockburn, a wooden platform behind Cockburn's house on which a Nordenfeldt gun was mounted, manned here by Sergeant J. Murphy, Royal Marines. Killie is the man standing at the rear of the group. This photograph was taken during the July truce. Reverend Stonehouse (dressed entirely in white) was later killed. *Photograph: C.A. Killie.*

Water gate under the wall of the Tartar City, Peking, through which British troops entered on 14 August 1900. *Photograph: Royal Engineers.*

Above: Russian soldiers at Tung Pien Men Gate, Peking, on 14 August 1900. *Photograph: C.F. O'Keefe.*

Left: A hole created by British troops in the wall of the Imperial City, very close to the British Legation compound. *Photograph: Royal Engineers.*

Ruins of the Legation Quarter, Peking, after the siege. *Photograph: Royal Engineers.*

The student interpreters' house at the British Legation, after the siege. *Photograph: C.A. Killie.*

The entrance to the British Legation compound after the siege. The barricade has been removed. The canal runs in the foreground. *Photograph: Royal Engineers.*

Sir Claude MacDonald, posed in the British Legation compound with Customs Volunteers – men from the Chinese Maritime Customs who had been active defenders during the siege. *Photograph: C.A. Killie.*

Group of American missionaries, in the British Legation compound, who had endured the siege. Miss Andrews is seated second from the right. *Photograph: C.A. Killie.*

British Staff at a Lama temple in Peking, after the siege. *Photograph: Royal Engineers.*

A Boxer standard-bearer, with spear and wicker shield, posed for a souvenir picture for the troops. *Photograph: Royal Engineers.*

Field Marshal Count Von Waldersee reviewing Allied troops on 1 January 1901. The troops paraded in front of the Imperial Palace. *Photograph: Royal Engineers.*

Officers' quarters of the British 12th Royal Field Artillery. The 12th Battery R.F.A. remained in Peking during the autumn of 1900 and winter of 1901. *Photograph: Royal Engineers.*

Troop 'L', 6th U.S. Cavalry in 1901 on a sightseeing expedition in the Avenue of Statues, Ming tombs, Peking. *Photograph: C.F. O'Keefe.*

New South Wales contingent leaving Tientsin, 26 March 1901. *Photograph: Nathan J. Sargent. Courtesy, Peabody Essex Museum, Salem, MA.*

hideously mutilated dead; the shells bursting in mid-air or exploding on the earth, while the plainly visible fragments flew up in a fan-shaped spread amid a cloud of driven sand; the quiet heroism of the officers, and the dash of the men; and added to all this there was the new element, the union of races alien until they met on the field, and the little acts of kindness between the white and the brown races where words could not be spoken. With all its horrors it was grand. On such a day the commonplace and the ordinary are driven from one's mind. The game is a mighty one and the stakes are life and death. Until one has seen men in battle it is impossible to truly understand the human race or grasp the fullness of words that speak the history of nations.

Sometimes a lull would come in the firing on one side or the other – a temporary lack of ammunition at the guns, or a pause for observation among officers directing the fire. But these intervals were of short duration, and the cracking of rifles, mingled with the heavier report of the ponderous muzzle-loading two-men guns which the Chinese used to help out their musketry, never ceased from dawn until sunset. Between ten and eleven it was reported at the gate that General Liscum was mortally wounded. Then came the report of his death. Next, Major Regan was reported hit, and Captain Davis, of the marines, killed. Not an hour went past without another name to the list. The Japanese loss was appalling. Terrible rows of dead and wounded were lying side by side behind the great mud wall. Pitiful attempts at shades were put up to keep away the rays of the merciless sun, that beat straight down on the burning sand. Ghastly patches of ravenous flies swarmed on every wound and every bandage. Every little bloody rag or drop of blood that had fallen on the sand was black with this living plague, and the air was alive when a movement disturbed their horrid feast.

In the afternoon General Dorward sent a detachment of Mohammedan infantry to further protect the flank from the distant enemy, which still hovered off in the southwest.

I did not see Lieutenant Lawton when he brought in the message from Major Lee to General Dorward. It was a daring thing, bravely done. When the first dash of the Ninth had brought them well up to the position which they finally held, Major Regan and Major Lee discussed the situation. General Liscum approached, and as Major Regan walked away he was hit. Then Major Lee went along the line to attend to his men. He turned to look for the general, and, not seeing him, called out to know where he was. Lieutenant Frazier answered: 'He is here, sir, wounded – badly wounded.' Then Major Lee took command. Some alterations were made in the disposition of the men, and they were crowded down in a curve, many of them in the mud and water. Even then a cross-fire reached some of the men. At this point a deep canal prevented the Ninth from rushing the enemy's position.

It was a desperate position, within a hundred yards of a dense cluster of houses swarming with Chinese. At three points along the bank of the canal on the Chinese side, behind sandbags, guns were placed. One was a machine-gun. The ammunition was running low, and it was feared the Chinese might find a way of crossing the canal. Retreat was impossible without a loss greater than the advance would cause. To retreat under the guns of this watchful enemy meant the annihilation of these two battalions of the Ninth. Major Lee decided that some attempt should be made to get news of the Ninth's situation to General Dorward. Lieutenant Lawton volunteered to go. About ten o'clock, accompanied by an orderly, he started across the fire-swept distance to the gate in the outer mud wall. Reckless exposure was useless, fatal; so he took advantage of every cover and delivered his message safely to the British general. The return journey was made in safety till the very last jump, when the bullets that stiffened his right arm and grazed his head found their mark. The orderly, Philip Hoyle, trumpeter of G company, made both journeys unhurt. The outcome of Lawton's message was that General Dorward sent a company of American marines, under Captain Fuller, and half a company of British blue-jackets to support the Ninth. That regiment did all that any troops could do; they lay tight, held their position, and sent in an effective fire at every yellow target. Between four and five in the afternoon Lieutenant-Colonel Coolidge arrived with two companies of the third battalion. He immediately saw General Dorward, and suggested taking in water and ammunition to relieve the men. General Dorward very wisely held that to send in new men only meant fresh and unnecessary losses, out of all proportion to the little good they could accomplish. It would be dusk in a few hours, and under cover of the darkness fresh troops could safely go in, cover the retreat, and assist in bringing off the wounded.

In a little while Captain Noyes came in alone. His was a pitiful tale. Wounded early in the day, he had lain in the shelter of a wrecked house. About three o'clock he decided that he would stand it no longer, and he had a strong hope that the information he could bring to General Dorward might be of use in devising a way to relieve the Ninth. He had been shot through the left leg and the right arm, yet he crawled into a ditch and for two weary hours paddled and crawled through the filthy water, taking cover from the mud banks, till at last he came out, pale and exhausted, and sat at the base of the mud wall among the wounded Japanese. He pointed out with a trembling hand to General Dorward, on a map, the exact position of the men and the possibility of trying to shell the Chinese out of the mud houses over the canal. But that idea had to be given up; it was too dangerous, since the Americans lay but a stone's-throw from the Chinese. To a gunner they were almost the same target. Nothing could be done but wait for the night. Captain Noyes was put in a rickshaw and taken down to the hospital, moving on the sheltered side of the mud wall.

The Japanese, the American and British marines, some French troops, the Welsh Fusiliers, and British blue-jackets held on in the same stubborn fashion. At nightfall nearly all the troops were withdrawn from their advanced position, except the Japanese, and placed along the mud wall. Japanese cavalry were thrown out to guard against a flank attack from the southwest during the night, and within the cavalry-line one company of French infantry and one company of British blue jackets were placed. The main force itself was massed along the wall, stretching from the gate by the arsenal to its western end.

Reviewing the fight during the evening, we were all despondent. On the face of it we had failed. We had withdrawn our forces, after a hard fight, with heavy loss. Then we had no knowledge of the terrible havoc our shell-fire had wrought among the Chinese, nor of their demoralized condition. These things considered, the splendid courage of the Japanese in holding on to their advanced position, and, during the early morning, creeping over to the very gates and blasting them down, stands out conspicuously. They are magnificent fighters. Neat and clean, well drilled, perfectly equipped, and dauntless under any fire, they are equal to, if not better than, any troops from other nations on the spot. In a fight all that is done counts, but there is always one conspicuous part played by some body of men that is the coup which wins the day. Not only had the Japanese borne a heavy portion of the fight during the day, infantry and artillery alike working with a vim and courage that never abated, despite the continual stream of dead and wounded, but they hung on to their advanced position, reached the gates in the darkness, and opened them with dynamite for the rest of the army to enter, victorious, on the morning of the 14th . . .

Tientsin, July 14th, 1900

On the 14th of July the Chinese city of Tientsin was strewn with corpses. Men had been killed in every act of life. In one house three corpses were jammed into a corner, one leaning against the other in almost peaceful attitudes. A table was overturned on top of them. Tea-cups and a broken tea-pot littered the floor among splintered wood, bricks, and mud. Their clothes were splashed with blood; over the dead and on the walls, the floor, everywhere, were swarms of flies, literally devouring the putrid flesh and laying their spawn of white worms in the ghastly eyes and between the bloated lips of these horrid faces, turned purple and green by the lyddite.

On the ramparts two corpses lay in sleep-like attitudes, hugging each other as companions would for warmth. Sometimes from a pile of débris a long pig-tail would arrest attention, and then a foot or a hand. One's nostrils were so full of the fetid smell of human flesh that the roar of disturbed flies and the killing stench were sometimes needed to keep one from trampling on the dead. I saw one man who had been killed entering a doorway, lying bent over the door sill. A woman with her spike-like feet in a narrow alley nearby hugged the gutter. Dead and wounded dogs were everywhere. One of the queerest dead animals that I saw was a mule killed in a Peking-cart. The shell had exploded over its head, and the concussion had knocked the brute to the earth, driving each fore-leg out at a right angle to its body. The cart was untouched.

But the terrible things were the human wrecks still alive. Just within the gate a strange creature sat. He was naked to the waist. His left arm above the elbow had a piece cut out to the bone. The wound was glutted with coagulated blood. His pelvis was smashed and his right thigh was crushed to a jelly. It was loose, and the lower leg seemed to hang to his body by some pulpy flesh and the bloody rags that were his clothes. He sat watching the rush of human beings through the burning streets with an imbecile smile, sometimes raising his arm with a gesture of appeal. It would have been mercy to have killed him, but the troops had seen their own like that, and mercy was not in their hearts. In two hours I came back and he was still there. When I passed a third time there was only the blood in the gutter and myriads of flies . . .

THE SIEGE OF PEKING

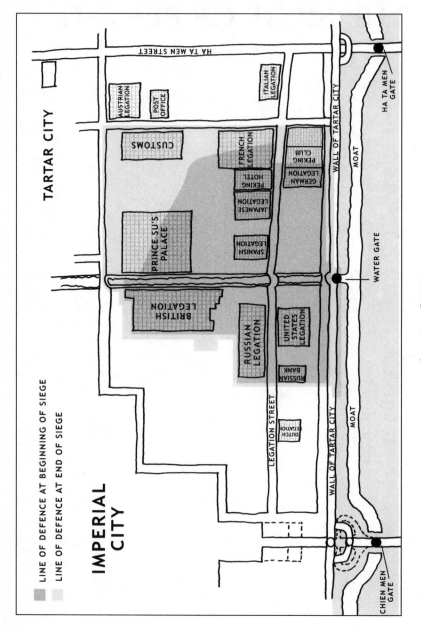

Legation Quarter

Introduction

After the murder of the German minister, von Ketteler, on 20 June 1900, the Allied leadership in Peking determined that the British Legation compound was the safest place for all foreigners to be located. It was spacious, had numerous buildings to accommodate the people, there was plenty of well water, and it was surrounded by defensible walls. By the end of that day there were approximately 900 people in residence within a compound which was meant to house 60 people!

The actual area to be defended was larger than the British Legation itself, taking in much of the Foreign Legation section of Peking. There were 415 marine guards from eight countries, and approximately 100 armed volunteers – some of whom had prior military experience. The balance of the population consisted of men unwilling or unable to bear arms, plus women and children. Many of those who did not actually fight were enlisted into various teams which supervised civilian needs ranging from medical and sanitation to food and water.

When Admiral Seymour's Expedition failed to reach Peking in mid-June the Allies were forced to make an urgent and concerted effort to send additional troops to China. They were not sure whether the diplomats and missionaries in Peking were safe or even alive, but they had to take charge of the situation.

Japan was able to get its troops to China in a short time. The British men came largely from India; American troops came from the Philippines and from San Francisco; and the Germans had to travel all the way from Europe.

The joint Allied Relief Expedition did not leave Tientsin until 4 August 1900. General Sir Alfred Gaselee, the British Commander, reported the troop strength as follows:

Japan	10,000
Russia	4,000
England	3,000
United States	2,000
France	800
Germany	200
Italy	200
Austria + Italy	100

His total estimate of 20,300 was probably over-stated by as much as 15%, which means that closer to 17,000 Allied troops actually marched to Peking.

After the siege it was noted that among the besieged 66 people died, of whom 6 were infants who died from malnutrition, the balance being men who died in the actual defense of the compound. No women died.

Account of Private Oscar Upham, American Marine

{*Private Upham was one of a group of marines transferred from the USS* Oregon *to the American flagship USS* Newark.}

May 24. Captain John T. Myers and twenty-five of the *Oregon*'s Marine Guard were transferred to the USS *Newark* for temporary duty at 6 pm; at 7.30 pm we got underway for Taku, China. A signal from *Oregon*'s whistle brought us to; her steam launch coming alongside brought two delinquent officers and a telegram. We soon left Nagasaki far behind.

May 25. At sea on a cattle boat, at least that is the name we christened her before we were aboard 24 hours. We were given the after-bridge to put our bags and hammocks on, and to make ourselves at home was the first order we received from Captain Myers. We sighted the southern coast of Korea this evening, hammocks were sounded at 7.30 pm, the watch was piped at 8 pm.

May 26. Arrived at Taku Light Ship at 1 pm and came to anchor about 15 miles from land in 8 fathoms of water. The coast is so low it can only be seen on a very clear day. It is necessary to take on a pilot to take the steam-launch to the landing at low tide which makes one trip a day. Two Chinese and one French cruisers are laying at anchor here.

May 27. The American Consul and Chinese Admiral made an official call on Admiral Kempff. Rumors of a landing party in the morning, all hands getting ready.

May 28. Everything quiet, rumor of yesterday was decidedly a fake.

May 29. At 4.30 am a tugboat came alongside with a telegram from Minister Conger, at Peking, to Admiral Kempff giving him instructions to land a guard at once and to proceed to Tientsin and wait further orders. All hands were called and after a hurried breakfast the *Oregon*'s detachment was ordered into the tug waiting at the gangway. As soon as Captain McCalla USN and Captain Myers USM came aboard, we cast off our bow and stern lines and headed for the beach followed later on by the *Newark*'s guard and a battalion of bluejackets with Colts Automatic and 3 in. field piece, in the ship's boats. We left the ship about 5.30 am; we got about 6 miles in when

153

we ran on a sand bar, we had to transfer to a couple of sampans, or native boats, to finish the journey. We made the landing about 12 o'clock; we took the steamer *Morning Star* to Tongku about 5 miles up the Peiho River. Arriving there we marched to the depot of the Imperial Railroad. Failing to get a train we went back to Taku, arriving there about 2 pm. We were joined there by the rest of the marines and the bluejackets. After having a lunch of canned beef and hard-tack we embarked on an old scow or cargo lighter and were towed to Tientsin by the *Peiho* under English colors.

As the boats belonged to an English firm we were kept below decks until we passed the Chinese forts, after which we were allowed to go on deck to admire the scenery, seeing some of the finest rice fields in the world, and the native villages along the river being made of dobe brick and plastered over with mud and grass. We also witnessed the natives irrigating their lands by hand and women and mules hitched to the same plow side by side working in the fields.

Shortly before reaching Tientsin we were ordered to stand by to land and in the confusion and darkness we came near having a fatal accident. Private Horton was having a quiet little nap and when the word was passed some one shook him up. Not being quite awake he walked overboard into the drink. He wasn't long in waking up and worked his way from under the bow of the lighter. One of the Chinese deck hands jumped overboard and rescued him as he could not swim a foot. Captain Myers asked him what he was doing down there; he quietly answered, 'Oh just getting wet.'

We landed about 10.30 pm at the English Concession and [were] escorted to the Temperance Hall by a Chinese band and a large number of Europeans. There was in the party Captain Myers, Captain [N.T.] Hall USMC, Ensigns Wurtzbaugh and McCourtney, Dr Lippett, 52 Marines and about 75 bluejackets. Admiral Kempff and staff came up by rail and quartered at the Astor House.

May 30. Mounted Guard at 8.30 am, the bluejackets relieving us as we did the guard duty last night. Captain Myers told us on the quiet to be ready to move at a minute's notice as we were going to Peking. There is an English Guard here that have been here since last winter. They were about ready to leave here when the Boxer movement started up and the British Consul held them awaiting developments.

May 31. The Marines mounted guard at 9 am and at 11.45 came hurry-up orders for us to be relieved; and fall in in 5 minutes. We were on our way to the depot without any dinner. Arriving at the station we unslung knapsacks, stacked arms and fell out. We waited till 4 o'clock before the guards of the other nations arrived; in the meantime we bulldozed the officials into letting us have a train which was made up of one gondola for baggage, ammunition and guns, and 10 coaches for the troops, which were made up of Americans, English, Russians, Japanese, Italians, Austrians and French. We arrived at the railroad terminus at Peking at about 6 pm, then came a forced march of 7 miles in heavy marching order to the Legation grounds. At the first gate Captain McCalla thought the Chinese would try to close the gates to keep us out. He gave us double time for about 300 yards Taking the place with a grandstand rush we kept up a rapid march until we reached the American Legation. We had a good supper awaiting us; we established our post for the night and turned in.

June 1–9. Established 3 posts and had the usual routine until June 10th.

June 10. Corporal Hunt and 9 privates were sent to the American Mission[1] to guard it; they arrived there at 6 pm. The mission is situated about $\frac{3}{4}$ of a mile from the US Legation and is a very nice place. The compound is about 100 yards long, the north end is about 100 yards and the south end about 300 yards wide; it is enclosed by a wall 12 ft high and contains 7 large dwelling houses, a fine church, one school and a hospital for treating charity patients. There is also a small inclosure west of the one we are in containing a girls' college for the Chinese girls, and another one called the *Bai-lo* with a college for the boys, east of us, which also contains an electric light plant and quarters for the Chinese servants. The missionaries are coming in from outside districts, some with only such articles of clothing as they could carry in their arms as they had to flee for their lives. The situation is getting more serious as the Boxers are gathering and getting more bold every hour, as the Chinese soldiers sent to guard foreign property are assisting the Boxers to loot the place.

June 11. The missionaries are doing everything for our comfort. Captain Hall, Corporal Dahlgren and 9 privates arrived at about 7 pm; this is quite an addition to our force. We are quartered in Dr Gamewell's house.[2] Some of the missionaries were all packed up to go to the United States but delayed too long and railroad connections being cut off, they had to stay.

June 12. More rumors coming in. General alarm sent in. All hands took up their positions expecting trouble; the alarm proved to be a false one.[3]

June 13. German Marines killed ten Boxers in the Southern City from the Tartar City Wall in the rear of the German Legation. Quite a crowd of the beggars gathered and howled and yelled till 11 pm, demanding the soldiers to open the gate to let them in and kill all the foreigners. The gate they wanted open was the Ha Ta Men, as this gate lay between us and the Legation. It made us get a move on. Captain Hall and Mr Tewksbury took a squad of marines down to the gate and relieved the keeper of the key to the gate so he could not use it.

June 14. Corporal Hunt and 4 marines went to the gate this morning with Mr Tewksbury to open it for the day, no Boxers could be seen, and returned by 6 am. The Boxers set fire to all shops selling foreign goods, burning a large area west of the Chien Men or Main Gate. They got the start of them and destroyed part of the gate house; this gate is only used by the Royal Family and leads direct to the Forbidden City and Palace grounds. The situation is growing worse, fires are burning every where. '*E Ho Twun*'[4] or Boxers are determined to exterminate everything foreign. Captain Hall has advised using the church as a last resort in case of a crisis; it has been loop-holed, its windows barricaded, and looks more like a fort than a house of worship.

June 15. Ten American Marines and twenty Russians from the Legations marched down to the Nan Tong (or South Church) and found some Boxers killing and torturing some Chinese Christians. Our boys killed about 50 and rescued 300 Christians, many of them wounded. Among the rescued was the blind mother of the Minister to France. We received word that [Admiral Seymour] at the head of 2000 foreign sailors and marines were on their way from Tientsin to relieve us.

June 16. Twenty British, five Japs and ten Yanks started out looking for trouble; they found plenty of it in a Boxer temple near the Russian Legation; they killed fifty-eight Boxers who were going through their exercises and incantations, and captured all of their arms without losing a man. The Boxers are getting more daring – they burned an old chapel within a hundred yards of the Mission this afternoon and were getting ready to charge down on us, when Captain Hall took ten men and met them half-way, scattering them in all directions.

June 18. We all attended Church today (may not get another chance). The usual routine of the day was carried out. The Boxers sent in word that they were going to gather 80,000 men to take our position as we were too strong for them, and fixed the date on the 27th of June. Our position is a very strong one but we have no food supplies in case of a siege.

June 19. The Foreign Ministers received 24 hours' notice to leave Peking, the Minister decided to go but asked for more time than 24 hours.

June 20. The German Minister[5] was killed and his interpreter[6] was badly wounded while on their way to the *Tsungli Yamen*. The interpreter made his way to our compound followed by a mob; our coolies however drove them off and brought him in to the mission. Word was sent down to the German Legation and the wounded man was escorted on a stretcher to the Legation. We received word to get ready to leave the mission at once. We had to take all of the converts with us, and posted guards along the streets leading to the Legations to protect them on the line of march; they carried everything they [could] lay their hands on with them. We arrived at the Legation about 2 o'clock; I was stationed in the rear of our Legation with Sergeant Fanning.

June 21. The Chinese soldiers have opened up the ball by an attack on the English and Russian Legations and succeeded in killing one Russian; they haven't bothered us yet, although they have been firing all along the line and at times quite heavily. We could see the smoke from the burning missions. I suppose it took them some time to loot the place as the buildings were well furnished and nearly everything was left behind when we left it.

June 22. The Boxers are coming our way at last. A large mob of them gathered near the Holland [Netherlands] Legation about 300 yards from our barricade in Legation Street and started to loot the place, it having been abandoned the day before. We opened fire on them with the Colts gun, soon clearing the street in our front. There are a few soldiers firing at us from an ally leading to the 'Mongol' Market; they keep well out of range, their shots doing no damage.

June 23. [The troops of General] Tang Foo Shiang and the Boxers combined in an attack on us from the west, looting and burning all the Chinese shops and houses on Legation Bank – which building we saved for the time being after a hard fight with the fire. The soldiers are firing at us from the Tartar City wall. Two of our men and one German Marine were posted on the roof of the Russian Bank building trying to pick off some sharpshooters who were giving us some trouble, when the German was shot through the side. He started to roll off the roof when one of our men caught him; they had some difficulty in getting him down as the Chinese had a good bead on them and were trying to assist them down. The German died before they could get him to the British Legation. The Chinese planted a three-inch field piece on the wall in the rear of the Bank and opened fire on us; they made a wreck of the Bank building but killed no one. The Russian Bank officials left their houses, taking refuge in the British Legation; they gave our boys permission to enter the buildings and make use of anything we thought we would need, as we had left our bedding on board the *Newark*. We were soon on the scout for some. I had just captured a fine blanket and was coming out through a narrow passageway leading to our quarters, when a 3-inch shrapnel came through the roof directly over my head and striking the wall about four feet from me, exploded tearing down half of the wall and covering me with dust and plaster; it was only a miracle that saved my life. I got out of there on the double-quick, with nothing more serious than a severe head-ache which lasted two days.

June 24. Well, they are after us early this [morning]. At about 6 am they opened up on us with their field piece and also advanced in numbers on Legation Street. Taking advantage of the ruin of the buildings burned yesterday, they planted their banners fifty feet from our barricade on the house tops and opened a galling fire on us. We received orders to get our things together and be ready to move over to the British Legation as the report came in that the other Legations were being abandoned. We fell in and marched over to the British Legation before we found out the mistake;

we left our knapsacks there and hurried back to our own Legation. The Bank was fired and there we lost our first man – Charles B. King; he was looking around the corner of the Bank and was shot through the head, dying almost instantly.

Our retreat did not lose us anything as the Chinese didn't know anything about [it] and did not advance on the Legation although they had advanced on the wall beyond us. The Germans made a sortie on the wall from their Legation and drove the Chinese back to the Chien Men, our men clearing the street. Shortly after we went on the wall with Captain Myers from the rear of the Germans and advanced down the wall to within 500 yards of the Chien Men under a heavy fire of small arms and their 3-inch field piece; we then retreated to the incline in the rear of our Legation without losing a man. After we gained the street Private Kehm was struck in the small of the back with a piece of shrapnel and was carried over to the British Legation Hospital. After 20 minutes' rest we were ordered up on the wall; again this time we took the Colts gun with us making the same trip over again without any loss on our side, only 20 men taking part in the sortie.

At 3 pm we made the third and last sortie on the wall as we intended to stay there. We gained the wall from the rear of our Legation and started to build a barricade across the top of the wall. We got it about 4 feet high and two-thirds the way across before the Chinese discovered us, as the smoke was blowing over the wall between us from the burning section. They started to make a big fuss blowing their war bugles and charging down the wall to drive us off but we didn't drive. They took up a position behind the ruins of an old stone house and dirt pile; we killed a large number before they took a hint to leave us alone. I was among those detailed to go below to do outpost duty for the night.

June 25. As soon as breakfast was over we went on the wall to relieve those men who spent the night there. At about 8 am they commenced to shell us and knocked down our barricade as fast as we could build it up; at 10 am the Italians sent us a 1 pounder and 2 gunners to work it to try and set fire to the gate house. Our first shot was a signal for them to open up on us with everything they had; there was all kinds of music in the air for a while. One of the Italians got hit in the head with a piece of brick and had to be taken below; the others lasted about ten minutes. A small scratch on the cheek took all of the fight out of him, then Mitchell who had charge of the Colts gun tried his luck at it, but he would no sooner get the gun trained when the Chinks would open up with a 3-inch and all hands would lie down till the shell landed. They soon placed another gun in position and Captain Hall ordered us to take the Colts and one-pounder below. The Chinese made a combined attack on the wall and rear street. Captain Hall ordered a retreat from the wall; we easily drove the Chinese back down the street.

Minister Conger and Captain Myers came down to where we were and as the Chinese had not taken advantage of our retreat, Captain Myers with seven men took the barricade. While reinforcements were going on the wall Private Mueller was wounded, the bullet striking his rifle at the magazine, breaking the rifle in two, and part of the bullet entered his leg just above the knee; it lodged on the bone but did not break it. Private Gold was wounded early this morning and one German killed.

June 26. Sergeant Fanning was killed between 12 and 1 o'clock this morning: he was shot through the head by a chance shot as it was too dark to take any accurate aim. The Chinks enjoyed themselves by firing at us all day long; we returned only a few shots as we had to make every shot tell. As soon as it got dark they opened up all around the Legations and raised H − l for about 4 hours and then they quieted down. They have succeeded in building a barricade about 100 yards from us; they are trying to burn us out but haven't made much headway since yesterday.

June 27. We were relieved this morning from the wall about 8 am but Captain Myers sent word for us to come up and let the other men go down again to get dinner as everything was quiet and they were foxy enough to stay down, leaving us to spend the worst night of the whole siege on the wall. A heavy storm came up about 10 pm, the rain coming down in torrents; a cold wind was blowing and the lightning was blinding. The Chinks seemed to go wild with delight and poured in a ton or two of lead at us. To make matters worse none of us went up prepared to spend the night as Captain Myers promised to have us relieved after supper.

June 28. We were relieved about 9 am. We were feeling more comfortable as the sun came out warm and dried our clothing; everything was quiet down below. The men on the wall had a little target practice: three Chinese soldiers came up the incline opposite to ours and tried to get over to their barricade; they didn't get far. Later in the day they made a bold attempt to take our position by storm, but changed their mind when our boys got to work on them. Dead Chinamen are getting very numerous up here.

June 29. Firing still continues. Dr Lippett, USN, was wounded in the thigh by a spent bullet as he was leaving Mr Conger's house this morning; the bone was badly shattered. We will miss him very much as he was generally on the wall or near at hand when anyone was hit. Dr Lowery[7] [*sic*] volunteered to take his place; he is one of the mission doctors and the boys think a great deal of him.

A Russian was killed at the next loophole to the one I was stationed at. He was smoking a cigarette and blowing the smoke out through the loophole. We told him to knock it off. One of the Chinese sharp shooters spotted him and put a slug through his head: he straightened up and turned towards me,

I saw the blood spurting from his head; he fell back into Private Moody's arms, dead. We buried him in the Russian Legation.

June 30. Sniping on our side and a continuous rifle fire from the Chinese varied once in a while with a shell or shrapnel to break the monotony. Private Schroeder was wounded at about 11 am. He was looking out of one loophole and had his arm resting in front of the same loophole the Russian was killed at yesterday, the two be[ing] about two feet apart. The bullet entered at the elbow making a severe wound. At 8 pm Private Tutcher was killed, being shot through the eye while looking through a loophole. Those Chinks have got it down pat; they can put 5 shots out of six through a loophole three inches square and don't need a field glass to do it either.

July 1. The Germans were driven from their position on the walls between us and the Ha Ta Men, in the rear of their Legation. The Chinese Artillery got their range down pat and shelled them out, wounding three men; they retreated to their Legation. The Chinese took possession of their barricade as soon as the Germans left it. When Captain Myers learned that the Germans had retreated and saw that his retreat would be cut off if the Chinese advanced any further, he ordered all hands off the wall. Mr Conger advised him to stay and Sir Claude MacDonald sent over 20 British Marines under Captain Wray to advance eastward along the wall to build a barricade. Captain Wray was slightly wounded in the shoulder; one of his men was hit in the side which proved to be very slight. Private Silvia of the *Newark's* guard volunteered to go and assist them and was hit in the arm making a very bad wound. The Chinese made another attempt to get us but failed. About 4 pm Private Kennedy was killed, being shot through the head while working on the rear barricade; and Private Hall wounded in the knee. Captain Hall relieved Captain Myers and he went below for the first time since the 25th of June; he was about worn out being up night and day watching the Chinese and they couldn't make a move but what he was dead on to them. They give us no rest at night; we can hear them working but will have to wait till morning to find out what they are doing. The flies swarming from the dead bodies give us no rest in the daytime.

July 2. The Chinese were not idle last night as they have a barricade extended from their incline half-way across the wall within 60 ft of us. We delay them some by sniping at them when they attempt to place a brick in place although they only show a hand. They started it from the incline and built the barricade so as to run it out into the Bastion on the south side of the wall. When Captain Myers and the relief came up at 7 pm the Chinese had extended their barricade into the middle of the Bastion and were throwing stones at us; we had no one hurt although several of the boys were struck by small stones.

July 3. At 1.30 am Captain Myers sent word down that the Chinks had built a tower to the south end of our barricade and were heaving large stones into our barricade. They held a council of war and decided to give the Chinese a surprise party. Our guard on the wall consisted of fifteen Americans, ten British, and seven Russians, and were reinforced by five British; making all told thirty-seven men, with Captain Myers in charge. At 2.30 am Captain Myers and eight men went over the barricade and lay down; the Chinese opened up such a hot fire that the rest of the men were delayed in getting over, one Russian being wounded in the leg. The firing soon ceased and then the charge was made – our men yelling like Indians, Privates Turner and Thomas being in the lead, and as they gained the rear of the Chinese barricade they received a volley. Our men soon had the Chinks on the run and shot down about sixty of them. Captain Myers received a spear wound on the leg, poor Turner was found shot through the head and Thomas was hit in the stomach. Captain Myers' wound though painful is not serious. Our men were quite busy throwing dead bodies over the wall into the Southern City.

The Chinese are very quiet this morning; they brought up one of their field pieces within 30 yards and opened up on us. The first shot went way up in the air, the second exploded before they were ready and knocked down part of their barricade. That settled it: they quit, evidently thinking their 'Joss' had deserted them. Privates Turner and Thomas were buried in the Russian Legation.

July 4. We celebrated the Glorious Fourth of July on the city wall of Peking, China. [With] Captain Percy Smith, a retired English officer in charge, we rustled up something to drink for the occasion. About 11 am, Private Moody was wounded through the leg; the bullet just missed the bone; he will be out inside of a week. The Chinese fired a few shots at our gate house in the Legation and succeeded in knocking our Flag down; no one hurt.

July 5. Everything quiet on the wall and in our Legation; of course the usual snipers are out trying to pick us off.

July 6. The Chinese have opened up again, but we are not wasting any ammunition on them: every shot fired, there is a Chinese funeral on hand. The Yanks gained another triumph today: one of our coolies discovered an old smooth bore of 3-inch calibre which we mounted on the Italian 1-pounder mount. The Russians brought up some shrapnel and common shell by mistake instead of rifle ammunition. We named it the 'International'. We took it over to the *Fu* where the Japs were having trouble of their own, with Mitchell our gunner's mate in charge who did very good work with it. Private Gold, one of the wounded men, returned to duty.

July 7. The firing still continues. 'Our friends the Enemy' have a gun mounted at the electric light plant; they are shelling the British Legation and the *Fu*. We fired about a dozen shots with the old International and did a lot of damage to the Chinese barricades.

July 8. The Imperial troops have mounted two guns on the Imperial City wall and have them trained on the British Legation, but we have the Colts gun located in a position to command these guns. When the Chinks try to load them we knock H – l out of them. They don't do much damage for most of their shots go so high that they land over in the Chinese City. They are working night and day on their barricades on the wall and do not trouble us much with the exception of an incessant rifle fire which they kept up all night.

July 9. Captain Myers is somewhat better; the Chinese got past the Japs and started to build a barricade across a street along the north wall of the *Fu*. The Japs got ladders and when the Chinks leaned their rifles against the wall to carry bricks the Japs reached over and gathered in all the guns. As they were getting the last one the Chinks saw them and made a break but the Japs got five before they could get to cover.

July 10. The Russian Military Attaché fixed up an acid shell to use on some buildings in the Imperial Carriage Park, which is occupied by the Boxers and soldiers. After loading the International, Private Young lit the fuse and took a sneak; the shell proved a failure, as it exploded just after leaving the muzzle of the gun, setting fire to some trees and sandbags inside of the British Legation. A couple of coolies and one student were slightly burned.

July 11. We have been working on our barricade and built a new one about thirty feet in the rear of the old one. They are using their artillery on the Legations; they seem to be afraid to use them on us on the wall for they can not get a good range. All the shells that go high, land in their barricades at the Ha Ta Men. The buildings in the German Legation and Peking Hotel are a sight to look at, the hotel having over 250 shot holes in it.

July 13. Another grand attempt to massacre us was made just before sundown today. A new camp of 500 men were stationed at the Ha Ta Men as reinforcements. After taking in the situation, they decided on a grand coup: the whole camp swarmed down the incline in the rear of the German Legation and advanced up the Wall Street towards us. The Germans let them pass, but some of our men on the wall let [shots] drive into them. They didn't seem to know where the shots were coming from and didn't know where to go. We had a regular picnic with them; they concluded that the wall was the best place to go and started for it on the jump, then the Germans got their work in. They started in to carry off the dead at dark and worked all night.

July 14. Two deserters came in from the enemy; one of them, a bugler, had his ear cut off for refusing to blow a charge. He said that the loss was nearly 300 killed and wounded. An attack was made on the French last night about 12 o'clock. The Chinks undermined and blew up two buildings, killing two Frenchmen. They gathered around to see how it was going to work; they saw to their sorrow, and spent the rest of the night hauling off their own dead and wounded. We can hear the Chinese digging in the barricade west of ours. I suppose they will put a mine in. Music Murphy was slightly wounded. We have advanced our position to the eastward about 200 yards and built a barricade two-thirds of the way cross the wall. We have to relieve the men on the wall at night as the Chinks have a clean sweep of the street which we have to cross in order to reach the wall. I and two others are detailed to go on the wall to build another barricade tonight.

We took twenty-three coolies up with us, each one carrying a sand bag. Captain Hall sent us out to a bastion about 200 yards in advance of our new barricade to start another, so as to command the canal. In case the troops come in they will have a place to come through the wall to our relief. Captain Hall sent out the coolies after we had the barricade started. We were getting along nicely when he sent word that the Germans wanted him to send a couple of volleys down at the Chinese barricade as they were trying to mount a big gun to play on the Germans. We were ordered to go into the bastion, then the fun commenced: our men started the ball to rolling, and we heard some of the prettiest music that was ever listened to as we were between two fires. We were somewhat anxious as we didn't know whether the Chinese were going to advance on us or not; if they had it would have been all up with us, for we were in a regular trap. As soon as the firing slacked up I ran over to the barricade to see if any advance was being made, and as there wasn't we commenced work again. The Chinese advanced their position towards us so that we are only 300 yards apart on the Ha Ta Men side and 300 yards on the Chien Men side.

July 16. We finished our work about four o'clock am, were relieved by Privates Fischer, Butts and Davis. Fischer was standing at one end of the barricade (it only extended two-thirds across the wall by order of Captain Hall). He was on watch when one of Chinks took a bead on him and let go, the bullet clipped a piece of brick out close to his head. Fischer muttered to himself, 'that's damn close'; he started to move in out of the way when he was hit in the chest, the bullet going through the right lung, coming out at the back, buried itself in the rear barricade. He lived about ten minutes. One of our messengers came in; he was captured and given a flogging by the Chinese soldiers and then sent in with offers of an armistice and a telegram from Secretary Hay to Mr Conger (it was about three weeks old and was sent in by the *Tsungli Yamen*). Secretary Hay was asking for tidings. Captain [B.M.] Strouts was killed and Dr Morrison was wounded while inspecting the Japs' position in the *Fu*.

July 17. Several of the *Yamen* [officials] came in today under a flag of truce and had a conference with the ministers. They said they were sorry that they could not control the Boxers and for God's sake keep our soldiers quiet; that if we could quit firing on them they would leave us alone. We are sitting on top of our barricades and talking with the Chinese soldiers. Those up at the Chien Men are taking the dead off the wall; it's about time as they have been lying there under our noses for near three weeks. As they lower them off the wall in straw matting we can see heads and limbs fall out and flatten when they hit the ground. We are very thankful to them for removing their dead as the stench has been something awful, for a dead Chinaman has a peculiar odor all his own. Some of the bodies were lying within 3 or 4 feet of our barricade and were quite an inducement to the flies – and I think all of the flies in Peking were here.

July 18. The conditions of the truce were that the Chinese were to cease firing on us, not make any advance or build any more barricades, and we to do the same. The Chinks started to build a barricade on Legation Street so we brought the 'Old International' over from the British Legation and trained it on them. We stuck up a large sign with Chinese characters on it telling them to knock off – which they refused to do, so we turned her loose and knocked part of their barricade down. They took the hint and quit. Last night it was so quiet we could hardly sleep; not a shot being fired as the Chinese continue to work on the wall. We are strengthening all of our barricades. Pekinese soldier told Col. Shiba[8] that the Allied forces were intending to leave Tientsin on the 20th of July and that the Taku Forts had been taken; a Swedish missionary named Nestigaard,[9] though better known as 'Nasty Guy', whose mind has been affected by the siege, escaped from the British Legation and joined the Boxers.

July 19. The Chinese soldiers are smuggling in a few eggs and selling them to the missionaries at fancy prices; everything is quiet.

July 20. Another day of rest. The Chinese got such a beating the other night that they are satisfied to take a rest and leave us alone. The truce just came in time as some of the forces here were almost out of ammunition and though we have plenty we will have to be saving, to help out the others. The *Yamen* sent in Old Nasty Guy today; he was glad to get back as he was nearly starved. Sir Claude asked him if he gave any information to the Chinese: he said that they asked him questions and he had to answer them. There was strong talk of shooting him but they put him in double irons in the brig with a Chinese prisoner instead, for safe keeping. The English Marines have orders to shoot if they see him trying to leave the Legation.

July 23. Everything quiet. We had a heavy rainstorm last night that will make hard travelling for the troops. We have our barricade in good condition and good shelters put up for the men on the wall.

July 25. The Holland Secretary, Mr [W.J.] van Duysberg, went over our west barricade last night and secured some ammunition left there by the Chinese in their retreat. He got about 250 rounds which he gave to the Japs as they are almost out; we let them have seven of our rifles and seventy rounds for each gun. The Chinese heard some noise last night and opened up all along our west line with a heavy rifle fire which lasted about forty-five minutes but did no damage.

July 26. The Chinese are very suspicious and kept burning rockets all night which illuminated the whole place; there was occasional firing all night.

July 27. The *Tsungli Yamen* sent in 200 melons, 150 pumpkins, and 200 lbs of flour. We got the report on the wall that Private Hobbs was very sick down at the Legation, where I went down at 6 pm to take charge of the outpost in one of the rear courts. I found a very sick man there all covered up with blankets; the boys told me that he had been coughing up large worms and a few snakes. I don't remember what else, but from the collection of empty bottles lying [around], I concluded that they had a glorious old time. Captain Hall came to the same conclusion and Mr Hobbs was told that he might sojourn on the wall for 48 hours until he got better.

July 28. Mr H.G. Squiers, the first Secretary to the Legation, had a turkey that he was saving for a rainy day. It rained last night and this morning Mr. Squiers got out a search warrant for his turkey; he put himself in charge of our stores at the beginning of the siege, and though we took enough canned fruit and vegetables and hams over to the general store house in the British Legation, he will not draw any for us although his own table is well supplied. We can get no satisfaction from Sir Claude as Mr Squiers was appointed his Aide-de-camp after Captain Strouts was killed. Whenever Sir Claude or Squiers comes on the wall they get a very chilly deal from the men; they are frequent visitors there now that there is no danger. When the firing was going on they shunned the wall like poison. Sir Claude sent up orders by Captain Wray for us to fire on any Chinese exposing themselves. I told Captain Wray that Sir Claude's orders 'didn't go' on the wall; even Captain Hall when giving any orders was careful not mention Sir Claude's name in connection with them for he knew how dearly we loved him.

July 29. The war is on again in earnest. The Chinese started it by picking off some of our coolies; we retaliated by picking a few of them off their roost. This brought on a general engagement. We feel better, having something to do, than we did during the truce.

July 30. The Chinese built a barricade across the bridge along the Imperial City Wall, under the nose of the English; I guess they were asleep last night. A Christian Chinese was killed on Legation Street bridge. One of the messengers came in from the *Yamen* today to the English Legation; when asked about the new barricade built last night, he claimed that our men killed a woman while crossing the bridge and that the barricade was put up for safety.

July 31. A large number of Chinese troops came in through the Chien Men this afternoon. There seems to be something in the wind; we are keeping a sharp lookout. They keep up their sniping all day but we have taught them to respect us (during the truce a Chinese Colonel in command on the wall was holding conversation with our officers; he eagerly asked who those men were that wore the big hats? On being told that they were American Marines, he shook his head and said, 'I don't understand them at all; they don't shoot very often, but when they do I lose a man; my men are afraid of them.')

The Chinese have a large gun playing on the Ri Tung.

Aug. 2. We heard heavy firing last night off to the southeast. A messenger arrived last night from Tientsin with a letter from the Japanese General and one from an English General saying that the troops would leave on the 28 or 29 of July, the delay being caused by failure to secure transportation of supplies, and that Mr Conger's telegram had reached the States and the French Ministers in France.

Aug. 3. Received some letters from the troops, among them one from Major Waller USM to Captain Myers, who is too sick with typhoid fever to receive it. It stated that Tientsin and the Taku Forts had been taken, and that a flying column of 10,000 would leave on the first of August to go to our relief, a larger force to follow on the third. There are 5000 Americans in China and that McKinley and Roosevelt had been nominated on the Republican ticket.

Aug. 4. Two Russian sailors were wounded at the Russian Bank where they were building a barricade; one was seriously hurt.

Aug. 5. Unofficial report that our troops had met the enemy and routed them, inflicting a heavy loss, at Laong Fung. One of the Russians wounded yesterday died this morning.

Aug. 6. Sniping still continues and at 2.30 am the monotony was broken by heavy rifle firing which lasted about 20 minutes, over in the Mongol Market; no news from the relief column yet.

Aug. 7. The weather is very warm: the thermometer registered 110° on the wall today. Not much wind stirring.

Aug. 10. Messengers from the Allied Forces arrived at the Japanese Legation and brought word that the troops would arrive here on the 13th or 14th at the very latest. He left them about 30 miles from here on the 6th. They had only two engagements that amounted to anything, routing them both times. They expected an engagement as soon as they arrived at Tung Chow, about 14 miles from here, as the enemy are reported enmassing their forces at that place, the city being enclosed by a large wall.

Aug. 11. We had quite a heavy rain storm last night with frequent showers during the day. The Chinese at the Ha Ta Men side opened fire on us for the first time since the 16th of July. The Chinese at the Chien Men side built a large tower in the rear of their front barricade; it is about 30 feet high. The Russians and our men stationed at that end have to keep up with the times and work on their barricade every night; they have it about 20 feet high and about 10 feet thick at the base. When it comes to hard work the Ruskies are OK but cannot be depended on in an emergency although they would go any place with our men and have as much faith in us as they have in their officers.

Aug. 12. The Chinese at the Ha Ta Men side opened up on us with a large smooth bore this morning. One of our men saw them place the gun in position; what they had it loaded with is more than we can tell. We saw the flash and smoke, but only the report reached us. We sent a couple of volleys into them and they quit for the rest of the day. As soon as it got dark they commenced to bombard the German Legation using solid shot. Captain Le Bouise of the French Army was killed tonight; he was making a tour of the world when he was caught in Peking. He volunteered his services which were gladly accepted. One German and two French soldiers were killed, and one Russian died of dysentery.

Aug. 13. At 5 o'clock this morning Corporal Dahlgren and party hoisted our colors at the Ha Ta Men, and I hoisted the Russian Flag at the Chien Men side; the American Flag was the first foreign flag hoisted on the Tartar City Wall. Corporal Dahlgren had the loopholes manned in case the Chinese fired on our flag. He intended to give them a 21 gun salute; however they took no notice of it. At 7 pm they made the usual night attack with rifle and artillery fire which they kept up almost all night. I was stationed at our incline with Private Zion and Drummer Murphy; we had orders to watch the incline at the German Legation where the Chinese had the old smooth bore planted. Our duties were to fire whenever they used this gun. We had a good range on them and kept them busy. The distance was 1000 yards. They soon stationed a couple of sharpshooters on their incline who kept up a continuous fire on us.

Princes Ching and Tuan and the *Tsungli Yamen* had made an engagement to meet the Foreign Ministers at the Spanish Legation, but failed to show up; they sent in a messenger with a note saying that as we had made an attack on them the night before, killing twenty-six men and an officer of high rank, they could not trust us. The facts of [the] matter are they made the attack and we did the rest.

Aug. 14. Good news, the best that we have heard yet. This messenger is the boom of artillery at the East Gate or Sha Wau Men and the steady crack of a Maxim gun; sometimes we can hear volleys. The Chinese cannot imitate no matter how hard they try. This did not seem to discourage the Chinese any, for they did not slack up on their fire but seemed to be more active than ever. I guess the troops must have stirred them up a little: as soon as daylight came we could see the shells bursting over the Imperial City, and the Chinese artillery firing from the east wall. We after learned that the Japanese were doing the bombarding.

At 2.15 pm we sighted the English Sikhs in the Southern City opposite our position on the wall. By our direction they came through the canal and were in the Legations before the Chinese were aware of it. The American troops were a close second, Company K of the 14th Infantry scaled the Southern City Wall under a heavy fire but only had two men wounded. The relief column had a hard time of it; some of the men were left by the way overcome by the heat. General Chaffee was in charge of our troops.

As soon as the Sikhs entered the Tartar City our men jumped over our west barricade and, joined by the Russians, made a rush for the Chinese position which we found deserted. We continued our way to the Chien Men; we could see hundreds of Chinese soldiers down at the next Gate House known as the Chang Go Men where they had retreated. The Chinese down in the street barricades and some others who were stationed in some shacks in front of the gate were somewhat surprised to see us at such close quarters; they seemed a little rattled and didn't know which way to run. We didn't do a thing. Then only one got away; he must have had a charmed life; he made a run with four others, of about 400 yards to shelter. We got three and fired 3 or 4 volleys at the other two; one of these was slightly wounded and fell behind a large stone gate post, the other got away. I killed one of them as he was trying to gain the archway of the Main Gate, the bullet must have went [sic] through his heart for he never moved after he fell. One of the Chinese had taken shelter behind the fence that faced Legation Street and was pumping away at us as fast as he could load. One of the 14th Infantry men spotted him and pointed him to me, and said, 'There he is! shoot him! shoot him!' I asked him why he didn't do a little shooting himself; he did [not] answer but kept jumping up and down and yelling 'shoot him!' I tried two shots without effect but the third did the business. He was afterward found with a bullet hole through his head.

We opened the gate for Reilly's battery[10] and they dropped a few shells into the Imperial City to where the majority of the Chinese soldiers have retreated. I was up in the gate house talking with an English Captain. He had a Maxim gun with him; I called his attention to some soldiers down at the Chang Go Men. They were advancing on us and were trying to place a field gun in position. We got the Maxim into action and soon had them on the run. I don't know how many men we killed for we had a fine range on them and could see them falling in every direction. The troops are camped just outside of the Chien Men in the Southern City with two Companies of infantry and Reilly's battery on the wall; there are with the Allied Forces the 9th and 14th Infantry, the 5th Artillery with 8 guns, Captain Reilly commanding, Troop L of the 5th Cavalry and two battalions of Marines, Major Waller in charge and General Chaffee in command of the Division; General Gaselee, being the ranking officer, was in command of the whole.

Aug. 15. The weather is fine and every one is in good spirits. To see them one would think they were in anticipation of going to a circus although we all know that we had a hard nut to crack before we reached the 'Forbidden City'. Captain Reilly had three guns mounted on the wall, two of these were working in the direction of the Chang Go Men and the other was playing on the Imperial City. Brave Captain Reilly while commanding the guns on the wall was shot, the bullet entering his mouth, as he was giving an order, and came out at the back of his head, killing him almost instantly.

There are four large gates to pass through to get into the Imperial City and each one is covered with steel. We battered open the first gate with our big guns by placing them within ten feet of the gate. As soon as they were open we received a volley from the Chinese who had taken a position in front of the second gate. Using a marble bridge for breastworks, our men started to go after them, but the firing was so hot they were ordered back; we had 15 men wounded inside of 10 seconds. After dropping a few shells into them we had no further trouble. We threw out a skirmish line and chased them into the Imperial City, our men taking the lead ... After searching the Gate leading to the Forbidden City, an altercation arose as to who should have the honor of entering first. General Chaffee became disgusted and ordered his men to return to their camps. After he left with his men the rest didn't seem to be so anxious to go in, and went into camp in different parts of the Imperial City. They wanted our men to do the work, and they take all the honors ...

All the siege is ended so I think that I will close hoping that we will soon have the extreme pleasure of greeting our shipmates once more – which I suppose will be a great surprise to them; all through the siege we had never held out any hopes of a rescue and never gave it a second thought.

Notes

[1] The Methodist Mission compound held missionaries of four mission boards: Presbyterian, Methodist, American, and London Missionary Society. Ultimately, they all moved to the British Legation compound.

[2] Dr Gamewell's house was in the Methodist Mission.

[3] Interestingly, Upham fails to make reference to the murder of Sugiyama Akira, secretary of the Japanese Legation, by soldiers of Dong Fuxiang (who were sympathetic to the Boxers) near the railway station on 12 June.

[4] *I Ho Chuan* or 'Fists of Righteous Harmony'.

[5] Baron Klemens von Ketteler, Envoy Extraordinary and Minister Plenipotentiary of the German Legation, was going to a meeting at the *Tsungli Yamen* when he was shot dead by a Chinese soldier.

[6] H. Cordes, Second Interpreter at the German Legation.

[7] Dr G.D.N. Lowry, Professor of Histology and Pathology at Peking University.

[8] Lieut. Col. Shiba, Military Attaché at the Japanese Legation.

[9] O.S. Nestigaard or Nestagaard, Lutheran missionary of the Norwegian Mission.

[10] Light Battery F, Fifth Artillery, commanded by Captain Henry J. Reilly.

Journal of Mary E. Andrews, American Missionary

Mary Elizabeth Andrews (1840–1936) was born in Cleveland, Ohio and set out for China in March 1868 to work as a missionary and teacher for the American Board of Commissioners for Foreign Missions (Congregational Church). She was assigned to a newly-established base at Tungchow where she would spend her entire working life. She retired in 1925, and died in Paotingfu at the age of 95.

On 8 June 1900 the American Board decided to evacuate all missionaries in Tungchow and move them to the American Methodist compound in Peking, where this account begins.

Peking, Saturday PM
June 16 1900

My Precious Sister –

I sent a letter to you yesterday. The situation today is practically unchanged. No more troops have appeared. We are in a state of semi-siege – no one goes out except on important business and then under guard. Even our servants going to make purchases for our table are guarded. Several attacks were made yesterday by foreign soldiers on [a] little company of Boxers, and a good many were killed. The work of burning still goes on. Heavy smoke is rising from the South City now, but no one knows what is being destroyed.

A bold thing was done by four of our missionaries[1] last night. Dr [J.H.] Ingram, Mr [Reverend E.G.] Tewksbury, Mr [Reverend C.E.] Ewing, and Dr [John] Inglis – they went armed with Winchester rifles to the city gate near us, leading into the South City, and demanded the key of the gate. In fear of the rifles the gate-keeper delivered it up – and they proceeded to close and lock the gate, and brought the key here for the night. Under ordinary circumstances it would have been a most lawless act, but this part of the city is under martial law. The Government is completely paralyzed, and anything that looks like self-protection is allowed. Of course with the key in our hands, no friends of the Boxers could open them and we had a quiet night. The officials begged the key might be returned to them this AM and it was, much to the disgust of some of those who took it, who thought we should have sent and opened the gate, but retained the key ourselves.

171

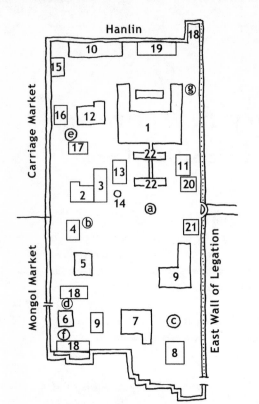

British Legation Compound

1. The Minister's house
2. Chinese Assistant Secretary (Mr. Ker.)
3. Doctor (Dr. Poole)
4. Chinese Secretary (Mr. Cockburn)
5. Accountant (Mr. Tours)
6. Escort quarters, stable yard, students
7. Chancery
8. First Secretary of Legation
9. Second Secretary of Legation
10. Students
11. Escort quarters, students
12. Theatre
13. Chapel
14. Bell-tower
15. Students' mess-room
16. Bowling Alley
17. Fives Court
18. Stables
19. Servants' quarters
20. Gate-house (Sergeant Herring)
21. Armoury
22. T'ing'rh open pavilion

a,b,c,e,g. Good drinking water wells.
d and f large wells of bitter water.

Later 16th. However they gave up the key again at evening and we had possession of this gate until we left. The day has been quiet except for one sudden alarm. While gathered for our noon prayer meeting, Dr Lowry[2] came and called all the gentlemen out. The mothers with little children, and ladies in charge of Chinese girls followed, and the call came to prepare to go to [the] chapel immediately for refuge. We made instant preparation and many of the Chinese had gathered there when word came the danger was over.

There is an encampment of soldiers not far from one corner of our compound, the least protected part, from whose presence we fear danger. A squad appeared as if intending an attack, but soon after the alarm was given, the guards were in place ready to receive them, that they turned off.

17th. I am sitting quietly in the chapel to write. We have not yet been driven here for protection, but it is a cool place to sit, quite different from what it will be when the hundreds of us are shut up within its walls. Everything possible is being done to make it habitable. The glass of the windows has been taken out − $\frac{2}{3}$ of the casements bricked up − and the rest filled with wire netting. Parapets have been thrown up on the roof for a protection for the marines and missionary soldiers who shall occupy that place. All the heavy trunks of those who have trunks are gathered in the vestibules to be piled against the doors in case of an attack. Large water *kangs* stand here and there, masses of canned goods and other provisions are piled on the pulpit platform. The girls of the 2 schools sleep here at night but spend the day at the schoolhouses across the way, marching back and forth with the escort of their teachers, with great decorum.

It is wonderful with the things here, that there is so little confusion and no panic, even in sudden cases of alarm. It shows what trust in the Lord can do, even for the Chinese who are so lacking in self-control. All through the courts the scene is a busy one, even on this Sabbath day; walls going up, and deep pits being dug everywhere to guard the approaches to the chapel from all directions. Everybody is pressed into the service – men, women, and little children carrying bricks and wielding pickax and shovel – guards of foreigners and Chinese take their turn in standing on guard armed night and day. We ladies too have our regular times of being on guard also day and night – to carry the word in case of sudden alarm, and attend to getting the women and children into the chapel. Everything is systematized and goes by the clock. Our great fear is that the strain of day work and night watching will prove too great for us all.

Mon. 18. I was on guard yesterday from 6 till 8 in the AM so had a quiet time with my Bible and the Lord. After breakfast we gathered our servants for prayers. By 'we' I mean the people in our house here, who are keeping house for us. Most of us Tung cho[3] people, but I was called to lead prayers in the next house, where there seemed no one to attend to it. After that I made the rounds of the refugees with Dr [Maud] Mackay – she to look after the sick ones, I to interpret for her and to speak words of cheer, or possibly of reproof, as needed. Later on we met in the chapel for worship and took that as a special answer to prayer, for the chaplain was unwilling to have us gather, thought it unwise. But we felt that our people needed the help of the Sabbath service, so we prayed and he was won over to give consent. Then those in charge of the work in the courts thought the work ought not to stop – but we felt sure it would do the men good to stop for an hour and get some nourishment, that they would work the better for it. That too the Lord brought about in answer to prayer. I had a meeting with the women in our courts in the PM then our own English service which I especially enjoyed. Mr Smith[4] gave a very strong helpful sermon on the 90 and 91 Psalms. After tea I went over to the other compound and had a meeting with the women there, out in the court as there is no room large enough for them to gather in. Later a delightful sing over at Mrs Walker's, all the marines who were off guard, coming in and seeming to enjoy it thoroughly.

Wed. 20th. We have passed another terrible night, a night of much prayer, for again we are facing the dreadful possibility of being obliged to leave all these dear native Christians to massacre or something worse. It seems as if we simply could not. To die with them would be easy, as compared with leaving them to their fate.

Monday was a comparatively quiet day, but yesterday a good many fires were started — one large one that burned most all day. All the foreign property has been burned except this one compound and Legation Street and they seem now to be burning stores that have kept foreign goods, the telegraph offices, and everything that is in any way connected with anything foreign. Yesterday reports came that the Legations and this place were to be attacked last night. Then in the evening a letter came from our Minister, Mr Conger, saying word had come from the palace that the Viceroy of Tientsin had sent word that the Admirals were to take possession of the Taku forts today, which would be a declaration of war on the part of the nations, and giving us 24 hours in which to leave.

English Legation, Thurs. 21st. Such a strange day yesterday. We were all called together after breakfast to hear the letters which had been sent to our Minister protesting against our being sent away leaving our native Christians to their fate — and his answer, which was that there seemed nothing else to do, since we were ordered away by the Chinese Government, that he should demand of them carts and an escort to take us to Tientsin, and that we should be ready to leave at the latest by next morning. It was such sad word to take to our women and children. They felt our danger in going was as great as theirs in staying, and had little hope of seeing us again here. We went to work to select from our little store of earthly goods those most important which we could take with us in our carts.

Then came another sudden call to be ready at once to go to the Legation on foot, taking with us only what we could carry in our hands. The [German] Minister had been killed on his way to the *Tsungli Yamen* and it seemed as if there were imminent danger for everybody. So our troops were to escort us to the Legation as the only place of safety. I went down again to see our people and say good bye to them, and was just turning away with a great sorrow of heart at the thought of leaving them at last, with no protection from their enemies, when word came suddenly that they were to be allowed to go with us, not to the Legation, but to a safe place opposite, which was also under the protection of the guns. That was another precious answer to prayer — we had been so pleading that we might not be obliged to leave them.

Well we walked over in the hot sun to the American Legation. But the quarters there were small and not so easily defensible as the English Legation and in the event of war it would be possible to hold only one — so after a hasty lunch which Mrs [Herbert] Squiers, the wife of the [American] Secretary of Legation, had prepared for us, we started again for the English Legation. Here we Americans are most of us quartered in the chapel, as close together as peas in a pod.

As soon as possible we went over to our people. We found them huddled together in groups under the trees, in a great open court. A large building, belonging to a prince who had fled,[5] was soon opened to them so that they have quite comfortable quarters. We stayed and helped them clean out the rooms and get them ready to shelter the mothers and babies. But a call came to come back at once to the Legation, and shortly after the Chinese opened fire on us, tho' without doing any harm. A sharp attack came in the evening and the bullets whistled through the trees over our heads. The Gatling guns answered, and the firing soon ceased, but it was renewed again and again during the night. Naturally sleep was not very sound or restful, though I did not at all realize we were being attacked. It seemed rather like 4th of July. I seem to be living in a dream these days and realize nothing. Today we have not been allowed to go over to our people, because of the danger of being fired on.

We hear this PM that our troops from Tientsin are at hand. I hope it is true. We found yesterday that to get away from here was simply impossible, since no cart could be hired. This AM word came from the officials that we need not leave.

Fri. evening, June 22nd. I keep on writing day after day, though there is no way of sending letters. We are quite cut off from the outside world – no communication by rail or telegraph, nor for many days by messenger.

Today I have sewed steadily on sand bags for fortifications, from breakfast until supper time, only stopping a few minutes for dinner. There have been several excitements during the day. All the AM firing was heavy and incessant – bullets falling about us, so it was not safe for us to step outside the chapel. A little later German, French, and Japanese troops came marching in, and the word spread that all the other Legations had been abandoned and the troops were concentrating here – that was sad word for us as it left the buildings where all our Chinese are gathered, wholly unprotected. But it seemed to me that after the Lord had answered so many prayers for them, making it possible to keep them with us and bring them to a place of safety, He would not forsake them now.

Only a little later a large number of troops were marched out again, and we learned they were sent purposely to protect those buildings. The English minister says those buildings will be protected to the very end, because it protects this Legation on that side – so our dear people are in the safest place possible thanks to God's loving care. At tea time the fire alarm sounded, buildings just next to us had been fired and the fear was that the flames might spread to us. Foreigners and Chinese men and women formed in lines to pass buckets of water, and after a time the fire was controlled. That exercise was a real rest to me after sitting still all day. Yesterday and today we have {not} been allowed to go over to the other court and I am a little homesick for our dear people – but it is good to know that they are safe.

Sat. eve. 23rd. Another weary day. Fire after fire has been started today just around us, with the evident intent of burning us out. Missionaries and native Christians are nearly worn out with fighting fires and fortifying. But the Lord has kept us thus far.

Tues. pm 26th. Just after that little word I went over to the scene of the latest fire – the Han Lin Yuan, the great Peking University.[6] Its library contained books of incalculable value, books which the Chinese were, and well might be, proud of – records of their empire from earliest ages. That even fanaticism could go to such lengths as to destroy anything so precious seems impossible. The books had been thrown out in a heap – a few of the most precious were gathered up by order of the English minister and brought over here. An immense pit was dug and the rest of the books and papers tumbled in and covered over by our people to save adding fuel to the flames. Evidently kerosene had been put on them to spread the flames. The fire started with the intention of setting fire to the rooms of the English Minister, as the wind was blowing in that direction. But at God's command and in answer to prayer it suddenly veered and blew the flames away from us; but for that we should all have been burned out. Saturday was a terrible day; firing all night, and in the AM the wounded and dead began to be brought in. Fires raged around us, so near it seemed as though we could not be saved. Evidently they were determined to burn us out. But still God's hand was over us and no harm came.

Once word came that the place where our Chinese were was attacked and could no longer be defended, and our people were hastily removed to room[s] in connection with our compound. But before the removal was finished the attack was repelled, and after a little they were moved back again. I did not see them for I was engaged in making bags and super-intending some Catholic women in the same work. The men who were fortifying were calling for more bags – and we could not stop. We have made thousands in these 4 days, and still the demand continues. Some of our men made a raid on deserted stores nearby and brought in quantities of cloth and thread for the purpose. Several sewing machines belonging to ladies in the Legation are in constant use. Most of those who are not at the machines sew by hand all day long. The Chinese women are busily working too.

Our position here is certainly an unheard-of one – all the foreigners in Pèking are gathered in the Legation,[7] most of them in this one – some thousands of native Christians, Protestants, Catholic and Greek are gathered here also. And here we are surrounded on all sides by our enemies, the Boxers and Chinese soldiers, who are determined to sweep us out of existence. They have 3 cannon on the city walls, and their men hidden every where, and balls and bullets whistle around and over us most of the time.

The last two nights a sharp determined attack has been made on all sides at midnight, and it has seemed as if all the hosts of hell were closing in around us. And yet we have been wonderfully held in the hollow of His hand. I think only 10 of our people, foreigners and Chinese, have been killed in all these days and some 20 wounded. Abbie[8] is in charge of the kitchen for the hospital and superintends the preparation of their food.

It is a strange life we are living and no one knows how it is to end. We are all the time hoping for the coming of foreign troops but none come. We know nothing of what is transpiring in the city – whether there is any government in existence or not. We are completely isolated. It seems strange to be on rations, to be able to eat just so much and no more, and to have to use water as sparingly as possible. We have had no meat, except a few tins of meat kept especially for the men, until yesterday when a horse was shot, and these two days we have been having meat. We have had no bread either until today, but I have found I could get on quite well without either. We have not suffered thus far from hunger or thirst, and I don't think we shall.

Wed. 27th. Another half day at bags but just now there is a lull in the work, so I take my writing. We had another sharp attack last night, and when it seemed as if Hell were let loose around us, but it lasted a much shorter time than the two nights before and no one was killed or wounded. Again the Lord's hand covered us in. It is terrible while it lasts and we ladies can only lie still and pray, while the incessant sharp reports make us quiver and the bullets and balls whistle around and above us.

I learned some things more last evening about the attack of the night before. The Boxers had evidently determined to get in at Tsu Wang Sen. They had torn down the outside of the walls leaving only the inner shell, and they had scaling ladders, and they expected by scaling or breaking down the walls to effect an entrance. Had they done so that whole company of native Christians would have been massacred. But the Japanese soldiers who were on guard discovered them, and they with the native Christians made a sortie and drove them away, capturing their ladders. One of our Tung cho Christians was slightly wounded.

Today the firing has been incessant and sharp. I am so tired of the sound. They say they were firing into the Tsu Wang Sen but I have heard of no harm done as yet. Last evening some of us went to one of the sentry boxes at the back of the place and with a glass looked out of a loophole on what is ordinarily one of the thronged busy streets of this crowded busy city. Bitterly desolate, not a living thing in sight – only a few dead horses and men scattered about and a sickening odor in the air. Oh this firing is terrible. It is just like the night attacks that have so tried us. They seem trying to batter down the walls at Tsu Wang Sen but I feel sure the Lord will not let them succeed.

Precious little sister, God help you and keep you from anxious care for me.

We all pray for the dear ones in the homeland, knowing how hard it must be for you. Such alarming telegrams as went home for a few days – and then this sudden silence. We have no possible way of getting any word to the outside world. But thank God we can still reach you by way of the throne, and our prayer is that your hearts may be kept in the Lord's own peace. I wonder if this long letter will ever reach you. I wonder what the end of all this will be. No one can tell. Whether we shall ever get out of this place alive or not seems quite uncertain. But the Lord holds our hearts quiet. Of course, we do not fear death. Yet such a death as would be our fate, if they should succeed in forcing an entrance, does seem terrible. Only we know that where the Lord leads, we can follow and that the end is home.

Thurs. evening 28th. We grew so utterly weary over the sharp incessant firing yesterday – nervously weary – that when at last silence and darkness fell, and we lay down to rest, it was almost impossible to sleep. Then about eleven came another sharp attack, making our hearts beat wildly. We are all so weary that these night attacks seem to grow harder and harder to bear. The one last night did not last long and afterward I went to sleep and slept until daylight. Today there has been less firing than yesterday, which has been a relief, but tonight they are shelling Tsu Wang Sen and arrangements are being made to move the Chinese over here in the night if it should be necessary. It is all so terrible – but the Lord reigns and He loves us and all our people.

Friday eve. 29th. I felt so weary and homesick last evening, so longed to be folded in and cuddled that I just wanted to cry. And I just told the Lord all about it, and I am sure He did fold me in, for I went to sleep and slept soundly until daylight and then awoke with such a grateful feeling that for one night there had been no sharp attack. Was quite surprised to hear that the sharp firing had been kept up a large part of the night, and many had hardly slept at all.

Today we have worked steadily on bags all day. I grew so weary this afternoon that I lay down and went to sleep a few minutes. The special attempt of the day on the part of our enemies has been to burn out Tsu Wang Sen. Some of the largest, finest buildings were fired, and the fire raged a long time, but the wind changed again and blew the flames away from the buildings occupied by our Christians and they were saved, though one of those buildings can no longer be occupied and the girls are to move over to the rooms to which they came on Saturday. It may be necessary for all the Christians to come over in the morning – Oh this is so terrible – Each day some lines are laid down – and the number in the hospital is increasing, but the Lord does wondrously cover us in, and I believe He will until relief comes. But I rather dread tonight. If I had some one to work for, if I could only be with our people helping them, it would be so much easier to bear. Good night my precious little sister. God keep your heart in peace.

Sat. eve. 30th. We had another hard night last night, unusually hard – about 10 oclock, just as we had lain down to sleep, a terrible attack began. The sharp incessant firing seemed so much nearer than ever before that it seemed as if they must really have effected an entrance and were surrounding the very rooms we were occupying. One bullet crashed through a pane of glass into the chapel, but no harm was done. I sleep on one of the seats usually, but when the firing began I slipped down on the floor, as the safest place. There came on a thunderstorm just in the fiercest of the attack, and we hoped it would stop it, but it did not. The cannonading lasted most of the night, and of course there was little sleep for any of us. Today has been a quiet day but a busy one for us. Steady work on sand bags all day. All our hand work is systematized, and today I was one of those whose business it was to clean the chapel. Seventy people take their meals in this one room, and about $\frac{2}{3}$ of them sleep here and it is a work of time to put it in order. It was to have a thorough cleaning for Saturday so [I] was occupied the most of the forenoon. After dinner I took up sand bags but was so sleepy that I could not keep my eyes open so lay down and went to sleep a few minutes. Then have given the rest of the day to the bags.

Sun. July 1st. Such a strange Sabbath, certainly not a day of rest. We had a more quiet night than usual. More or less of firing all night, but no sharp attack and no harm done. But today more lives have been lost and more men wounded than any day before. Our troops on the walls, both American and German, were obliged to give up their position this morning because the Chinese were attacking on both sides and they had a fortification only on one side. Later they took up sand bags for a new rampart and retook their position at least the American troops did, but in the attempt a good many were killed and wounded, among them seven of our Chinese who were acting as coolies, carrying bags. Just after breakfast this morning I took time to write a little letter in Chinese to our Chinese Christian women over in Tsu Wang Sen as I haven't been able to see them since the day we came here. But before it was finished there came a call, first for 400 and then 2000 bags as soon as possible. So the whole day has been a rush with bags. During a little lull while waiting for material I went over and had a little meeting with a company of Catholic women, who are quartered in a little pavilion close by the chapel. We have had no regular service today, but after we Congregationalists had had our tea, and before the Presbyterians had started in with theirs, we took the time and room to have a little time of prayer together. It has not seemed at all like Sabbath and I am tired. Abbie and the others at work in the hospital have the hardest time, caring for the wounded dying and dead.

Abbie said today it seemed as if she should never see anything again but wounds and blood. We wait and pray for the coming of troops from Tientsin and wonder at the long delay. Our soldiers are so few, and the number grows less from day to day. They cannot fight because the Chinese fire only from behind walls and fortifications or from loopholes in houses and never come out for open battle, and our troops have no artillery for battering down walls and so cannot get at them. Many of these troops have been at Manila and in war at other places, but they say they never went through such a hard experience as this.

Mon. July 2nd. We had another quiet night – at least there was no general attack, but some firing all night. Today too has been a remarkably quiet day, though there has been some heavy firing on Tsu Wang Sen and one Japanese soldier was killed and another wounded. No one understands the lull in the firing. Some think that the Chinese soldiers know that our troops are near and have gone out to meet and retard their coming; others that their ammunition is nearly exhausted so that they can no longer keep up this continuous fire; and still another and more alarming theory is that they are busy mining and mean to destroy us from underneath, since they do not succeed from above. I am not concerned about it, for though we do not know what they are doing and do know that they are using every endeavor to get us out of the way, it is enough that the Lord knows all about it, and that we are in His care.

It is strange how one grows accustomed even to bullets flying all around, to balls whistling over our heads, and to shells bursting here and there, and goes quietly on with one's work, as if nothing was happening. Again I have been busy all day. I was one of the cooks today with Mrs Tewksbury, and we have had charge of the meals for our own mission, some 35 to cater for. Of course we have a Chinese cook and several other men to help, but it still takes a good deal of our time – but it has been easier than sewing bags all day.

This forenoon as there was no material for bags I took the time to do a little bit of sewing for myself. Of the few things I brought from Tung cho, two thirds or more were left at the Methodist Mission when we came over here. I meant to bring one complete change of underclothing but in the confusion and rush, some things were forgotten. I found after getting here that I had not a single nightdress. Among things that were picked up and brought over here later on, was one nightdress which nobody claimed, so it was given to me. But it was evidently made for some one much larger than I, and needed to be reduced in size. We do not, most of us, undress these nights so that nightdresses are not a necessity, but we live in the hope that this state of things may not last long.

There have been reports again and again all through these weeks of rockets and flash lights – signals seen by one and another, and supposed to indicate the near approach of our expected troops. Today the British Minister testified to having seen such signals in the night last night. Reports and rumors, opinions and theories, are so constant and numberless, that I take little account of them. But I do hope our troops may come soon. Even when they come I don't know what will be done.

Tues. 3rd. We had rather a hard night. There were several sharp attacks during the night, but no harm was done apart from the general alarm and sleeplessness. I slept through the first two attacks. While this was going on a party of our soldiers, Austrian and American, made a charge on the barricade of the Chinese on the wall, and carried it, scattering the Chinese and capturing their guns – but they did not succeed in getting possession of the cannon which they especially wanted. Two brave men were killed and one, the captain wounded – but now they hold a part of the wall commanding our Legation, which was especially dangerous to have in the hands of the Chinese.

Today the rainy season seems fairly upon us. It has been a little rainy for several days past, but today it rains steadily and some of the time heavily. Things are quiet today, very little of firing. The rain keeps all of the children indoors, which of course adds to the general noise and confusion.

Wed. 4th. Such a strange 4th of July. We had a terrible night, one sharp attack following another nearly all night long – The ordinary racket of the night before the 4th of July was nothing to it. Of course there was little sleep and it has been a tired day. We had no way of celebrating, except that we sang 'America', 'Battle Hymn of the Republic', and 'Oh say can you see' this morning, and most of us are wearing little badges of red white and blue sewing silk. The American flag was draped [on] the altar, which is our sideboard. We had more material brought in today, so I have given much of the day as usual to making sandbags. Went to sleep a little while this afternoon. A great deal of firing has been going on all day and we learn that one [girl] at Tsu Wang Sen was struck by a fragment of shell, making a bad wound in her knee. Just now Major Conger, our minister, brought over for us to see the copy of the Declaration of Independence which had been hanging in his study. He took it down to read today and found that a bullet had been fired through it and lay on the mantel behind it.

Thurs. 5th. We had a more than usually quiet night with no sharp attacks, and I slept a good deal. Today has been quiet too most of the time, though a cannonading was opened from a new point this afternoon and for a time we were obliged to stay closely under shelter.

This afternoon I went over to the court where the school girls are living, just to see them a few minutes – but they asked me to have a little meeting with them, so we gathered in the large room, and I had a very pleasant time with them. Then I went across to the smaller room and there the girls said they had not been able to get into the large room, and outside the door could not hear what I said, so wanted a meeting there. So I lingered for a second meeting and was a little late in getting home for supper. I feel troubled about our women and children over at the Tsu Wang Sen. They say there is a great deal of sickness among them. Three little children were buried yesterday and one today. The last one of our Tung cho babies, and a good many of the older people, are sick too.

Just now word has come to us that Gilbert Reid[9] has been wounded. They say it is only a slight flesh wound, a bullet passing through the calf of the leg. His brave little wife took the word very quietly and has gone to put her baby to bed that she may go to him. He has been taken to the hospital to have the wound dressed. This is the first wound in our missionary circle. Surely we are covered by the Lord's own hand. The gentlemen just go everywhere, superintending all the various kinds of work. We have a mill for grinding wheat, a blacksmith's shop, a bakery, and a laundry, and all this work, besides the fortifying, is under the oversight of the missionaries and they are here and there and everywhere all the time. On guard too, by day and by night – and it has seemed indeed a miracle that they have thus far passed among the bullets and shells unharmed.

Friday 6th. We had another hard night last night – two sharp attacks and a good deal of firing all night prevented much sleep. This morning I received a note from our Station Class teacher or Hana, begging me to speak to Mr Tewksbury and have all their family moved over here, as she heard other families had been moved over. It is not to our Legation Court but to vacant houses this side the moat, where it is possible for us to go to them now and then. I felt I could not ask for that one family, what so many other families want and need just as much. Besides I can't bear to have the leaders among our women come away and leave the ignorant and helpless ones, with no one to strengthen, or help, or encourage them in their sore trouble and danger and fear – so the first thing after breakfast, I wrote a letter to her, explaining why I could not ask the favor for them. I suppose they will feel hurt, but I cannot do a thing which would seem to the Chinese like partiality or favoritism. They are all well, while many are sick and need to come far more. But all the same it hurts one to refuse. Afterward I wrote a line to all our Christians over there and sent them some Bible verses to think about, then read Chinese until nearly dinner time. At noon I learned that [—] Nainai, our Bible reader and Hana's mother, had just been wounded by a bullet which passed through her foot. I don't know how serious the wound is and of course I cannot go to her, but I feel so sorry for her and wish she was now within my reach. The Japanese who are guarding Tsu Wang Sen with some of the Chinese made a sally to take a cannon which was troubling them.

They drove the Chinese away but they took the cannon with them and three of the Japanese and one of the Chinese were killed. There are more or less killed every day lately.

Sat. eve. 7th. We had no general attack last night – but a fully constant firing from two o'clock on, so that I slept but little. Today there was a heavy cannonading about noon and the balls crashed through the English Minister's dining room and demolished the table set for dinner. I think some harm was done to the French Legation also. Tsu Wang Sen was heavily attacked at the same time, but I don't know that any one was injured.

I hear today that two of our Tung cho babies have died. I knew of one before. There is a terrible state of things over there, so much sickness and cases of smallpox, scarlet fever and diphtheria among them. More and more of our people are being removed to other places to relieve the crowd there, but none are in places where I can go to them. I wrote a letter to [—] Nainai the first thing after breakfast. She is better and the family have been allowed to come over to this side. After that worked on bags until dinner time – and then some time after dinner, and as the material was old tents etc., very dirty and very heavy, I grew very weary over it, and when the work was finished lay down to rest a while. After that I finished a shirtwaist I have been at work on in the intervals between bags for more than a week. I have only one shirtwaist with me but several thin light-colored waists that get soiled so soon, and it is so hard to get my washing done here. I had several with me at the Methodist Mission, but all except this one had been put into the wash and had not come out when we made the sudden move over here, and so were lost. Miss Brown[10] had some material on hand and gave me a piece of dark print, but I have not before had time to make it. Mrs Fenn of the Presbyterian Mission was injured by a brick, while a Chinese cannon was battering down one of our barricades.

Sat. eve. 8th. This has been a busy day, but not in the same way as the last two Sabbaths. No bag-making today, indeed no material. I was on as housekeeper today so was busy at mealtimes. After breakfast I sat down to prepare for a meeting with the girls, then we had our own English service, a precious prayer meeting. Then came the preparation for dinner and the serving and cleaning up afterward for our party of 33 and then I went over to Miss Douw's[11] – Abbie and I for a quiet dinner with their little party of four. It did seem so good to sit down once more at an orderly well-appointed table. We have our great crowd, and the rush to get through to make way for the other parties whose meals follow ours. We can do nothing in a homelike way – we sit on the chapel seats on the platform or the floor, as we can, and often with our plates in our laps. The confusion, and rush and disorder are rather trying, and the food is not always appetizing – but still we get on very well, and thus far know nothing of real hardship. Today we have been obliged to shut down on butter, condensed milk, and indeed all canned goods. It is a little absurd but the one thing I especially miss, I mean about meals, is a napkin, for we have no table linen. How could refugees have such luxuries.

Well after dinner I went over for my meeting with my school girls, Abbie having a meeting at the same time with another company of them, for there is no room large enough for them all. Coming back we had a pleasant little Bible study, and then came the rush for tea. We had two furious attacks in the night and one cannon ball struck the roof of our chapel knocking off one of the little stone lions that adorn it, but no harm was done. There has been another persistent attempt to burn out Tsu Wang Sen. Another of our Yang cho people was wounded today, our chapel keeper, but the wound is not serious. I found last night that the court to which [—] Nainai and a good many of our people were removed yesterday, is where we can reach it without much danger, and I went over to see her.

Mon. 9th. Such a hot day. A hot night too. I could not sleep for the heat. Two fierce attacks before midnight. The children were unusually restless and cried a good deal and as usual the myriads of flies began to torment us with the first break of day – and altogether the night was a weary one. Today we have been at work on sand bags again, and this evening I have been over with Mrs Tewskbury to see our women – as many of them as we can reach. All the rest of our people, except two or three who are sick with contagious diseases, have been brought over from Tsu Wang Sen and are quartered in courts connected with the American Legation; but we cannot go to them.

Tues. 10th. Another day passed in this monotonous way and so far as we can see no more prospect of relief. We wonder and wonder why the troops do not come but have no way of knowing anything about them or indeed anything of the outside world. What became of the friends at Pao ting fu, at Kalgan or Shantung, and Shonai – we know nothing. Probably from Luntim and Peitaihoh[12] they escaped early to Shanghai and Japan – or perhaps to the homeland if war is really declared. But of that too we do not know. And then we think of all our dear native Christians scattered – of whose whereabouts and circumstances we know nothing.

Such terrible stories came to us from Tung cho, while we were still at the Methodist Mission; one of our faithful deacons we hear was cut to pieces, and his wife and two dear little girls. My West Gate scholars jumped into the river to escape a worse fate. The family at the East Gate – to whose home I have gone for meetings and for teaching all these years – are reported as all massacred. I know nothing about the dear Too Hoh people. They had all escaped from their homes just as the terrible outburst came, but whether they succeeded in hiding or not is doubtful, for the Boxers and soldiers seemed determined to search out and utterly destroy not only every

Christian, but everybody who had anything to do with us. I had had no word of the West Suburb people, the dear little Too Tang circle, and the people at the other villages of the Lang pa people, the teacher's family and several other families out here, including the larger part of my scholars.

Last night was a weary night. The summer heat is upon us and last night was quite too hot for any quiet sleep. Then just before midnight came a furious attack, the cannonading shook the building and one rifle bullet came into the chapel and struck Mrs Tewksbury – but it was a spent bullet and she was not harmed. Today has been full, as usual. I was housekeeper again today and so busy at meal times, and in the intervals I have worked on bags, though I did take time this afternoon for a little nap. This evening I went over with Mrs. Goodrich[13] to see our women and was delighted to find that holes had been dug through walls separating different courts, so that we could reach half a dozen families whom I have not seen before since the day we came here, three weeks ago.

Wed. 11th. Another hot night, so that it was hard work to sleep, though there was much less firing than usual. A hot day too, most of it spent on bags. It is a weary way of living, and yet we have much to thank God for. I wish I could somehow send you a message just to let you know how well I am, and how safely the Lord folds us in and shields us from our enemies who are bent on our destruction. God bless my precious little sister, and keep her heart in peace. It seems an age since I heard from you last or could send to you. I fear the last letters I sent you from the Methodist Mission were never sent or were lost by the way.

Friday 13th. I did not write yesterday. The night before had been an almost sleepless night and I was too weary in the morning to do anything. Indeed I could not keep my eyes open, and soon after breakfast I went over to the ballroom where a good many of our ladies sleep, and where it is cool and quiet usually at that hour, and went to sleep and had a good nap. Most of the day was given as usual to sand bags, and at evening I went over to see our women and to lead prayers with the London Mission women and at Miss Smith's[14] request. It grew a little cooler toward evening and the night was not so hot as the past three or four have been. So I got a good deal of sleep notwithstanding several sharp attacks which of course awoke everybody.

This morning soon after breakfast I went over to the courts beyond the American Legation to see the rest of our women, those whom I have not before seen. Some more holes dug in the walls made it possible for me to go to them without much danger and it was so good to see them again, and they seemed so glad to see me. Afterward I lingered to lead prayers with another group of London Mission and our own women, so that it was dinnertime before I got back to our chapel, which I call home these days.

Sat. 14th. Just as I was writing last evening a furious attack began which lasted two hours or more. The most furious and long-continued we have ever had. I was so glad it was not in the night. From one direction it was aimed especially at the French Legation – the Chinese had mined under the house of the Secretary of Legation and blew it up, killing a number of their own people and burying two of the French in the ruins, and injuring several others. A great fire was started which burned several buildings and the French were obliged to give up about half of their premises and fall back to another barricade. At the same time we were attacked from another direction, and the rifle firing and cannonading were fearful, bullets, balls, and shells falling in all directions. In the midst of the general confusion a large company of Chinese – some 200-were discovered creeping along close to the wall toward the American Legation. They were fired upon by our troops and 30 or 40 were killed. If we could at all realize the situation it would be a fearful thing to feel oneself in the focus of all this murderous hate and deviltry. As it is we feel held in the hollow of the Lord's hand and so safe.

This afternoon one of our messengers sent out some days ago to find the troops returned with a letter purporting to come from Prince Ching and others, the most audacious and absurd letter that ever was written. The writer utterly ignores the fact that Government soldiers have been cannonading us day and night the past three and a half weeks, assumes that relations are friendly, and desires to maintain them so, hence wishes to protect us. They have devised the following plan. They request the foreign ministers, with their families and staff officers, to leave the legation and come in detachments to the *Tsungli Yamen*, the government sending trusty men to protect them – but on no account to allow a single armed soldier to accompany them. They to be kept for the present in the *Tsungli Yamen*, till arrangements are made for sending them home. They request an answer today. They say no other plan can be devised and if the ministers refuse to accede to this request – even their 'affection' can do nothing to help us.

One wonders what their idea is in sending such a letter. They cannot be fools enough to expect us to accede to such a request. The messenger was a Catholic. He was seized just outside the city, his letter written to the captain of the troops, which was hidden in his mouth, was taken from him and he was beaten 80 blows, but his life was spared that he might bring us this letter and take back our answer.

Sabbath 15th. Today has been more like Sabbath than any we have spent here. We have not been making bags and we have had a good many meetings among ourselves and for our people. They are so scattered now that there is no opportunity to gather them together, even if there were any room large enough to hold them, but we arranged meetings in various places for them. I led the Lang pa group, and it did seem so good to have a meeting with our women once more. We had an English service this morning and another this afternoon and a few of us had a quiet little sing at bedtime. There has been some excitement today over the answer sent by the English Minister, Sir Claude MacDonald,[15] to Prince Ching's letter. In substance it stated that the attacks complained of had been made by their troops, not ours, who are simply defending our lives and property against Chinese government troops; also that the ministers declined to leave their legations and go to the *Yamen* as they proposed.

Mon. 16th. A terrible cannonading in the night, and bullets, solid shot, and shells fell every where – but no one was hurt. Today, however, while things were apparently quiet, several lives were lost by stray shot. Captain Strouts,[16] the commander of all the English forces here, was shot in the morning, and Mr Fisher, an American Marine; both wounds mortal; while others were wounded before and died in the night, and he and Captain S. were buried in one grave just at evening.

There has been little firing during the day. Some excitement over another letter from Prince Ching regretting the decision of the ministers, and requesting that if their troops stopped firing, ours should do the same. Another messenger brought a telegram in cypher to Major Conger without date or signature, saying only 'Communicate by bearer'. There are various surmises as to what it all means, but no one knows. It may be that the Chinese Government is divided against itself – Prince Ching and [General] Jung Lu and his troops really wishing to protect us, Prince Tuan with [General] Tung Fu Hsiang and his troops determined to destroy us. It may be the Chinese know that our troops are at hand and sincerely wish to make overtures of peace before their arrival.

Tues. 17th. Only a slight attack last night, and today has been very quiet – hardly any firing at all, all day. Several men, probably Boxers, and spies, have been captured and brought in today – but I put no faith in anything they tell us. Another letter from Prince Ching to the English minister laying the blame of all this warfare upon us and wanting it stopped. Evidently for some unknown reason – perhaps because our troops are near – the Chinese, at least a part of them, want to make peace, or else they want to delay matters while they are secretly mining.

Another letter came also to Major Conger, in answer to his inquiring in regard to the strange telegram of the day before. They say it comes from Washington and was accompanied by a telegram not in cypher from the Chinese minister in Washington. A copy of the telegram was sent. It says that the Secretary of State instructs him to telegraph that America will gladly help China – also to inquire after the welfare of Minister Conger. I have no faith in the authenticity of the telegram. Don't believe such a message could possibly be sent by our government – after the telegrams we sent home more than a month ago, telling of the burning of all our property, the massacre of all our Christians and our own danger.

Wed. 18th. Almost no firing yesterday, and none at all late in the night. But for the mosquitoes I might have slept, but they [pester] me so and I have no netting so the night was a weary one and today I am very tired.

Today has come the first reliable word from the outside world which we have had for weeks and weeks. A messenger sent out June 6th with a letter to the captain of the troops did succeed in reaching Tientsin and came back today with a letter and news of various kinds. The foreign settlement there had not been burned, but chapels in the Chinese city had been destroyed. The missionaries had all gone 'home' it was said – but very likely not further than Shanghai or Japan. Consuls and other officials, and very likely merchants, [are] still there. The Taku forts were taken a month ago by foreign troops and a few days ago Tientsin itself. The Chinese city was also taken after a two-days battle, with heavy loss to the Chinese. The letter says that 33,500 troops would start about the 20th to the relief of Pekin. So it will probably be ten days or more before they reach here – it may be very much longer. Still after all these weeks with nothing but rumors, it is good to hear something that can be depended upon. Today has been quiet, no firing at all.

Thurs. July 19th. Another perfectly quiet day. Yesterday I got hold of a piece of netting, and today I have made me a tiny mosquito net, so I hope to sleep tonight. I have come almost to the end of my strength through loss of sleep, so that for two or three days past I have been ready to cry through weariness and it has been hard work to keep cheery and pleasant, and I fear I have not succeeded very well. There have been messengers in from the *Tsungli Yamen* today, but there is no word worth writing except that since the foreign ministers decline to go to the *Yamen* for protection they are requested to go to Tientsin – of course, under Chinese 'protection'. Of course they will not for a moment think of going.

Friday 20th. We are wondering if the troops really started today. We have had another quiet day and night. No special news today. Some amusing things – among others, a cartload of watermelons sent to the foreign ministers, with a card purporting to be from the Emperor Huang Hsu, saying he feared they might not be able to get them here and wished to make them a present of them. It is true that we get no fruit or vegetables of any kind. A few hucksters have ventured to come into our lines with things to sell but we hear that their heads were taken off in consequence. However a few eggs are smuggled in so that the sick ones and the little children can have them.

Some copies of the *Pekin Gazette* were brought in today containing various government edicts – they are posted upon the bell tower, but so many have been around them reading and copying that I have not yet had opportunity to get within reading distance.

My mosquito net was a great success and not a mosquito nor fly came near me all night. Consequently I overslept this morning, and found it necessary to hasten to be ready for my duties of getting breakfast, for I was one of the housekeepers again today. I have risen about 4 ever since we came here, partly because the flies would not let me sleep after that hour, and partly because it is only at that early hour that I can be sure of a place in the bath room long enough for the sponge bath which seems quite essential to my comfort and health. Since the cessation of the firing, so that we are free from the constant thought of danger to life, I find that I am getting very tired of living in a crowd with no opportunity for a moment of quiet – very tired, too, of keeping the few things I have in a bag, so that I have to go to the bottom of it for every little thing I need. Very trifles to care about to be sure.

Mon. 23rd. We have been having terribly hot nights of late so that sleep has been quite impossible, but last night came a pouring rain, and I slept soundly most of the night and so am not so weary today as I have been of late. But the day is intensely sultry and hard to bear. The perfect quiet, so far as any firing is concerned, still continues day and night. I think the Chinese authorities are most anxious to put the blame of all this upon the Boxers, and to pose as our protectors when the troops shall come. But the Imperial Edicts in the *Pekin Gazettes* in our hands show plainly, if we needed to be shown, how the government and the Boxers worked together in the attempt to drive us all out and to root out the Christian church from this land. I am not going to copy the Edicts here for they have all been printed off and I shall send you a copy, unless I go home myself to take it.

Now that we look forward to the coming of the troops soon, we cannot help thinking some of what is to come afterward. No one can foresee what is to be and I for one do not know at all what ought to be done, that the Christian church may be protected in the years to come, that China may be saved and God glorified. People prophesy this and that and tell what ought to be done, but I am sure of only one thing – and that is that the Lord has a plan for China, and whatever her friends or her enemies may wish for her, the Lord's plan is surely best and He will surely carry [it] out – I wait to see how. As to what I shall myself do when we are released, it will depend upon circumstances. If there is any hope of going back to Tung cho in the autumn to begin our work over again, then I want to stay on, but if, as is more likely it will be a year or two before we can go back there, then I want to take my furlough now, so as to come back and be ready to begin work as soon as the way is open. In that case I shall start for home as soon as possible, after we get out of here. Perhaps the same steamer that takes this letter will also take me.

I do not forget, darling, how hard this waiting time must be for you, especially if, as I fear, we are all supposed to be killed, and that word has been sent home. Mr Tewksbury tried to send a telegram to the Board Rooms yesterday, telling them of our safety and asking them to notify our friends. We dare not trust the Chinese authorities to send it, and the plan was to send a messenger to Tientsin and it was all arranged for – but I hear today that he finally declined to go, so the effort failed.

Yesterday was quite like Sabbath. The Chinese men all let off from work at 11 oclock, and in the afternoon Dr Goodrich[17] held a general service for them, much to their joy, the first service they have had since coming over here. We had our own preaching service in the morning and a Bible study in the afternoon and between times I had prayer meetings with two groups of our women. At evening we had a sad little funeral service. Dr Inglis of the Presbyterian Mission laid his little one to rest, a darling girlie in whom the hearts of father and mother were bound up. This siege is proving very hard on the little ones; this is the fourth death among the foreign children since we came here. Another of our Lang pa little ones, I mean of the Chinese, passed away the night before and was laid to rest in the early morning.

We are still at work at fortifications and as we fear the Chinese are occupying the quiet time in mining, we are doing some counter-mining. We dare not trust their professions, though we hope the quiet may continue until the troops come.

Wed. am 25th. I did not write yesterday. The night before was almost sleepless because of the heat and yesterday I seemed to have come to the end of my strength. I lay down and went to sleep for a little while in the forenoon and did nothing of any importance all day. Indeed I didn't feel equal to anything. Mr Cockburn, who has some position in the Legation[18] so that his home is here, has opened his library to us lately and I have rested my mind and taken it away from present surroundings for a little by reading two or three stories, so I read yesterday. For all the first weeks of our stay here, there was nothing whatever to read and it seemed so strange to be living absolutely without any books or papers. Of all my beautiful library I saved only my Bible, and that is the case with many of us. I do think of my books, and of all my Bible study notes and of the beautiful pictures, gifts of you and other friends, with something of regret, and indeed of the dear home where so large a part of my life has been spent, my bedroom furniture, the gift of our SS people so long ago – in which Mr Perkins was so much interested. I find that I did care for my possessions now that they are in ashes. Though their loss does not make me unhappy, and I am so glad that the really precious things cannot be lost, of course if we get indemnity from the Chinese Government, as we may, many things can be replaced, but it will be beginning everything anew. I cannot even get home without making some additions to my wardrobe and I haven't the least little thing for autumn and winter wear. Ah well, I am not troubled about that.

Yesterday just at evening came word – whether true or not I don't know – that on the 17th our troops took possession of Yang Tsun, a town on the river, one quarter the way from Tientsin to Tung cho, that on the 19th a great battle occurred not far from there, in which many of the Chinese were wounded. Wounded soldiers had begun to come in to Peking and when they started, our troops were some 18 miles this side of Yang Tsun. If it be true, they cannot be very far away now. Last night, after more than a week of quiet, there was a sharp attack made in the night not of cannon but of musketry. The night was a little cooler, and except at the time of the firing I slept soundly, so feel like myself again today.

Sat. eve. 26th. The days pass monotonously and there is little to report. The nights are so weary with heat, insect bites, and the worrying of the little children who are half sick and as uncomfortable as the older folks, and besides more or less of firing, that I have come to quite dread them. Yesterday I was not feeling quite well, just a touch of bowel trouble, caused probably by the heat and the sleeplessness, so I lay still a good deal of the day, and today I am all right again. Various rumors have come in these last days, of battles at Hohshihwo,[19] Motou[20] and Chongu[21] [—], but I do not put much faith in them, and only hope the troops may come soon. I am growing so weary of the confusion of this life and yet there is always so much to thank God for all of the time. I should not mind things so much but for the intense heat which takes all the life out of me. This morning one of our messengers sent out July 4th, a little boy, disguised as a beggar, came back with a letter from the Consul at Tientsin, but it is not very encouraging. It was dated the 22nd and evidently our troops had not started then, though the letter said plainly our troops were on the way, if only we could make our food supply hold out. I was sadly disappointed over it, and found it very hard to be really glad in God's will, even though it be a longer waiting time. Tears have been very near the surface all day, tears of weariness, and I have just cried to the Lord for grace to welcome gladly God's will.

Tues. 31st. I have written nothing since Saturday. There came a rain on Sabbath and it is a little cooler now. Last night I slept better than for many nights before, so feel more like myself. Sabbath our people had a rest day and two general services, and I had a little prayer meeting with our group of women. We ourselves had communion in the morning and a praise service in the afternoon, and just at bedtime a few of us ladies got together for a little prayer meeting.

All sorts of reports are coming in all of the time of the movements of the troops, but we do not know at all what to believe. Today our troops are reported at Chang-Chia-Wan,[22] 10 miles from Tung cho. They seem to be having to fight their way all the way. What will happen when they reach here no one can predict. Our people fear that we shall all be sent away and they left helpless. Dr Goodrich has the same fear, that before the city is attacked we shall be taken away. But I feel sure that prayer will again be answered, as so many times before, and that we shall not be separated from our people.

Friday Aug. 3rd. So much to write. On Wednesday we had another messenger from Tientsin with a letter dated July 26th which said the troops had been delayed in starting, owing to difficulty of transport, but hoped to start in two or three days. So all the reports brought in as to the battles along the way have been false, and we could not know that they had even started. Last evening came another messenger with several letters, one from Mr Ed. Lowery[23] to his wife, who is here with us. He had been away on business for months before these troubles broke out and since has not been able to get back – but is coming with the troops as interpreter. He wrote definite word in regard to the Methodist missionaries, which was a great relief to their friends here, especially several gentlemen whose families were in Peitaiho or at other places, but there was no word in regard to our missionaries, who I suppose left Tientsin long ago; nor was there any word from Pao-ting-fu or Shantung, so we still have no idea what has become of our friends there. Some of the troops had already left Tientsin when those letters were written July 30th, but the main body was to move the next day, and Mr Lowery wrote that he hoped they might reach us in a week. They had a very hard time in Tientsin. The Chinese troops shelled the foreign settlement for 30 days and hardly a house remained uninjured. The foreign troops who started for our relief so long ago were surrounded by Chinese soldiers and could not even get back to Tientsin until a larger party went to their relief – so it was useless to make another attempt to reach Peking without a much larger force and it took time to gather them from the Philippines and other places. In the meantime they had given up all hope in Tientsin of being able to save us, supposing we had long since been murdered. I fear such word went home.

This letter of Mr Lowery's is the first which has been received in Peking for nearly two months, except the two or three official letters, and it was a joy to everybody when Mrs Lowry received her letter. Where all our letters and papers are and when, if ever, they will reach us, no one can tell. We feel so utterly separated from all the world and can but think anxiously of all the anxiety of home friends for us. The messenger who brought back those last letters was the one who took a telegram for the American Board down to Tientsin telling of our safety, so we know that telegram went through and hope the word reached you and relieved your anxiety.

Thurs. 9th. Nearly a week since I wrote last, darling. The days are full even here, and many days I do not find time to write – I am keeping well, but somehow the strength seems all to have dropped out. It is not strange with such a throng of us shut up — not only in this dirtiest of dirty cities for all summer, but within the walls of the Legation as well, with no possibility of getting out or even seeing out, how can one keep strong? Then too at the very time when one needs to be living on fresh fruit and vegetables, to be wholly cut off from them is not healthful, to say the least. I am better off than most for my stomach does not protest against our fare, so I am able to eat — as many cannot. If I could only sleep as well, I should be all right; but the nights are very weary, and every morning by the time breakfast and the morning duties and prayers are over I feel as if I had reached the very end of my strength and could not longer hold my head up. Often I lie down and sleep until dinner time, but it is very hot, and whether by day or by night sleep is not very refreshing.

Friday 10th. Still no reliable word from our troops, and we have no idea where they are nor when we shall see them. We are facing the danger of a food supply if they delay much longer, but I am not troubled. I am sure the Lord will somehow supply that need as he has every need so far. We hear that the Chinese over at Tsu Wang Sen are suffering for food, having only one meal a day. It seems that when there was an opportunity for getting the food supplies, they failed to improve it and instead gathered in silver ornaments and beautiful garments and other things with which to enrich themselves, and then while they had food were very wasteful of it — and so are feeling the pressure earlier than we.

Just this moment there has come in word from the troops, a special messenger with a letter from General [Sir Alfred] Gaselee, the commander of the English forces. He is leading the 2nd Division of the forces, and when the messenger left was this side of Hoh-shih-wu, the midway point between Tientsin and Tung cho, the 1st Division being of course in advance of that point. They had two sharp engagements with Chinese troops, victorious in each case, and he hoped to get here four or five days from yesterday. So glad to hear.

There is great mortality among the little Chinese children and several are laid to rest every day. Kao-Chih lost his little one two days ago, and Tsui-Fui his youngest two or three days before, and several others of our little Tung cho babies cannot last much longer. Measles, scarlet fever, and bowel troubles are making sad havoc with the little lives.

So many things come to fill the days. One day last week I gave the entire day to patching and darning, a little for myself and a good deal for others. Some of our gentlemen here without their wives have rather a hard time of it when their clothes give out. One day I gave a large part of the afternoon to writing out telegrams in cypher, because the numbers needed to be written as small as possible in order that the telegram might be the more easily concealed on the person of the messenger and I seemed able to make smaller figures than any one else. One day this week I gave all the afternoon to helping prepare a little coffin for a dear little Swiss baby who had just died. The poor father and mother were very lonely, there being no other family of that nationality here. I give a good deal of time to going about among our people, though there is little that I can do for them. I have little meetings here and there for little groups of them now and then, and I try to show my sympathy and give the little help I can in their sicknesses and troubles. The nights are very wearisome. I am able to sleep so little, but I get a little sleep in the day time sometimes and so keep up. This forenoon I slept soundly for two hours and it did me good. This afternoon I have been trying to make out a list and valuation of property destroyed to send in for indemnity.

The farce of a truce is over and for four or five nights past we have had sharp attacks of musketry every night – sometimes one attack following another most of the night. The bullets whiz past our windows, and now and then there is a crash as something is hit, but very little real harm is done. There are no cannon shots and we hear that a large part of the soldiers have gone out to meet our troops.

Sat. 12th. Just a line to you before tea. Besides the letter from the English Commander of which I wrote on Friday, the same messenger brought another from the Japanese Commander giving a more definite idea of their hope and plan in regard to reaching here. Their hope was to reach Chang-chia-wan yesterday, Tung cho today and Peking tomorrow or the next day. Word came today of a great battle and a great defeat of the Chinese troops at Chang-chia-wan yesterday but I don't know how reliable the word is. The messenger brought word from Tung cho that a Boxer flag was over every store in the city and a man had been impressed from every one to join the Boxer army. They were systematically hunting out and murdering all Christians. He himself is one of the family at Kuo-chia-ching which I have been in the habit of visiting. He made inquiries in regard to his own family and learned that they had nearly all been murdered, two only having escaped – hiding I suppose somewhere.

A fierce attack was made in the night last night upon the German and French Legations – one man being killed and one wounded. We too were attacked and the bullets whistled past our windows but no harm was done. We have had our usual Sabbath services today. This afternoon a very precious experience, meeting, telling one another the lessons the Lord had been teaching us during these weeks of stress and storm, and the things for which we thank the Lord. The Chinese have had their meetings as usual and Miss Evans[24] had a meeting with our group of women. I wanted to meet another group, but it has been so fearfully hot that I thought I would wait till after tea. Later a fierce attack came just after tea and the bullets were so flying everywhere that I delayed my meeting till the firing stopped. Then it was so far to the group I wanted to reach, and so many sick ones to see by the way, that I was finally obliged to give up my meeting as the darkness was already gathering. Just as I started back another terrific attack began and I was rather afraid to come back, but I could not know how long it would last and dared not wait lest it be dark, so I rushed and asked the Lord as I went to cover me with his hand and He did. As soon as I got within the walls of the English Legation – our people are scattered about among all the Legation – I went into the first house I came to, in which Miss Douw and the ladies of her Mission are staying, and waited there until there was a lull in the firing. There have been five distinct attacks today, in one of which the French commander was killed.

Mon. 13th – Wed. 15th. I didn't finally write Monday and now at last, darling, there is opportunity to send letters tonight so I must hasten to finish. Will you ever find the time to read such a long letter? I wonder how you have borne the suspense of the long waiting. I could only reach you by way of the throne and I have asked for you day by day strength of faith to trust for me and comfort for the heartache if, as I fear, our home friends supposed we were all to be massacred. It lacks only two days of two months since my last was sent and I fear several of the last sent from the Methodist Mission failed to reach you, and it is more than two months since I heard last from you. And now finally our troops have come and we are free – though when we shall be able to leave the Legation and where we shall go when we do leave, we do not at all know. We wait for leading.

Night before last was such a hard night. A furious attack lasted nearly all night, answered by our cannon at intervals. And then in the middle of the night we heard in the distance another and different sound – the firing of foreign cannon – and knew our troops could not be very far off. And then in the morning came the pounding of cannon against the walls and gate of the city.

I couldn't have believed it possible that I could ever find delight in such a sound knowing how much it must mean of havoc and probably of slaughter, but it was music to us all, because we knew well that only so could deliverance come to us, and only so salvation to China. We didn't think it possible that the troops could get in before night, if indeed before today. But in the middle of the afternoon suddenly came the word that they had come. I was writing cypher telegrams for Dr Reid but everybody dropped everything and there was a wild rush for the gate at which they would come in. After all the pounding on the Chi-hua-men had been only a feint to divert attention, and meantime they had battered down a less strongly protected gate and entered, and then by the water gate into the Legations.

Our American Marines had opened the gate but they did not get in first as they had other plans. The first to march in were the Bengal Lancers (Sikhs) with their big turbans, strange costumes, long lances, their splendid physique, sparkling eyes, and jolly faces. They came in with a hurrah and were wildly cheered. Of course, they were under English officers and soon after the English troops followed – but with less of dash – and still later our Americans, bearing our beautiful flag. They had gone to the Chien Men and scaled the wall, the Chinese soldiers who have fired so persistently upon us flying before them. The rest of the afternoon was full of the wildest excitement and joy. Mr Ed. Lowry had come with the troops, also Mr Lewis of the YMCA[25] and Mr Brown of the Methodist mission[26] and from them we learned many things about Tung cho, Tientsin and other parts of our Mission.

There was no battle at Tung cho, the troops simply took possession of the city without resistance, and are in possession now, 700: of whom 400 are Japanese, and 100 each English, American and Russian. Not a Boxer was to be found. They had simply thrown aside their red girdles and other marks and were transformed into good citizens. A large part of the people had left the city. The destruction of all our property was complete, not even a whole brick left – either in the city or at the college – even the foundations dug up and carried away. We learn that at Pang chuang all the houses were burnt and the missionaries driven out, but no one knows what has become of the native Christians. The word from Pao-ting-fu is dubious – but the fear is that all the missionaries there were killed. No word from Kalgan or Shensi.

Well today the troops have been shelling the Forbidden City and the Palace and have effected an entrance. What will be done by or with the Government no one knows. What we shall do is equally uncertain. If we can go back to Tung cho with our people, search out the scattered ones and begin our work anew, I want to stay and help. If we must stay in Peking and most of our missionaries go home, I want to stay. But if there are enough left to care for the people and do the work which is open, I shall go home as soon as possible.

At all events, darling little sister, whether I go or stay, I love you and long to see you. A few days will decide the matter and if there is opportunity to send again I will let you know –

With a whole – [end of MS]

Notes

[1] Mr Ingram, Reverend Tewksbury, and Reverend Ewing were from the American Board; Dr Inglis was an American Presbyterian missionary.

[2] Dr G.D.N. Lowry, Methodist Episcopal missionary.

[3] Also referred to as Tungchow, Tungchau, or Tungchou.

[4] Rev. T. Howard Smith, London Missionary Society.

[5] Peking Residence of Prince Su, known as *Su Wang Fu*. It was seized by the Allies on 15 June as a refuge for Chinese converts.

[6] National Academy, highest place of learning in China.

[7] British Legation compound.

[8] Miss Abbie G. Chapin, a close friend, had served in Tung chau at the American Board compound and accompanied Miss Andrews to the British Legation compound. Miss Chapin was placed in charge of the hospital's kitchen; for her distinguished services she was later awarded the Order of the Red Cross by King Edward VII.

[9] Dr Gilbert Reid had been attached to the American Presbyterian Mission. In 1900 he was engaged in independent work in Peking among Chinese scholars and officials, trying to interest them in reform and in science. He also served as a correspondent for *The Shanghai Mercury*, which published his own account of the siege (including accounts of others) in the fall of 1900.

[10] Miss Amy Brown, Christian Alliance.

[11] Miss D.M. Douw, Christian Alliance.

[12] Peitiaho was a seaside resort community; many prominent missionaries had summer homes there.

[13] Wife of Rev. Chauncey Goodrich, American Board missionary.

[14] Of the London Missionary Society.

[15] MacDonald was the commander for the entire beseiged legation compound.

[16] Captain B.M. Strouts, Royal Marines.

[17] Rev. Chauncey Goodrich, DD.

[18] Henry Cockburn was the Chinese Secretary of the British Legation. He occupied a large and handsome house which is frequently depicted in siege photographs, its balconies covered in sandbags.

[19] Ho-hsi-wu.

[20] Matou.

[21] Tongku.

[22] Chang-chiao-wan, located on the Peiho River between Matou and Tung chau.

[23] Edward K. Lowery of the Methodist Episcopal Mission, youngest son of Reverend H.H. Lowery, DD, who was formerly superintendent of the Methodist Episcopal Mission in North China. Edward Lowery had been absent from Peking on Mission business when the siege started. His wife was besieged, and he wanted desperately to reach her; he had marched in vain with the failed Seymour Expedition. General Chaffee engaged him as an interpreter with the American Army on the march to Peking.

[24] Miss Jane Gertrude Evans, American Board.

[25] Robert E. Lewis, Secretary of the Young Men's Christian Association, was based in Shanghai but carried responsibliity for all of North China. He arrived at Tientsin on 13 July 1900 and at once established a YMCA headquarters near the 9th US Infantry barracks. Lewis marched to Peking with the 14th US Infantry. After the relief of the city, he organised correspondence paper, envelopes, and reading material for the troops.

[26] Reverend Frederick Brown of the Methodist Episcopal Mission in Tientsin was officially appointed on 20 July 1900 to the Intelligence Department of the China Expeditionary Force and accompanied the British soldiers to Peking. He had stopped in Tung chau to obtain local intelligence, and observed of the site of the American Board compound, 'we found only a heap of broken bricks. The foundations had been dug up and the good bricks stolen.' (*Tientsin to Peking*, page 103.)

Account of
Private Harry J. Dill,
US Army

Harry J. Dill arrived with the 14th US Infantry from the Philippines. A resident of Atlantic City, New Jersey, he had enlisted for service in 1899, aged 18.

[Tientsin
31 July 1900]

We arrived off Taku on July 26th about one o'clock in the afternoon. Companies E and F's goods were loaded onto lighters and at two o'clock on the morning of the 27th started for Taku. We passed the forts at the mouth of the Peiho, which were bombarded and captured by the allied fleet and in which it is said 5000 Chinese were killed, about daylight. About 7 o'clock we had landed at Tongku. Both Taku and Tongku are in ruins. The houses that were not blown to pieces were burned down. This is the landing place of all nations. The inhabited part of the town is one vast hospital. Several American marines are here wounded.

At Tongku we unloaded our goods from the boat and put them on to the cars. At noon we boarded the train and started toward Tientsin. The advance can plainly be seen for everything, town, crops, bridges etc., are ruined. The rail way is one line of troops, mostly Russians. The distance from Tongku to Tientsin is about thirty-five miles, but it took us over three hours to make the trip. About 3.30 we pulled through the wall surrounding the city and as far as eye could see was one mass of ruined buildings.

Some had been completely blown to bits by exploding shells, others burned. Here and there lay a dead Chinese, some killed by small bullets. others torn up by shell fire. The station [is] perhaps the most interesting place, for here the Japs and Chinese fought at fifty yards with large and small arms. There is not one foot of surface that has not a shot of some size in it. The Russians are quartered in this part of the town.

The river divides the native from the foreign city. For twenty days the two armies battered each other till the Chinese were driven out with a loss estimated from 8,000 to 30,000. The Japs and Russians lost the heaviest of the allies.

The Ninth United States Infantry on July 13th had a battalion engaged in an attack on a gate and lost twenty killed and a lot wounded beside having their colonel[1] killed. On the evening of the 27th we went into camp along side of the Ninth.[2] We had to wash in the river which was fairly crowded with dead Chinos.

On the 28th we took quarters in the American Board Mission's grounds[3] and are still there. The Japs and the Russians have been fighting daily with the Boxers and in a couple of cases were driven back. Today we start for Lord knows where, but I think on the way to Peking. The Boxers are intrenched about ten miles from here and I think this will be our first stop.

We are getting fine food here. The boys go foraging every day and get all kinds of vegetables. The climate is fine. In the winter there is not over four inches of snow.

I am in fine health and expect to be in the States before a year for in a few months this trouble will be over and they will send us home

Peking
5 September 1900

We started on August 4, and on the 14th forced the first wall [of the Chinese City] and planted the stars and stripes, the first foreign flag to wave over Peking in the present war. The flag was planted by a bugler of E Company [Trumpeter Calvin P. Titus] after the color bearer had been killed.

On the 5th and 6th we had stiff fights with the Chinese [at Peit-tsang and Yang-tsun respectively], the engagement on the latter date being especially severe. They had four batteries of artillery throwing shrapnel, and 3000 other men engaged. The Americans, the Fourteenth Infantry and Fifth Artillery, did all the work in routing them, and the Fourteenth's loss was fourteen killed outright and fifty-six wounded. Some of the latter died subsequently.

At 3 o'clock on the morning of the 6th we started from Pei-tsang, the town we had helped the Japs to capture on the 5th, and after a march of between fourteen and fifteen miles through a country ankle-deep in sand and with a broiling sun pouring down (and the officers wouldn't allow us to get water), went into the fight. The advance guard sighted the enemy ahead and we were deployed in line of battle. For the next two hours we were under as heavy a fire as was probably ever poured upon any body of troops. The rifle balls were coming like rain, throwing up little puffs of dust, and the shrapnel was dropping everywhere. I saw one shell knock over sixteen men, though only seven were injured. A part of it carried away a piece of my hat brim. We advanced with a yell and were for nearly three-quarters of an hour in the open where we encountered an awful fire. We pressed on, however, and carried the trenches at the point of the bayonet. Some of the men were overcome by the heat and a few went raving insane.

An old English colonel said: 'I have been in the Queen's service many years and have been in many campaigns where strong forts and positions were taken, but I never saw a fire that equaled that of today. I have also seen the troops of several nations in action, but the Americans are champions. They are wonders.'

The Japs are America's best friends. They are as bold as lions. The Russians are not much account. They were driven back at the city wall which we carried with not half as many men. The Germans are fighters from the heart. We joined with the Japs in capturing Tung-Chou, a walled city about fifteen miles from Pekin. Our troops on the 15th took the second wall and four gates, let out the missionaries and would have forced the secret city [Forbidden City] had we not been recalled.

The hardships of the campaign were all forgotten when we saw the people of the legations. They actually cried with joy. They did not look as though they had suffered, being in good health and actually fat. On the other hand our poor boys looked like skeletons. They had marched through all kinds of country under a broiling sun for ten days, sometimes without food. At night it was almost freezing cold and we sometimes slept in mud puddles.

There is all kinds of loot here. Gold and silver watches, gold and silver coins, ivory, silks, bicycles, furs, horses and wagons, silver plate, costly stones and in fact everything one might name. If we had any means of transporting the stuff we could all come home rich. I have seen boys wiping mess plates with silk worth $1.00 a yard. Fur coats of fox and seal skins are used for bed coverings. Nearly every man in my company has half a dozen watches and some ten or fifteen. We are at present camped between the first and second walls. The city is nearly ruined, the damage having been done very largely by the Chinese. Around the legations everything had been burned.

I am in good health. Some men who were strong and healthy when we left Tientsin have been reduced to human wrecks, while I – a sparrow, the boys call me – am as well prepared as any to go through the same thing again. I have carried strong men's guns when they had been played out, and the captain once threatened to send me back to Tientsin if I didn't stop it, saying that if the big fellows couldn't carry their own loads what could I do with theirs and mine too.

Our total loss in the advance was between 80 and 90 killed and wounded, without counting several more who died from heat and sickness.

CHRONOLOGY: RELIEF EXPEDITION FROM TIENTSIN TO PEKING

4 August (Saturday)	Depart Tientsin at 2:30 pm; bivouac at Sin-ku.
5 August (Sunday)	Capture of Hsi-ku Arsenal and Pei-tsang; bivouac at Tao-Wa-She.
6 August (Monday)	Capture of Yang-tsun; bivouac at Yang-tsun.
7 August (Tuesday)	Bivouac at Yang-tsun.
8 August (Wednesday)	Depart Yang-tsun at 5 am; bivouac at Tsai-tsun.
9 August (Thursday)	Depart at 7:30 am; brief battle at Hosiwu. Bivouac at Peh-Meaou.
10 August (Friday)	Late departure from Hosiwu, due to extreme exhaustion of troops. Bivouac at Tsun-ping and Matou.
11 August (Saturday)	Entire day in bivouac at Matou. Departure at 5:30 pm. Bivouac at Chang-chai-wan.
12 August (Sunday)	Advance to Tung-chou, which was captured without any fight. Bivouac at Tung-chou.
13 August (Monday)	Reconnaissance of Peking. Some troops bivouac at Tung-chou, while others advance to Kai-Pei-Tien.
14 August (Tuesday)	Relief of Peking

Notes

[1] Colonel Emerson H. Liscum.

[2] Camp site in German Concession.

[3] Located on Taku Road. Reverend J. Walter Lowrie of the American Presbyterian Mission gave permission to the Fourteenth US Infantry to camp on the grounds of the Mission. Rev. Lowrie had been stationed in Peking, but was assigned to Pao-ting-fu in 1900; however, he was in Tientsin when the trouble in Pao-ting-fu erupted. (Official US reports refer to him as having escaped just before the massacre and living at the American Board compound in Tientsin when US troops arrived.)

Account of
Lieutenant Roger Keyes,
Royal Navy

Roger John Brownlow Keyes (1872–1945) was born at Tundiani Fort on India's Northwest Frontier. His family had distinguished itself in the military, and his ancestors had served kings of England since 1203.

Keyes entered the Royal Navy in 1885. In 1900 he was the Commander of HMS Fame, a Torpedo Boat Destroyer attached to the China Station. He accompanied the Allied Relief Expedition as Naval ADC to General Gaselee. His advance in the Navy was rapid; he ultimately became the Admiral of the Fleet and the first Baron Keyes.

That he wrote similar letters to other friends is suggested by the fact that his report on the condition of those imprisoned at the British Legation was published by one of his corespondents in Hong Kong in September 1900. His description of the assembled foreign colony looking like a 'garden party' caused him considerable embarrassment with the English community at a time when world public opinion was lionising the survivors.

British Legation, Peking
September 6th

No one to tell me how to spell so I've no doubt there are endless mistakes!

Dear Miss Bee,
I have been meaning to write to you for ages, ever since I got your letter – and I feel rather guilty for having left it so long unanswered, but just about then I tumbled into the most extraordinary piece of luck and really haven't had many opportunities of writing. I hope you will forgive me when I tell you this is absolutely the first letter I have written to England except one or two hasty scrawls to my people.

After Tientsin City had fallen, and the little scrap I came in for there, I was beginning to make up my mind as far as I was concerned the whole show was over and to reconcile myself to the deadly dull fate of remaining a ferry from the fleet to Taku, Tongku, Chefoo or Newchang – when Sir Alfred

Gaselee[1] arrived, said he was an old friend of my father's – had served under him as a little boy – and asked for me for his naval Aide-de-Camp. Jimmy Bruce[2] let me go at once without Sir E.'s[3] permission – put Tomkinson in command of the *Fame* (it was a great shame they had appointed a man of 14 years seniority to command the *Taku*) but before we started from Tientsin, after I had been on the staff about a week, a wire came from Sir E. saying he didn't approve of my going – I couldn't be spared from the *Fame*. J.B. [Bruce] forwarded this to General Gaselee but said he wasn't going to recall me, and Sir Alfred telegraphed applying for my appointment, and Sir E. apparently gave in but we didn't hear anything about that until we arrived here. I don't believe I am supposed to know about this. But what a good little friend J.B. is, isn't he! So is Edward really, but I expect he was harassed and worried and was in a bad temper when he first got the application. It was a stroke of luck for me his going to Shanghai just before the General arrived.

You will have read about the march up. It was dreadfully hot and dusty and the men suffered horribly, natives and Europeans alike, from sunstroke – several dead. The Americans, thanks to the silly felt hat they wear, had an awful time. We had one good fight to ourselves, and the men behaved splendidly – hardly any of them, officers or men, had been under shell fire before, their service being all on the Indian frontier, and we were heavily peppered with quick firing guns large and small – the former being larger than our 12 Pounders which unfortunately that day weren't able to get up in time owing to the bad road, but as they found in South Africa, shell fire is not dangerous in the open if the ranks are kept properly extended – which they always are. The Americans suffered much more than we did comparatively considering the rather back seat they took in the show, they hung in bunches and didn't advance while our men dashed through the dangerous zone.

I galloped down their advance with a message to the American general and I must say saw an awful lot of scrimshanking in the same regiment which behaved so badly at the capture of Tientsin and was extricated by some of the *Barfleur's* Naval Brigade. Gibbs the midshipman, you will remember, distinguished himself on that occasion and was mentioned in the American and British despatches. I must admit a few of our men were playing the same game.

At Pei-tsung, the fight before, we were only supporting the Japs and the only other force except them engaged. We only lost 4 killed and 21 wounded – they had over 300 casualties and did splendidly. At Yang-tsun, thanks to the excellently kept open order, we only had 11 killed, 30-odd wounded – the Americans had 10 or 12 killed and 40 wounded.

There was practically no more fighting until Peking was reached. When we arrived at Tung-chau as far as the River route goes the whole force was cooked and wanted rest badly; but Sir Alfred was very strong on the necessity of keeping the Chinese on the move and said we ought to go on the next day – Monday. The Russians said they couldn't, the Japs were for it, the Americans said they would if we would – so it was agreed that we all except the Russians should send forward about seven miles a strong reconnoitering force which should bivouack and the whole force should concentrate on Tuesday and attack on Wednesday.

The Russians said their whole force would move out on Tuesday but they couldn't do anything before. All that evening they quietly moved out troops and tried to get in by themselves and claim to have been on the wall at 2 am on Tuesday. It was a lie – they weren't – but they were repulsed and they fell back and asked the Japs who had concentrated all Monday, meaning I really believe to play the game by us but not intending to be left by the Russians.

So they advanced and were also kept in check all day, losing 50 killed and about 100 wounded in one or two rather hopeless but very gallant attempts to blow open the East gate of the Tartar City – so they contented themselves by keeping up a futile bombardment until the evening when they finally got in at 10 pm. The Russians did much the same and got in [at] 9 pm losing 50 killed and about 100 wounded. The Americans got an inkling of what was going on and moved out at 5 pm on Monday [13 August].

General Gaselee stuck to the agreed time and we left at 3 am on Tuesday; about 7 am came up with our advance bivouak, 10 am found the Americans engaged on our right (we were on the extreme left, they next, Japs other side of the canal, and Russians on the right) and what seemed a great battle going on on our extreme right. We pushed on and after a slight skirmish battered in the East gate of the Chinese City, went along parallel to the Tartar City wall through the Chinese City, crossed the canal or drain bed at the water sluice gate under the legations under a heavy but ill-directed fire and into the legations at 2.45 pm. The Americans got in the same way at 5 pm. You can imagine the sickness of the foreigners! We only had 4 or 5 wounded.

What really happened was the very premature attack on the right (Chinese left) made the Chinese think there would be no attack on the left especially as the former went on for 10 hours before we arrived. They withdrew everyone from their right to strengthen their left so the Russians caught a Tartar and we practically marched in unopposed.

The scene coming onto the British Legation lawn was extraordinary. We were never more hopeless of finding them alive than when we actually [arrived] in the Chinese City. We had the best evidence to prove they had been bombarded all night (which they were, but their defences were so excellent it was quite futile) and the only hope we had of finding them alive was that the Chinese were keeping them as a last card which it was pretty clear by then they didn't intend to play as we had no overtures.

It looked like a garden party. All the ladies looked nice in clean white and light-coloured dresses, strolling about on the lawn. Some of the men who had run in from the barricades looked rather fierce with arms of sorts festooned round them but most were in flannels having a quiet afternoon off. A very enthusiastic and friendly garden party – they all wanted to shake hands with us – a very dust[y] and disreputable-looking lot of ruffians. Lady MacDonald[4] looked very charming and nice and might have been hostess – said to Pell,[5] one of the Aides de Camp and me who went up to her, she didn't know who we were but was simply delighted to see us.

Then the Chinese all over the place appear to have discovered we were in, and the band or its equivalent began to play – the bullets went zipping overhead, occasionally breaking twigs off the trees – others went phutting against the walls and roof – but no one seemed to mind; they all strolled about as casually as ever until a Sikh was hit on the lawn and a French lady was the only women touched all through the siege. So then they went in under cover as one would out of a shower of rain. A gun also brought a shell or two into the courtyard. So the field battery galloped through the water sluice and up the most impossible place and very soon silenced it. As did the infantry the people who were annoying us with rifles.

In the early part of the siege they must have had an awful time and the anticipation of what might happen must have been appauling [sic]. Their casualties were 60 killed and about 100 wounded – but for the last few weeks, thanks to their excellent barricades and defences, they had hardly had any losses; and except that their meat was mule and pony they had plenty to eat, excellent brown bread, lots of rice and many luxuries. As long as they could keep off starvation I don't think there was the slightest chance of their being captured; the Chinese – though plucky in defence – haven't got it in them to attack. And the Legation is so excellently placed it is almost impossible to shell it except from a very near distance, which the Chinese didn't seem to realise.

The French Roman Catholic Cathedral, *Pei tang,* had an infinitely worse time and the defence was marvellous – only 50 French and Italian sailors. Of course they hadn't such a big line to defend – but they were much more exposed to shell fire.

Please excuse this pencil scrawl but I am more or less in bed recovering from rather a bad go of diptheria. I believe I nearly croaked. So the doctor tells me. I didn't feel the least inclined to! It would have been a dull way of departing this life! And I feel most eternally grateful to the Almighty for sparing me from it! By the most extraordinary act of providence a German doctor here had some anti-toxin I think they call it which they injected into me with marvellous results.

The Naval Brigade have all gone back and I hope to soon. I must say I am rather bored up here and am beginning to long for my *Fame* again.

The General is a good sort and has been a good friend to me; it was a stroke of luck coming up like this. I have seen all there has been to see in the way of fighting (we could have done with a little more!) which the Naval Brigade, I am sorry to say, haven't except at Pei-tsung when they did good work. And they arrived here a day late thanks to an impossible road.

I hear from O.B. occasionally. She tells me you aren't coming out which is very sad except that if I go home this winter – and which is possible, it will be very nice finding you there! Your Father and Sister will be nearly at Hong Kong by the time you get this and I expect I shall see them pretty soon. Murray Stewart, as no doubt you have heard, came up here as the Times Correspondent. He looked very thin and seedy at one time and I didn't think he would be able to stand it but he went back a few days ago very fit. He is quite an old soldier and most delightfully cool under fire. He was sitting with his back to a stone wall looking through his glasses when a huge single ball went smack up against it about a foot from his head and he never moved or took his glasses down which rather fetched some Japs and Americans who were near!

Poor little Selwyn[6] hasn't seen much of the show. He was very soon invalided to Weihaiwei from Guntsen and when he came back he was too seedy to go up with us so he was left with a small detachment, as was Mr Rotherham, [7] at Tientsin. Captain Richards[8] nearly died of sunstroke the day we got here but is all right again. Colonel Bertie[9] looks better than he ever did at Hong Kong and looks very fit. Higgin and Bancroft[10] stayed at Hong Kong with their two Moses' brides. And poor Captain Berger[11] was left behind and is out of it once again. I am sorry for him.

Is your sister married yet? I haven't seen a paper for ages. Please remember me to her and to your people, and give my love to Miss Dot.

Yours very sincerely
Roger Keyes

Notes

[1] General Sir Alfred Gaselee (1844–1918), commanded the British Expeditionary Force during the relief of the legations.

[2] Rear Admiral James A.T. Bruce, second in command to Seymour, on board the battleship, HMS *Barfleur*.

[3] Commander-in-Chief of Her Britannic Majesty's Squadron in China and Japan, Vice-

Admiral Sir Edward Hobart Seymour, KCB (1840–1929). He commanded the international naval brigade during the Boxer rising.

[4] Lady Ethel MacDonald, wife of Sir Claude MacDonald (1852–1915), the British minister at Peking.

[5] Captain Beauchamp Tyndall Pell, Queen's Royal West Surrey Regiment. Born in 1866, he joined the regiment in 1887. He was ADC to General Officer Commanding China Expedition, 26 June 1900–20 July 1901, seeing action at Pei-tsung, Yang-tsun and Peking. Was mentioned in despatches, 14 May 1901 and received the Distinguished Service Order.

[6] Major Charles Henry Selwyn, Indian Staff Corps. Formerly of the Connaught Rangers. Served with the Burmese Expedition in 1886–87. He was on Special Service with the China Expeditionary Force, and shortly after became Assistant Secretary to the Government of India Military Department.

[7] Captain Henry Rotherham, Royal Welch Fusiliers. Served during the Peking relief expedition and was invalided out. The Royal Welch Fusiliers were attached to the First Brigade China Expeditionary Force under Brigadier-General Sir Norman Stewart. They had arrived at Taku aboard HMS *Terrible* on 21 June 21 1900.

[8] Lieutenant Henry Meredyth Richards, Royal Welch Fusiliers. Richards recovered sufficiently to take part in a parade at Hong Kong on 3 November 1900.

[9] Lieutenant-Colonel the Hon. Reginald Henry Bertie, Royal Welch Fusiliers. Served in the occupation of Crete in 1897–98 with the Second Battalion, and commanded the battalion during the relief of Peking. Colonel Bertie kept a diary of the expedition, extracts of which were published in *Regimental Records of the Royal Welch Fusiliers*, Vol. II.

[10] Captain Charles Edward Bancroft, Royal Welch Fusiliers.

[11] Possibly Captain Ernest Lewis Corbett Berger, Thirtieth Bombay Infantry, serving on the Indian Staff Corps.

THE ALLIED OCCUPATION OF PEKING

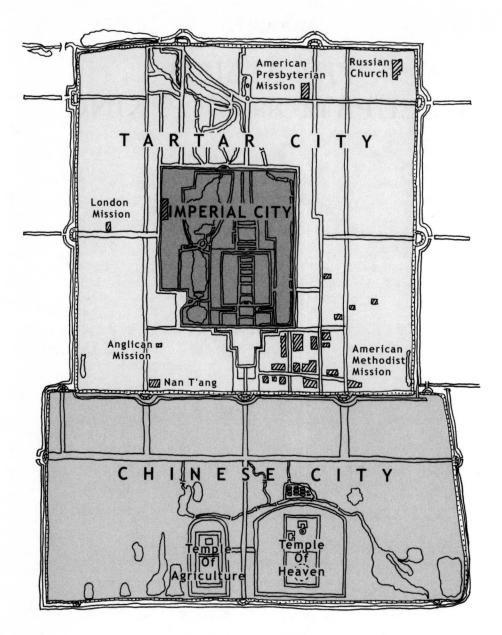

Plan of the City of Peking

Introduction

On 14 August 1900 the Allied troops found themselves in Peking – a devastated city which was largely abandoned by the native population. Shops were closed, streets were deserted but for the bodies everywhere – many Chinese had been victims of their own countrymen.

The city was divided into zones of occupation, each under the control of one of the eight Allied nations. There was no way to distinguish a hated Boxer from any other Chinese, and the Allied soldiers took out their desire for vengeance – and loot – on anyone. Looting was prevalent, not only among the soldiers but even more so among the westerners who had spent 55 days besieged in the Legation Quarter. The diplomats were often the worst offenders.

There was an enormous influx of Allied soldiers. By September, the American troops numbered approximately 5000 and the British and Germans approximately 20,000 each. The German leader, Count Alfred von Waldersee, was designated by the Allies as Supreme Commander of all Allied troops. He and his East Asia Regiment had been sent to China by Kaiser Wilhelm with specific instructions to avenge the murder of Minister von Ketteler.

Von Waldersee had not even departed from Berlin until 18 August and reached Tientsin only on 27 September. His troops, who arrived too late to participate in the actual relief, now thirsted for action. Under their leadership, the Allies occupied not only Peking but also surrounding sections of Chihli Province, and embarked on a series of punitive expeditions designed to eradicate any and all pockets of Boxer sympathisers.

The official report of numbers of Allied troops in North China on 1 April 1901 shows the size of the occupying force:

Austria	300
England	18,181
France	15,670
Germany	21,295
Italy	2,155
Japan	6,408
Russia	2,900
USA	1,750
Total:	68,659

Account of Jasper Whiting
American War
Correspondent

Jasper Whiting (1868–1941) was born in Charlestown, Massachusetts. After graduating from the Massachusetts Institute of Technology in 1889 with a degree in engineering, he moved to Chicago to work for the Illinois Steel Company. There he invented the process for making Portland cement from the waste products of blast furnace slag.

In the spring of 1900 Whiting decided to retire and travel. Arriving in London early in July, he found the entire city outraged by events taking place in China. He decided to proceed directly there. He realised that as a private citizen he would see little of the action, so he obtained an appointment from the Westminster Gazette *of London as their Special Correspondent.*

He left London on 18 July 1900. He had been travelling for seven weeks when we join him in Taku.

Taku is not, strictly speaking, a coast city. It lies near the mouth of the Peiho River, the entrance to which is protected by forts. This river empties into what is known as the inner harbor – separated from the outer harbor by a sand bar over which only steamers of moderate draught can pass even at high tide. Beyond this bar, a distance of about eleven miles from the forts, is, therefore, the real harbor of Taku, and in this harbor at the time of our arrival were anchored no less than forty men-of-war, and nearly one hundred transports, representing practically every great power of the world. Not since the Queen's jubilee has such a cosmopolitan and formidable fleet of boats been gathered together, and it was a sight which well repaid us for the discomforts of the previous few days. In a conspicuous position was Admiral Bruce's flagship, *Barfleur*, and nearby our own *Brooklyn*, easily distinguished by her tall and stately stacks and businesslike appearance. We also made out the flags of Italy, Germany, France, Austria, Russia, and Japan, and over one little craft proudly floated the banner of the Netherlands. Every vessel saluted us as we passed, and several sent special messengers to us in launches to ask the latest news from civilization. Altogether it was a most impressive sight – one none of us, I think, will soon forget.

TAKU TO TIENTSIN: *September 4 to 11*

The *Haean,* at high water on September 4th, passed over the bar, entered the inner harbor of Taku, and made fast alongside the dock. As I stepped ashore with Scott I felt that a very disagreeable chapter in my journey had ended, and I breathed a sigh of relief. Scott, being a true Britisher, had a raft of things with him, and all had to be transported to the railway station, a distance of half a mile. First we hired a sampan by which the luggage was carried to within a hundred yards of its destination; then an army of coolies was engaged and it deposited the boxes on the platform of the station; then the station hands took hold and carried the pieces into the car. Altogether I figured we employed sixty-eight men to get our traps aboard the train. My boy Ying (who was engaged at Shanghai and of whom much should be written) was *generalissimo* of the operations and conducted the march with signal success. When everything was over he came to me for further instructions and before I sent him away I told him I liked the way he had worked. He grunted and disappeared, and I was afraid that my words of appreciation had not been understood until I overheard him say to Scott's Indian servant: 'My master belong velly good. He number one man. He no think I bloody fool.'

In going from Taku to Tientsin I got my first insight into the seriousness of the trouble which had drawn us toward that city. The railway by which we travelled was guarded by a double line of pickets throughout its entire length. Russian soldiers patrolled the inner line, and Japs the outer. Everywhere were evidences of the havoc wrought by the invading armies. The car in which I rode had a hole through its side made by a well-aimed shell. The station at Taku was badly damaged, and occasionally from the windows of the car we could see the dead and now rapidly decomposing bodies of men who had paid the full penalty of their lawlessness, or had won everlasting glory for their patriotism, according as their acts were viewed by foe or friend. Now and then we passed what was once a native village but was now a mass of ruins; only a collection of roofless houses remaining to tell very eloquently the story of indescribable misery and suffering experienced by those who had dwelt within their walls. A few weeks before, the country between Taku and Tientsin had supported a population of more than four millions; but now only rarely did we see a Chinaman, so thoroughly were the villages destroyed and vacated.

Tientsin, at the time of my arrival, was probably the most cosmopolitan place in the world, and the Astor House of that town, where I put up, was the center of its interest. Never have I seen so interesting a company gathered under one roof. In the first place it was the headquarters for the Russian staff officers, twenty or so stalwart ruffians, each of whom was accompanied by a ruffian servant of the same nationality, and by a camp wife. Some of these latter were very attractive, and all were bubbling over with spirits, so that there were times when things moved at a pretty swift pace. The place was also filled with war correspondents, some of them being battle-scarred heroes with medals on their breasts, and records of which anyone might well be proud. One of them was a woman, 'The Widow', of *Town Topics,* a person who knows the skeletons in the closets of nearly every family of prominence in America. The Astor House was a common ground, moreover, for officers of every nationality to meet and discuss the problems of the hour, and consequently it was a place teeming with interest from morning until very late.

I used to sit on the veranda of the Hotel and watch the passersby. It was as good as going to the midway of the Chicago Fair. Soldiers of every nation of consequence passed in review before this grandstand. Englishmen and Frenchmen, Germans, Italians, Austrians, Americans and Russians; men from Korea and men from Japan, and men from a half-dozen different nations of India, all came and went. Many were in uniform; some carried swords or lances, and not a few were mounted upon high-stepping thoroughbred horses. Martial music was to be heard at all hours of the day until after sunset when the distant sound of the bugle told of coming night. Then the tramp, tramp, tramp, ceased upon the street. The soldiers went to their tents; the officers reassembled at the Astor House, to drink, to sing, to make merry, and finally, to sleep.

I had not been in Tientsin long before I began to hear on all sides the story of the siege – and a most exciting story it was. From the 16th of June to the 14th of July the city was practically shut off from communication with the outside world, and during that time the Chinese poured shot and shell in an intermittent stream into the foreign settlement, destroying lives and property and causing consternation and havoc indescribable. During this time the people lived in cellars, only venturing out in cases of the direst necessity. Many suffered untold hardships from lack of sleep and proper food, but nearly all bore the privations with wonderful courage and patience.

The stories of heroism exhibited during that time are many, but one deed stands alone above all the others – the famous ride of Jim Watts to Taku through the very heart of the hostile country. Alone, Watts volunteered to undertake the perilous journey in search of relief; alone he travelled the distance – but not alone did he return, for he brought with him an armed force which promptly relieved the town, and captured and burned the native city itself. Had it not been for the information received through Watts, the commander of the Allied Troops would have waited for reinforcements before attempting the relief, and there are grave doubts as to whether the city could have held out that long. Therefore, Jim Watts' name is in every mouth, and Jim Watts' fame will last forever in Tientsin.

Most of the damage done during the siege was sustained by the French settlement, where several of the buildings, including the Consular and Government offices, were riddled with shells or destroyed by fire, resulting from the bombardment. I walked through several of the houses which had been hit, and it was remarkable to note the extent of the havoc which one small shell will cause if successfully discharged. The Astor House itself was hit by several shells, and the room in which I lived had a broken door and a torn wall, eloquent evidences of the accuracy of Chinese marksmanship.

Soon after my arrival I went all through the native city. Many of the Chinamen who had fled had returned, and more were constantly returning. A provisional government had been set up by the foreigners, in which every important nation was represented, and headquarters were opened in the *Yamen* of the Viceroy, formerly the residence of Li Hung Chang. It was strange indeed to see white men working among such surroundings. In one of the reception rooms the Secretary of the Provisional Government sat and labored. About him were Chinese idols and ornaments and filigree – evidences of the old regime – while by his side was an up-to-date American typewriter, the operator being an even more up-to-date American maiden.

The reception rooms were all turned into offices for the other members of the Council, and the great audience chamber became the court-room of the acting magistrate. This official performed his multitudinous duties in a way which would have made Pooh Bah green with envy. On his way to the Court, if he saw a disturbance he would personally arrest the offender, and conduct the culprit by his queue to the court-room. Here he was at once judge, jury, advocate, and sometimes even sheriff as well. Before him the Chinese prisoners were brought in a continuous stream, each one kneeling and knocking his head three times on the floor before the great man, who, with the aid of an interpreter and a few street cossacks, examined them, passed sentence upon them, and if found guilty, had the punishment inflicted then and there. All this was done with such rapidity and precision that even my head swam. It must have seemed little short of supernatural to the poor wretches brought before the bar.

The utilization of palaces and sacred buildings was not alone confined to the native city, however. In the outskirts of the foreign settlement many temples and residences of prominent Chinese were turned into barracks or hospitals or commissary headquarters. These residences as a rule, were unharmed by the bombardment, and therefore the furniture and hangings in them were practically the same as when the owners left. Never before, I believe, have soldiers slept on such magnificent couches and eaten from such delicate and exquisite china as many of them are doing in Tientsin today.

One wild Irishman with a bullet through his leg remarked to me as he lay on his back, eating his midday meal – 'Sure, I never expected to be feeding off the Emperor of China's plate nor a-sleeping on his bed; – Bedad, this is the country for me.'

TIENTSIN TO PEKING: *September 11 to 19*

By great good fortune I was enabled to make the journey to Peking with a British surveying column under command of Major T.F.B. Renny-Tailyour;[1] R.E. Scott was also of the company, the remainder consisting of Indian surveyors, a dozen servants, and an escort of Indian troops. Scott and I, together with his two servants and the only Ying, two ponies and two grooms or *mafoos,* went by rail to Yang-tsun, where we met the Major and his party who had preceded us by a day, travelling on foot. Two junks had been provided to carry us up river and these were well stocked with tents and camp furniture, with things to eat and things to smoke and many, many things to drink.

The journey from Yang-tsun to Tung-chow, where we were to leave the river and proceed overland to Peking, was to take us six days but from the appearance of the kit one would have supposed we were provided for an outing of at least a month.

Major Renny-Tailyour was [a] delightful host. In appearance he is a British Army officer of the best type – tall, broad-shouldered, erect and athletic, and above all, a gentleman born and bred.

Our march to Peking began about two weeks behind the relief column, but as our route was a little different from that taken by the first troops we expected to have more than one scrap with our Boxer enemies. On this march I got my first insight into the terrors of war as experienced by British Indian officers. On the first day we marched about fifteen miles; when we reached the end I saw an American flag flying in the distance, so I thought I would ride over and talk with the officers of the post while our camp was being pitched. I must have been gone about two hours. When I returned I was met by one of the Major's servants who announced that dinner was served. A moment later I found myself, not sitting upon a box eating a meal of bacon and beef and bread and tea, as I had expected, but inside a spacious dining tent in which were several camp chairs, a well-built camp table covered with a spotless cloth, knives, plates, forks, etc.

Upon this table also stood three ice cold Manhattan cocktails which had been mixed by a master hand. These cocktails were indicative of the whole meal. The dinner was of six courses, well cooked and well served by four Indian servants exactly as if we were dining in Calcutta instead of in North China in the heart of a hostile country. We had two kinds of wine, cigars, and a liqueur, and we sat and talked over our black coffee as if we were dining at home. Nor was this for the first night only. Every evening of the march to Peking was spent in this way.

Very different was the meal I had two days later at an American post a little farther on. Bacon and hardtack, potatoes and hot black coffee, was the menu, and we ate off the proverbial tall box, sitting on shorter boxes and helped ourselves as best we could. The American officer prides himself upon the fact that he lives exactly as do the men in the ranks. Between the fare of the British Army officer and that of the private there is no similarity whatsoever.

The next morning the tents and supplies were all loaded aboard the boats, and taking only our ponies and two or three extra servants to carry the luncheon, and a small guard, we started off on foot, the *mafoos* leading the ponies and the others following. It was delightful walking along the winding road in the early morning, often following the very path that the relief troops had taken a few days before. Everywhere were evidences of the devastation wrought by the invading armies. Corn fields and crops were going to waste. Villages were deserted and destroyed, and occasionally a dead body marked only too plainly the path of the avenging hosts. Occasionally we mounted our ponies and rode for a way; occasionally we sat down beside a well and refreshed ourselves with a cooling drink and a pipe, but it was not until we reached Tsai-tsun, after travelling fifteen miles, that we stopped and had luncheon.

Tsai-tsun must have been a rather important village and at the time of our arrival it was not only deserted and destroyed, but looted of everything valuable. We camped in the garden of the Mandarin and went all over what was once his magnificent *Yamen*. The building covered several acres of ground, and though only one storey high it looked very impressive with its beautiful facade crowned with a pagoda-like roof. Inside, everything was in confusion and ruins. Pieces of exquisite china covered the floors. Remnants of choice silks and furs were scattered about, and fragments of beautifully carved furniture lay in heaps about the place. We found little of value, for many had been before us, but much of interest remained. Among the debris I picked up a badly torn, but exquisitely embroidered lady's shoe about four inches long which, if the history could have been learned, might have been well worth keeping. I also found some childrens' toys and several mutilated dolls, each almost shouting to me a story so full of misery that for a moment I forgot the atrocities that had been committed at Peking and felt only pity for those who had not only been driven from their homes but had had their dearest household goods destroyed.

Late in the afternoon we were joined by two British officers: Major Steele, of the 2nd Bengal Lancers, and Captain J.R. Douglass, of the same troop, both bound for Peking with a train of carts and coolies. That evening we all dined together very well and very beautifully, and then with our chairs thrown far back, our toes tipped up, and our pipes lighted, we talked late into the night. Stories were told of life in India and in England – of people of the North and people of the South – of the gaieties of Simla and of Paris; of the hardships of poverty and the pleasures of prosperity, of horses, of dogs, of birds of the field and beasts of the jungle; of hairbreadth escapes and fool-hardy performances; of everything under the sun except of China. Not even the stray bullets which occasionally whizzed over our heads disturbed us. We talked and talked and talked, and at the very end we rose and drank one toast – 'To Her' [Queen Victoria].

The next day was a repetition of the first. I dined that evening at Hohsi-wu with Lieutenant Brown of the 9th US Infantry, who entertained me with an account of the taking of Tientsin, in which he was actively engaged. It was an exciting tale.

The following day we sent our ponies on to Tungchow by land in charge of the *mafoos,* boarded our junks and settled ourselves for a three or four days' journey by water. Travelling up stream by water is not a very exciting diversion. We averaged a little over a mile an hour, our two crafts being pulled against a strong current by Chinese coolies, five to each boat. Each junk was provided with a mast on which hung a sail of the characteristic Chinese cut, and in the characteristic Chinese condition, that is, in tatters and shreds. To the tip of the mast was fastened a long rope leading to the shore, and this rope the coolies pulled, walking along a sort of two path. Almost every three hours our boatmen would stop and gather in a little knot on the shore and eat rice and curry, or drink tea. It was not a pretty sight (their table manners were not pleasing) but it was interesting, so interesting that I used up several of my precious films endeavoring to obtain a good photograph of the operation. In the early morning the coolies worked well and looked fairly respectable, but as the sun rose they gradually discarded their clothing piece by piece, until by noontime each boat was towed by five absolutely naked bipeds.

The first night after boarding her we slept on board the junk but we found the quarters so uncomfortable that we decided next morning to do so no more. The second night we again pitched our tents and lived like white men. This was at Ma-tau. Here we met Captain Brown, of the 1st B.L., who was in charge of a small British camp. He was an interesting chap and regaled us with an exciting story of how he, with twenty men, rode forth a week before and routed a force of four hundred armed Boxers, killing fifty or more, and burning the town they occupied. The tale sounded more like a slaughter than a fight. The Captain admitted that the affair was not at all to his liking.

Tung-chow, the end of our water journey, was reached on the evening of the 15th. Here we were to unload our things from the boats and carry them on mules overland to Peking, a distance of fifteen miles. Major T.E. Scott, DSO, of the Third Sikhs (the first man to enter Peking with the relief force), arranged to give us transportation, and early the next morning we began our march. It was good to get on our ponies again, and the ride to the city of our destination was very enjoyable in spite of the horrible condition of the roads and the intense glare of the sun. We reached Peking a little after one o'clock, and after saying 'Thank you' most heartily to Major Renny-Tailyour, Scott and I started forth in search of an abode.

PEKING TO TIENTSIN: *September 19 to October 3*

When we entered Peking we found the city swarming with foreign troops but deserted by the Chinese. Evidences of shot and shell and fire were to be seen on all sides. Acres upon acres of a once thickly-populated city had been burnt to the ground. Temples and palaces and towers were pierced with shells or destroyed, and miles upon miles of houses had been sacked of all things valuable they once contained. It was, consequently, not easy to find a place to sleep at the time of our arrival. Scott and I first went to a mass of debris formerly known as the Hotel, and were told that no place worthy the name of sleeping apartment was available. We then tried two other establishments with like result, but finally, by means of much bribery and corruption, induced a Chinaman to let us occupy his master's room during that gentleman's absence from town. It was a little 8 × 10 affair, just big enough to hold our two camp beds, but it was far better than the street or a roofless Chinese house, and we were quite content. Our dinner that night – the first meal that we had had since morning – consisted of eggs and tongue and water; absolutely nothing else, not even tea or bread. I have had things in America that have tasted far worse, but never before have I paid so much for so little. The tongue I brought in my saddle-bags with me; the eggs were fifty cents each. The meal cost Scott and me six dollars.

The next day I interviewed the hotel man again, and by means of more bribery induced him to clean two places which had been rooms and allow us to put our beds in them. The side of my room is literally shot away; the windows and doors are all gone, and in the walls and ceiling I have counted over two hundred holes made by Chinese shot and shell. It rained the first night and I was wet through. It blew half a gale another night, and my cot was nearly upset – yet we are the proud possessors of the best apartments in Peking outside the Legations and, as I said before, are quite content.

The condition of the Hotel at Peking is indicative of the whole foreign city. It is as much worse than Tientsin as Tientsin is worse than Shanghai. Nothing foreign remains uninjured; even the British Legation bears innumerable evidences of the frightful state of affairs which has existed. Cannon are planted over the gates of the city; breastworks have been thrown up; everywhere are fortifications. Even on the walls of the Legations are many impromptu barricades. During the trouble every pillow case in town was used to make a sandbag, even silk embroidered ones, and more than one fur coat and nightrobe had its sleeves sewed up and filled with earth to help afford protection to the panic-stricken and almost helpless people besieged. The only places remaining uninjured are those held sacred by the Chinese: the Imperial Palaces, the Temple of Heaven, the Temple of Agriculture, Lama Temple, Coal Hill, and a few other places are as they always have been – otherwise the central section of the city is damaged almost beyond recognition. Only the indescribably muddy streets remain to identify beyond dispute the capital of China.

Within the sacred temples and inclosures the foreign troops are quartered, and very comfortably quartered too. The Temple of Agriculture is situated in a beautiful park containing, besides the main edifice, a dozen or more lesser temples, each surrounded by trees and foliage, by statuary and by symbolic walls and arches. Here the Americans have pitched their camp – the common soldiers occupying the grounds, the officers the lesser buildings, while the commanding General, with his staff, is luxuriously settled in the main edifice. It is a singular sight, indeed, to go within the sacred temple and see standing beside elaborately carved golden gods and graven images, American cot beds and blankets, haversacks and canteens, pistols and swords and rifles.

But if the Temple of Agriculture is desecrated, the same cannot so truly be said of the Temple of Heaven – the enclosure which houses the main portion of the British troops. Here the lesser temples are occupied by officers, but the main edifice remains untouched – the most impressive Chinese building I have yet seen. The approach to this temple is by way of a long broad avenue running from the main street, terminating in a second avenue extending at right angles to it. This approach is very thickly wooded, so thickly that the temple itself is completely hidden until the last avenue is reached; then, in its full glory, it bursts suddenly into view – a massive pile of brilliant blue and dazzling white magnificently placed upon a base of pure marble and surmounted by a beautifully shaped dome crowned with a ball of gold. Never before have I seen such contrasts of color harmonizing so well; never a building the design of which so appealed to my sense of fitness and of beauty.

Within the temple, the same effect of chastity, simplicity and magnificence, is carried out. No ornamentation spoils the purity of design; no mingling of colors the richness of the tone. A raised platform of white marble in the center forms the only variation – this platform being the Holy of

Holies – the shrine to which the Emperor, or Son of Heaven, was wont to
come each year and spend alone a whole day in fasting and in prayer.
Everything is in keeping with the surroundings; nothing jars one's sense of
propriety and fitness, and what is most remarkable of all, in view of the fact
that it is Chinese, there is nothing trivial or tawdry in any way connected
with the edifice. My first and last thought was one of gratitude to the British
commander for not allowing this beautiful Temple to be desecrated by
Tommy Atkins and his kind.

On my return to my room after my visit to the Temple of Heaven, I found
my boy Ying in a very bad way. He was doubled up over a chair, moaning
and saying over and over – 'Peking side no belong ploper; me velly sick; me
makey die.' I questioned him and found too many green pears to be the
direct cause of his trouble, so I opened my medicine chest and prescribed a
cure. He took the pills from my hands and disappeared. In an hour he came
back somewhat better and told me he had been to a Chinese doctor who had
given him a tiger's tooth to hold, and some frog's skin to chew, both of
which were working wonders. He had thrown away my precious pills
because 'Chinese doctor say what can do for foreign master velly bad for
Chinee boy.' Since then Ying has never been seen without his tiger's tooth,
and a piece of frog's skin is generally stowed away in some inner recess of his
mouth.

When the allied troops entered the city there were two great pieces of
work to be done: first, the relief of the British Legation, where all the foreigners of prominence were housed, and second, the relief of the *Pei tsang*
cathedral, where about a dozen French Catholic missionaries and eight
hundred Chinese Christians had been besieged for more than two months.
The Legation was relieved according to programme, but as soon as this was
accomplished the Allied Troops forgot the other, and in some regards the
greater, work – so great was their desire to lay their hands upon the many
valuable things within arm's reach. For more than two days the courageous
band of half-starved missionaries and Chinese were forced to exist after the
troops had entered the city, but I am glad to say that they were finally
relieved by American troops aided by those from Japan.

I thought the looting of Peking was the most extraordinary as well as the
most outrageous proceeding connected with the Boxer troubles. It was not
confined, however, to any set of individuals or to any nationality, nor was it
confined to the men. I was told upon the best authority that it was started by
women. Within five minutes after the doors of the British Legation had been
thrown open to admit the Allied Troops, two French ladies who had been
sheltered in the British Legation, rushed out of the gate and raced each other
to a certain shop in Legation Street, which they had frequented in calmer
times, and which they knew to be deserted. In ten minutes they were back,

their arms loaded down with silks and embroideries and furs and jade, a triumphal smile upon their faces, both well repaid for the privations they had endured during the past few weeks.

It is not surprising that the common soldiers looted when one considers the example set them by their officers and by the high officials of the Legations. The best collection of loot which was obtained is said to be that of Lady MacDonald, the wife of the British minister, and the next best that of Mr Squiers, First Secretary of the American Legation. I saw part of Lady MacDonald's collection myself, and I can testify if there is anything better it was not in evidence at the time of my arrival. She had then eighty-seven large packing cases filled with most valuable treasures, and I personally heard her say that she 'had not begun to pack'.

Japanese and Russians got the most of the silver and gold that was taken away. The Japs in one day removed thirteen million dollars worth of silver from the Treasury. Our own troops were not far behind the others in looting, however. Soon after I arrived I inquired of an old resident where I could purchase some of the treasures myself, and was advised to go to the camp of the American soldiers. I did so; and among other things purchased a sable fur coat for $1.50, and a number of less valuable furs at corresponding figures.

But it is not just to condemn the looters thoughtlessly. Nobody who was not there is competent to judge those who were on the subject. It was a disease. Everybody, I think, without exception, who had been through the city, looted; and those who came after, those who were most eloquent in their denunciation of the practice on the day of their arrival, soon could not resist seeing their friends bring in from their daily jaunts treasures of priceless value and even greater interest. The one excuse offered was, 'If I don't take the things somebody else will.' It was some weeks after, and not until all the best things had been removed, that the authorities took precautions to stop the proceedings; then things had to be purchased; but this was only another method of looting, for a Chinaman will dispose of his choicest possessions for a song if he is allowed to inspect at close range the muzzle of a loaded revolver.

The British controlled looting better than any of the others, though they legalized it, which cannot be charged to the rest. In the section of the city guarded by them, everything of value was collected and taken to a store-house within the Legation grounds, and there sold at auction to the highest bidder, the proceeds being divided equitably among the troops. These auction sales were the chief diversion in Peking at the time of my arrival. To them every afternoon went men and women of many nationalities, all eager to buy the treasures offered for sale. Some of the things, such as furs and cloaks and silks, sold very reasonably. Heavy mandarin decorations, and

huge Chinese clocks and curios, went at ridiculously low prices – not because
they would not be appreciated at home, but because of the very great difficulty of transporting them to and across the seas.

I purchased a few things and submitted the lot to the inspection of the
incomparable Ying. His eyes watered when he saw a fur coat and he said
'Velly good.' They grew large and brilliant when he beheld a mandarin's
cloak, and he remarked, 'Number one ploper', but when he looked upon a
bit of yellow Imperial china I had bought, he danced up and down with
excitement and joy but was quite speechless. To be so closely associated with
royalty was far beyond his highest hopes. First he made a motion to touch
the bit, but drew back as if unworthy of such an honor. I thrust it into his
hands and then beheld an exhibition of faith which would have done credit
to the saints of history. Ying was radiant! Pigeon English flowed from his
lips like water from a geyser. He was well again, he said, quite well. No harm
could come to him so long as he held that bit of china close to his breast.
Bullets would not pierce, flames would not destroy, the fortunate one who
possessed the sacred treasure. The plate possessed strange inherent powers as
well. Food would never spoil if placed upon it. Cold things would keep cold,
and hot things hot, if served thereon, and he who possessed it need have no
fear of famine. All this I learned from Ying's excited lips, and as I listened I
marveled at the faith of men in general, and at the credulity of Chinese
coolies in particular.

The streets of the native city of Peking, as they are at present, are worth a
long journey to see. They are, as I have said, in chaos. There is no government, not even a uniform military one. Within the outer walls the city is
divided off into sections, each section being under the control of a different
nationality, the Imperial Palace alone being considered neutral ground into
which no one is supposed to enter. But if one were to judge the place from
the appearance of the streets, he might easily believe the city had lately put
on gala attire in celebration of some great international festival, for over
every house floats a flag which, though not always elegant, is highly colored
and decorative. Most of the flags are improvised affairs, few being of the
regulation dimensions and colors, and a greater collection of nondescript
banners would be very hard to find. The colors have run on most of them.
Others were made by painting the design on a bit of white cambric, while
still more especially the emblems of the United States were ludicrous in the
extreme, they were so far from being correct in design.

The only Chinese about the city when I arrived were those who had been
commandeered by the troops and made to work. All these wore a placard on
their coats, or carried a card on which was written the name of the protector
of the individual. Gradually, however, some of the more adventurous of
Peking's former inhabitants returned, and in order to insure immunity from

interference they would at once approach some soldier or civilian and indicate by signs their desire for a protecting placard. The request was seldom refused, but few could withstand the temptation to play a joke on the unsuspecting Celestial. Here are some of the placards I read: 'I am a Boxer; give me H – !' 'Please give me a swift kick.' 'I am a loafer – make me work.' 'Please jerk my queue off', etc.

For similar reasons, over the doors of some of the Chinese houses are tacked cards on which appeals are made to the reader to refrain from destroying the property. Some of these are pathetic, others are disgusting, but most are only amusing: 'May I come under the protection of your flag?' is a common one. 'I protected a missionary; please protect me' is another often seen; but the one which appealed strongest to me read, 'I am a damned good Christian.'

The scarcest things in Peking just at present are sheets and pillow cases and table linen. All material of this sort was either destroyed during the siege or used for the making of sand bags. As a substitute everyone is using silk, bought or looted from the Chinese houses. My sheets are of bright yellow, and my pillow case is of a beautiful pale blue color. It will seem rather commonplace getting back to ordinary linen again.

I called on our minister, Mr E.H. Conger, soon after my arrival, and found him very much as I had understood him to be – shrewd, egotistical, and extremely unobliging and unhospitable. He did go so far as to ask me to 'drop around at the house' (an expression which amused Scott – himself a trained diplomat – immensely), but I did not do so for several reasons, one being that I caught sight of his wife and daughters on the street. They looked as if they had just come off the farm.

General James H. Wilson, commanding our 1st Brigade, was exceedingly cordial when I went to see him. We had a long talk together on the situation.

TIENTSIN TO PAOTING-FU: *October 5 to 21*

During the time I had been away from Tientsin the city had changed a good deal. More troops had arrived; communication with the outside world had been perfected and the natives had returned to their homes in swarms. The place was crowded – jammed to the doors – and if it was cosmopolitan and interesting before it was doubly so now. I had the greatest difficulty in getting the manager of the Astor House to give me even a cot for the night, and as he absolutely refused to let me remain permanently, on the following day I again packed my boxes and moved to the house of Judge W.S. Emens (the magistrate of the Provisional Government), whose acquaintance I had made during my first visit, and who very kindly offered to put me up. Here I spent a week in comfort and quiet, and very refreshing it was to be around the corner from where the band was playing all day and all night.

On the 12th of October I started with the British troops for Paoting-fu, the capital of the province of Chihli. Paoting-fu is situated about ninety miles west of Tientsin, and about eighty miles south of Peking – lines connecting the cities forming an almost equilateral triangle embracing the heart of the Boxer territory. It was the richest city in North China and the home of many of the most influential men of the nation. Moreover, there had been several known cases of outrages committed upon foreign residents by the Chinese of the place, and there still remained in the city a few missionaries whose lives seemed in constant peril. It was, therefore, determined to take the city, and in order to cut off all chance of escape it was also determined to make the approach from several directions at once.

The main column, consisting of British, French, German, and a few Italian troops, all under the personal command of Lieutenant General Sir Alfred Gazalee, was to move from Peking. Another combined force of French and Germans was to march from Tientsin and approach the city from the east, and a British column under command of Major General Lorne Campbell was to leave Tientsin on the 12th, and by making a detour, approach the city from the south. It was expected that this column would meet with resistance on the way, and it was largely the hope of seeing a little fighting as well as the desire to keep in touch with the British element that made me decide to join this force.

I had little time to prepare for the journey and very little knowledge of what was required for so indefinite a trip. Several schemes suggested themselves. I didn't have a suitable tent and none could be bought; I didn't have pack mules, and above all I didn't want to put myself under obligations at the very beginning, to my newly-made friends, so I finally decided to get a two-wheeled covered Peking cart and live in that, and thus be independent of everybody. The cart was strong and was provided with two mules. In it I had loaded besides things to wear and things to sleep in, things to eat and things to drink and things to smoke; a charcoal stove and cooking utensils and a box containing writing materials, and a lot of odds and ends – Ying was to do the cooking. My Peking *mafoo* was to go to look after my pony, and another Chinaman, the owner of the cart and mules, was also to go to drive the vehicle and look after his own animals. Everything seemed quite complete and I started off feeling that I was not only in for a lot of interesting experiences, but that I was provided with everything I might need for an excursion of more than a month.

But the best-laid plans sometimes fail. The first trouble was due to the eggs. I had laid in a store of three dozen of these delicacies, and had instructed Ying to see that one half of them were hard boiled and packed in my luncheon basket – the others to be carefully placed in a box containing feed for the pony. Ying boiled the eggs according to program, but got the packages mixed, with the natural result that everything in the cart was soon more or less covered with a layer of raw egg. When the catastrophe was discovered the boy was crestfallen, and I hot, but the column had started and there was no time to spend in regrets or punishments, so we travelled on, but for a while a certain coolness existed in the relations between my servant and me.

The British column with which I travelled was made up of fifteen hundred [and] fifty fighting men and was, as I have said, under command of Major General Lorne Campbell. There were besides these fighting men about fourteen hundred other men, which included the transport, hospital, and commissary corps, but was in reality largely made up of personal servants of the officers. The commonest subaltern in the British Indian service never travels without at least three servants; captains have from five to ten; colonels fifteen or more; and General Campbell had so many about him that it was impossible for me to estimate the number. As a result, in order to get fifteen hundred fighting men forward it was necessary to move a column containing approximately three thousand men, to say nothing of the horses and carts, and in consequence the column was extremely unwieldy and hard to move with despatch.

We left Tientsin on a cold, crisp, typical New England autumn day, and everything went smoothly. The troops had no difficulty in marching fifteen miles and when we had pitched camp on the outskirts of a small village called Liu Chang, they seemed little the worse for their exercise. I had my cart stationed just outside the camp of the Australian contingent and within a half hour after we stopped tea was served to me by Ying in a very inviting way. Everything in the cart had been taken out, the shafts placed upon a prop so as to bring the floor of the vehicle level, and cloth spread thereon. I sat in a chair looted from the village and enjoyed my four o'clock beverage exceedingly. At seven I dined in the same way and soon after I drew myself into a fur-lined rug I had brought with me, laid down on the floor of the cart and for nine solid hours slept the sleep of the reasonably just.

It will be a long time before I forget the march to Paoting-fu. After the first day I used to leave my cart in charge of Ying and together with my *mafoo* would ride at the head of the column with the advance guard, mounted on a little Chinese pony. Most of the country through which we passed at first was deserted, but as we got into the interior we came upon villages which were more or less peopled, and these received us with great ceremony and a show of hospitality. It was a curious sight, when approaching a village, to see a crowd of Chinamen come forward bearing cards of the officials and bowing low in recognition of our authority as they advanced. These cards were received by Colonel Phayre,[2] in charge of the advance, and after being translated by.the interpreters their owners would be instructed to appear. Then came forward the mandarins themselves, sometimes walking under high and highly-colored umbrellas, sometimes being borne in state in great sedan-chairs, but all anxious to do homage to the commander of the approaching host. Colonel Phayre received them coldly, and through an interpreter submitted them to a short cross-examination, after which they were generally told to return to their homes and collect within an hour a certain amount of provisions such as eggs, chickens, sheep, bullocks, etc., with which to feed the troops, threatening total destruction of the village in case of disobedience. Each high official who came in state returned in haste to fulfill the command, and by the time our transport came up we were fully provisioned for the next twenty-four hours. No looting was permitted.

Occasionally a detachment of troops was delegated to visit a village known to have been hostile and search it for firearms and ammunition. These villages were generally small and contained little of value. The men invariably fled at our approach, but there remained in them always many terror-stricken women and children to receive us. I shall never forget the abject submission and fright on the faces of the poor unfortunates who were left behind. Many fell on the ground before us; many kissed our feet, uttering all the while unintelligible sounds, while others hid their faces in their arms, hugged their babies to their breasts, and groaned and wept, expecting evidently to be murdered within the next few moments.

I remember going into one house alone and finding there a woman of about forty or so, nursing a small child who was evidently very ill. The woman was terror-stricken, tears were in her eyes, and her whole frame trembled. When she saw me she fell upon her face, bared her breast, and moaned, as if she wished me to shoot her and spare the child. The child was almost naked; its ribs stood out clearly like those of a skeleton; its eyes rolled as if it were delirious, which doubtless it was. The woman was terror stricken, yet after the first notice of me she turned towards the child and thought only of it. A more pitiable, a more heart-rendering sight I shall never see. I put my pistol away; I slipped a coin into the woman's hand, and the look of surprise and gratitude that overspread her features was wonderful indeed. She tried to thank me but I hurried away. We found little in this particular village, but in the next one examined we found guns, ammunition and Boxer flags, and it was immediately burned to the ground.

A day or two later I again joined the advance guard and had rather an exciting experience. The galloping cavalry after the first hour or so proved quite too much for my pony, and in spite of urging him to the utmost, I fell behind. The main column was a mile or so in the rear of the advance, so almost before I knew it I was alone and abreast of rather a good-sized village. My *mafoo*, who never left me, at this juncture suggested that we go into the village and get water for our ponies, and thinking there would be no danger in visiting a place that our cavalry had just passed through, I acquiesced.

We entered by a side gate and immediately found ourselves in the main thoroughfare of the town. The street was crowded with men and women all bent on packing their things into carts and getting away into the grain fields before the arrival of the troops. I saw at once that the advance guard had not passed through the village, but around it, and that I was its first arrival. I pulled up, levelled my revolver, and shouted 'Kow tow.'

Many people at once fell on their knees, but one man, with a savage look on his face, ran into a house in evident excitement. I jumped from my pony, and giving the reins to my *mafoo*, ran after the man and discovered him in an outhouse, searching for something under old straw. With a whip I lashed him across the head and motioned him to bring forth the article, and to my surprise he handed me, not silver or jewels or treasure, but a muzzle-loaded gun ready for firing. I grabbed it, and at the same time grabbed the man by the pigtail and attempted to make my way out, but the people had crowded about, and it was almost impossible. Sticks and stones fell about my head like hail. I could not manage both the man and the gun, so I dropped the pigtail and ran outside. Here I found a mob of one hundred, at least, so I threw the gun to my *mafoo* and jumped to my pony and galloped off. Then I turned and after firing a shot over the heads of the crowd I had my *mafoo* shout that I would return in five minutes with the army and if the owner of the gun was not produced the town would be burned.

Then I rode away, reported the case to the Colonel, handed over the gun and returned towards the village again. When I approached the second time my reception was quite different. The culprit had flown, but the mandarins had come in person to explain the situation. The Colonel listened, examined the gun, decided it was a Boxer weapon, and ordered the village burned. Then we rode on, but this time I kept pretty close to the main column.

After twelve days of marching we arrived at Paoting-fu, the last column to reach its destination, and camped just outside the walls of the city. Captain Tickell, of the Australians, had asked me to mess with them some days earlier, an invitation I accepted most gladly, and as soon as we had pitched a camp he insisted on my sharing his own spacious tent with him. This was not only agreeable, but gave me an excellent opportunity of studying at close range this very remarkable body of men. They, were, in fact, the unique feature of the column.

At the outbreak of the trouble in China, Victoria volunteered to send a full ship's company of men to the front, bearing all the expense of the undertaking, and when the offer was accepted by the War Office, they pulled together the men, provisioned and equipped them, and were ready to start within a week after receiving the summons. I tell this simply to show the quality of the men in the camp. Each is full-blooded and able, and a credit to Victoria and Australia. In many ways they are like Americans – they are big strapping fellows, alert and keen, and to use an expression often heard among them, they are 'handy'. They can do anything – they have no servants – everything is done within themselves by themselves. Among them are cooks, carpenters, armorers, engineers, telegraphers, signal men, tailors, sailmakers, blacksmiths, horsemen, bakers, butchers, saddlers, gunners, divers and many other artisans who have forsaken good, permanent positions for the glory of being part of the body of men who were to represent their country in China.

Above all, every man in the contingent is self-reliant. He has faith in his ability to compete with men of other nationalities. He has full confidence in his own worth. In these respects he is like the American, but he differs in one marked characteristic – he is never above the position he occupies. A better-disciplined set of men I have never seen, and I may further add I have never been thrown into contact with a body of men whose officers had such a firm hold upon their subordinates, and at the same time permitted a familiarity that bespoke almost social equality. The four commissioned officers of the contingent are men well and favorably known in their country. The never speak loudly, they never use profane language so common among Americans. They never speak slightingly of their subordinates; they know the ins and outs of every man with whom they have to deal, and above all, they have the unqualified respect, not only of every one within their authority, but of their English associates as well. Moreover, they are popular. Our mess, after dinner, was always crowded with visitors, and many stayed late into the night. It will be a long time before I shall forget the songs that were sung and the tales that were told during the evenings of those memorable days.

PAOTING-FU; PAOTING-FU TO TIENTSIN: *October 21 to November 6*

We were the last column to reach Paoting-fu. When we arrived the city had not only been entered by the other troops, but had been divided into four sections, the French controlling one section, the Germans another, the Italians another, and the British the one remaining. General Gazelee, as senior officer, had established his headquarters in the *Yamen* of the Viceroy; the French General, who was next in rank, taking the Governor's *Yamen*; and the Italian and German commanders, other buildings of importance. The Australians were camped outside the north gate of the city, not far from the British headquarters.

On the day following our arrival I went into the city and found, to my surprise, that business was being carried on in the shops and upon the streets almost as if nothing unusual were occurring. The Chinese officials, with their usual duplicity, had endeavored to deceive the people a little longer as to the true state of affairs. A proclamation had been issued to the effect that the foreign troops within their walls were military guests of the city – come at the invitation of the Throne – and directed that they be treated with great deference and hospitality. Moreover, an order had been sent out by the Lieutenant General commanding, prohibiting all looting, and as this order was enforced there was little reason for the inhabitants to close their doors.

But though Paoting-fu itself seemed quiet, the country round about was in a very disturbed state, so much so that no one was allowed outside camp limits. Occasionally, however, small detachments of cavalry would be sent out on reconnoitering expeditions. On one of these expeditions I saw my first fighting. A party had been out the day before and while passing a town was fired upon, and one of the soldiers wounded. It turned, charged, entered the city and killed a number of men, and then rode back to headquarters to report. The following day General Campbell ordered a larger detachment of cavalry to proceed against the town and destroy it. I went along.

There were about eighty mounted Indian troops in the attacking party. We found the town walled and fortified and the gates locked, and as we approached a volley was fired, wounding one man. The captain in charge divided the column in two detachments, and encircling the walls, each entered at a weak point and found approximately one thousand men armed with muzzle-loading guns, with bows and arrows, with spears and antiquated swords, all intent on defending the town. One charge of the Indian Lancers settled the business. The sight of the horses evidently terrified the Chinese, for they fell on their faces and offered no resistance; it was simply a matter of riding over the hundreds of Chinese men lying and kneeling on the ground, and either killing them by the lance or with a sword. The command had been total destruction, but after five minutes' work the Indian soldiers themselves refused to kill more, and it was decided to leave the scene with the job half done. This was a sample of the fighting of the Allied Troops in China after the first week; the Chinese would fire one shot, and then if resistance was made they would fall on their knees and wait until their heads were cut off.

We stayed in Paoting-fu six days. During those six days I felt stronger and healthier and in many ways happier than I had for years. The camp was comfortable, the scenery beautiful, and the weather glorious. We lived on the fat of the land and spent most of our time in congratulating each other on being alive. Then one quiet morning we folded our tents and silently moved away. It had been decided to return to our base, Tientsin, in a leisurely manner, going first to a walled and fortified town seventeen miles south of Paoting-fu, supposed to contain many Boxers and much treasure.

The plan was to destroy the town, capture the treasure, and then move on to other towns not previously visited by the troops. The expedition was supposed to be secret. The other powers were not advised of our intentions; but on the day of our departure we found that our purpose had leaked out and that the French were already on their way to the same spot, twenty-four hours ahead of us. This is only one instance of many I noticed in which the British were outwitted by another power – in fact, the regularity with which the British troops in China arrived behind time became almost a byword.

Little of interest happened during the first day of our homeward journey. We marched through a beautiful, fertile farming country, passed many little deserted villages, and finally camped for the night at a point about six miles from the supposed hostile city. The next morning, as usual, I joined the advance, and as usual, expected to spend the first hour riding beside Colonel Phayre, listening to his stories of Indian life.

We had not gone far, however, when in the distance we saw galloping toward us a horse covered with foam, its rider urging him to the utmost, and waving in his right hand a paper. A few moments later we made the horseman out to be a French soldier, and when he came up and handed Colonel Phayre the paper he carried, talking at the same time excitedly in patois French, there were none of us about, I think, who did not feel trouble ahead. The document said that the French column that had preceded us had been attacked the day before by a large force of Boxers, that a battle had ensued in which the casualties on both sides were heavy, and that at the end the Chinese had retreated to within a strongly walled and fortified city just beyond. In view of this the French commander did not wish to make the attack without reinforcements, and he therefore prayed that we hurry forward with all possible despatch.

In an instant Colonel Phayre changed from a raconteur of Indian stories into an executive whirlwind. By his swiftest aide he sent the message back to General Campbell, he despatched scouts ahead, to the right and to the left, and he gave a dozen orders to be followed in case of attack. Within an incredibly short time the aide was back from headquarters with the General's command that the cavalry and light artillery push forward with all possible despatch. A moment later we were riding at a fast trot toward the enemy, my pony panting, my *mafoo* beside me trembling like an autumn leaf, and I – well, I was not feeling over cheerful. For a half hour we rode on, on – then we met another messenger hurrying towards us. His despatch read, 'We are all ready to make attack. Waiting only for heavy artillery. Hurry!' Again this was sent to the rear, and the order came back, 'Push forward the Royal Horse Artillery.' Major Blaine, commanding the RHA, was present when the order came, and spurring his horse to the rear, he was soon with his Battery, urging it on at breakneck speed.

We drew to one side to let it go past, and as each heavy gun, drawn by six 'whalers' on the dead run, went thundering by, it made my heart, at least, jump into my mouth. On and on we pushed, each second seeming a minute, and each minute an hour, until in the distance we could make out the French troops drawn up in line of attack on a large field a mile or so in front of the walled city. Then we halted, and General Campbell and his staff, who had come up, rode over to the French force for a conference with its commander. It appeared that our allies had had a brush with the Chinese the day before, and that the latter had retreated before much harm was done, although several French soldiers had been killed or wounded. The enemy was seen to go within the walled city, and as the strength of the city was an unknown quantity it was deemed wise to wait for reinforcement before making an attack – hence the messenger and messages.

Various schemes of approach were then discussed but none decided upon until, at last, Colonel Phayre suggested that it might be well to send out scouts before proceeding with the main body of troops, which suggestion (strange to say) was approved. In ten minutes the four men despatched were back, and on the face of each was a broad grin. They had ridden to the rear gate of the city, had found it wide open, and upon investigation, had ascertained the place to be destitute of inhabitants. The Chinese had decamped in a body during the night and nobody had known a thing about it.

I shall not try to describe our weary march home. It was one long series of expectations raised but never realized – of hopes deferred and blasted. We travelled through a series of deserted villages. We saw little of interest; we met with no resistance, and to crown all the weather became cold and damp and extremely disagreeable. For two days we were in the center of a North China dust storm, the wind blowing a hurricane and carrying with it clouds of sharp, fine sand, which cut our faces, filled up our throats, and so impeded our progress that we could make but five miles per day. During the storm I fell ill with fever, and for two days had to be carried in the ambulance or *doolie*. These days were long and dreary ones. I lay on my back with nothing but my thoughts for company and they were very poor companions indeed. But the doctor was a good one, and the men very kind in their attentions. Ying never left me after we got into camp. His devotion was wonderful and did much to bring me round.

When we arrived at Tuliu we were joined by the junks, and it was decided that I had better make the rest of the journey in the hospital boat, so I was carried to the place where she was moored. My quarters were not quite ready, so the *doolie* in which I was lying was set down about thirty paces from a pile of articles captured from the Chinese and just taken off the boats. There was a crowd of men around looking at these articles, which consisted of silks and furs, guns and gunpowder, and old Chinese swords and lances. Suddenly there was a terrific explosion, followed by a second shot and a stampede of horses and mules in my direction. I sprang up, weak as I was, and saw forty or more flaming men running frantically about, shrieking and yelling like mad. Never have I seen so terrible a sight. Somebody had dropped a spark into the gunpowder and it had exploded. Most of the crowd were to windward or the loss would have been several hundred. As it was, thirty men, mostly Chinamen and Indian soldiers, died. Of the agony they suffered as they slowly expired before our eyes I shall not speak. It was unspeakable, but the odor of the burning flesh, the terrorizing shrieks of the dying, and the expressions on the faces of the suffering wretches will haunt me in my waking and sleeping dreams as long as I exist. It will be long, very long, before I forget that terrible half-hour.

As a result of the accident, I saw that the hospital boat would be crowded and so insisted upon going back to camp and continuing with the troops. The rest of the journey was uneventful. I reached Tientsin about noon on the sixth of November, and went straight to the house of Judge Emens. A few days of quiet and rest – a few meals of white men's food, and a few nights of sleep in a real bed, soon straightened me out.

Notes

[1] Thomas Francis Bruce Renny-Tailyour was born 8 June 1863 and was promoted to Major, Royal Engineers, 1 April 1900.

[2] Lieutenant Colonel Arthur Phayre was born 23 February 1856, and served in the Indian Army.

Account of Lieutenant Bernard Frederick Roper Holbrooke, British Army

Bernard Frederick Roper Holbrooke (1871–?) was made Second Lieutenant in the Indian Army on 28 June 1893 and promoted to First Lieutenant two years later. He was serving on the Northwest Frontier of India in June 1900 when he was suddenly ordered to proceed to China via Quetta and Karachi. He disembarked at Taku on 4 August, too late to join the Relief Expedition which had already departed from Tientsin.

He remained in China until the spring of 1901 before being sent to South Africa.

26th Baluchistan Regiment
Peking, August 23, 1900[1]

Dear Papa

We arrived here on August 17th but have been too busy to write before.

After leaving Hong Kong (July 30) we went to Weihaiwei where we stopped one day – not much of a place. We then went on to Taku at the mouth of the river Peiho. We got there at daybreak and were met by a splendid sight. The allied fleet of all nations was at anchor – English, French, Russian, German, Italian, Austrian, Japanese and American. It was a grand sight – over seventy ships. We were here transferred to a smaller steamer, as no large ones can approach near the shore. We steamed past the celebrated Taku Forts – which were now in our possession – to about fifteen miles up the river to where the British have a landing stage. All the Powers are very jealous of each other, and each has a separate landing place. There we were transferred to a train and went to Tientsin where we arrived at 9 pm. Eighteen hours solid work including unloading two steamers and loading and unloading the trains with our kit, ammunition, etc.

Tientsin is or rather was a beautiful city full of big houses, hotels, etc. but it is now a mass of burnt ruins. It was defended by Admiral Seymour against the Chinese and they burnt the whole place, to be quits however – the allies stormed and looted the Chinese city about 5 miles off. It is reported that over one million pounds worth of loot was taken, mainly by the Russians and Americans. The English did not get much. We are very virtuous on such occasions.

We were in Tientsin three days. The Relief Force started the morning we arrived. The General in command of the Base would not let us catch them up much to our disgust but kept us three days and then we started off with a large convoy. It is eight marches from Tientsin to Peking and we could not catch them up. The number of animals in the convoy was too large to move fast. We however had various little shows of our own en route and lost about nine men – mostly in night attacks. There are few or no Chinamen to be seen on the way – everybody has fled.

Peking, if properly defended, is impregnable. It is divided into four cities. Outside is the Chinese City; the wall is sixty feet high and sixty feet thick. Inside that is the Tartar City, the walls being equally massive. Inside this is the Imperial City – and inside that the Forbidden City. We are quartered in the Tartar city. The Forbidden City has not yet been entered. It is the Emperor's private residence, etc. and is about one mile square. It is doubtful whether it will be entered – there is too much jealousy amongst the different forces. We spend our day in looting – organised parties of twenty non-commissioned officers and men and one officer go into the Imperial City and all the loot they collect is brought back and put into a big central Depôt which is being sold for the benefit of the troops. Of course on the q.t. we loot for ourselves a little as well and I have some most valuable Tartar silk dresses which I will send home if possible; also some curios – but the great difficulty is transport. We were only allowed 40 lbs of kit all told coming here and no tents.

Peking is mostly in ruins. The Legations are absolutely in ruins. I don't know how they managed to hold out so long – they were eating mules and dogs. Their strength all told was only about 950 Europeans of whom over 500 were women and children, and the losses were (out of a little over 400) 200 killed and wounded – not a single woman or child was hit. It beats Ladysmith altogether – as the Legations stand in streets and the Chinese were often only a yard or two away from our people. They also took to mining. We unfortunately had no powder, so could not countermine – we could only bluff – also they tried to burn the place – they could not possibly have held out another week. They only had about 250 men left for duty against 10,000 fanatics. In fact if the Chinese had had any pluck they could have rushed the place any time within the last ten days. However there are not 20,000 Chinese left now in the whole city in the place of over 1,000,000 (a million). The Emperor has fled. We shall probably get more stores etc. up here and then march after the Boxers who cannot be many miles off.

About the different troops composing the Force – the Americans are a magnificent body of men, slight and tall – few under 5'10" – but they have not much discipline. There are no German or Austrian soldiers but their sailors are a good lot of men – not very smart but very hard-working and polite. The Russians are an awful lot – no discipline – they are simply hordes of men – know little about their rifles – loot everything and everywhere – shoot everybody – they shoot all day long any defenseless Chinaman. They are nothing more than savages and the Cossacks rather worse – the stories told about them in camp are fearful.

But if the Russians are bad so are the French – dirty – slovenly – lot of men wear the filthiest uniform imaginable – take no notice of their own or any other officer – no sanitary arrangements – their camp stinks – they are the contempt of all the other nations even including the Russians.

The Japs are the last in the list and the best; their arrangements are perfect – everybody knows his work – they are as plucky as could be – in fact they are perfect in every particular but one and that is their formations are much too cumbersome. They have lost very heavily in consequence. They move 3 or 4 deep; against the Boers they would have been annihilated.

About the enemy. They fought well at Tientsin but lost so terrifically there they have been quite demoralized since. At the best however they are not the equal of the Boers except in artillery. They have hundreds of guns and their practice is wonderful; also their shells and fuses good – all our losses are nearly due to artillery fire. They always run when we get within 700 yards of them.

This is a most interesting show – although we are having a bad time of it. No tents, food scarce, stinks awful. Peking is full of dead Chinamen and horses and the stench is awful.

Give love to all,
Bernard
P.S. We are living on Tommy rations intended for daily 1 lb. bread 1 lb. meat etc. etc. No tents and only 40 lbs. of kit. So you can imagine we are having a hard time of it – but we are very fit.

Peking, Feb. 10th 1901

Dear Papa
Since last I wrote to you a much-belated mail has arrived and no less than four letters from you and also 2 very nice vests from A & N stores. It has been so beastly cold here, they were most welcome. Our Field post office has

not been playing up well here. Up to Nov. 1 we got our letters very regularly. They came by P & O to the Base Post office Hong Kong, where they were redirected to the different brigades and then sent up here by the transports which were running every week with provisions and supplies. But since the beginning of November the port of Taku has been quite frozen and the transports have ceased running, the mails being sent up once a month or so per local steamer. The worst part is that the Chinese Imperial Post Office beats us hollow. Sir Robert Hart has started it again. The letters are sent to Chefoo by steamer and then come per 'courier' overland to Peking every week, so all civilians etc. in Peking are getting their letters weeks before us. It is a beastly piece of red tape-ism on the part of the military authorities because they could easily do the same. Our Field Post Office Department has had more practice than any other nation in the world as we are always at war somewhere or other.

We had a most impressive parade here on Feb 2nd, the day of the funeral of the Queen. The artillery fired 101 guns and the whole of the British garrison formed up and the funeral service was read; the pipers played dirges, etc. Count Waldersee and all the foreign officers were present and each nation sent a detachment of troops limited to 250 per nation. They all sent their picked troops, and we had French Zouaves in their picturesque uniform, Italian Basagheri, German Jagers, Japanese, Cossacks, Austrians and Americans. The weather has been warmer of late but the river is still frozen, it has been frozen now for 3 months – there is still 1 foot of snow on the ground and 20 to 30 degrees of frost every night.

The Peking garrison is now about 60 to 70 thousand men. We are about 10,000 strong, the Germans and French about the same, Italians 5000, Americans 5000, Russians 2000, Austrians 1000 and Japs 6000. On the whole we are very friendly with each other. Of course we are great 'pals' with the Americans and we are fairly friendly with Germans and Italians but see very little of any of the others. There have been a few international rows and fracas generally with the French who are certainly the biggest brutes going – they refuse to hobnob with anybody and keep entirely to themselves; which is the best thing perhaps, on the whole.

We have absolutely no information as to when we are going away from here, it is simply a matter of diplomacy now and getting the various ministers to agree with each other, a very difficult thing as the Russian and French ministers seem determined to put as many difficulties in the way as possible.

The climate is absolutely ripping except for its coldness. Everybody is awfully fit and I have not had 5 minutes sickness since I have been in China. The Germans are suffering a great deal from enteric amongst their junior officers and men but every other nation is fitter here than in their own country.

No more news. Sorry for poor old Gerry. Could not get a commission. One of our officers, [Lieut. C.A.] Orton by name, has a brother [Capt. E.F. Orton] in the Cape Mounted Rifles who has just been given a commission in the Royal Artillery and allowed to count half his service in the ranks.

Love to all,
Bernard

Note

[1] Holbrooke was writing to his father, who lived in Andover, Hampshire. Reverend F.G. Holbrooke noted on this letter that it arrived on 13 October; a transit time of 51 days!

The Photographers' Perspective

The Photographers' Perspective

Much attention has been lavished on a handful of early Western photographers of Imperial China, such as John Thomson and Felice Beato. However, the events of 1900 created opportunities that resulted in important documentary images as well as occasional images of a high artistic level – all taken by men and women who, by and large, have remained obscure.

There was a curious mix of professional and amateur photographers whose work must be considered. Some were equipped with their own personal, hand-held Kodak cameras, which used rolled film and were easy to carry and easy to use. Others were equipped with larger cameras which used glass plates of various sizes. Motion picture cameras were also present.

Categorising the photographers is an important first step in understanding their work as well as their motivation. Many photographs were taken simply to record people and places; others were taken with a clear recognition that they would be memorials to important historic events.

Civilian Photographers: Journalists, Missionaries, Tourists, Diplomats

Newspaper correspondents were a large and important group, whose work was widely circulated in contemporary publications. They all carried cameras as part of the reporting process, often providing visual evidence for their written observations. Some, such as James A. Ricalton and John C. Hemment, were professional photographers; others, such as Henry Savage Landor and George Lynch, were professional journalists; still others, such as Sydney Adamson, John Schonberg, and Fred Whiting, were professional artists.

The emerging field of motion picture photography was represented by two teams of photographers sent by the American Mutoscope and Biograph Company of New York City. This company was organised in 1896 specifically to record historic events. Their professionals had already covered military campaigns in Cuba (1898), the Philippines and South Africa (1899). Travelling to China in 1900, they produced footage of ceremonial troop reviews – in Shanghai, Tientsin and Peking – as well as some action scenes which could have been live or posed. The company trade catalogue dated November 1902 lists 28 different China titles, with film footage ranging from 25 to 92 feet. Two pertain to the relief of Peking: 'Charge of Reilly's Battery' and 'Assault on the South Gate'.

It is not widely known that there were numerous missionary photographers in China in 1900. These men and women combined an intimate knowledge of the country with a deep sympathy for its people. Photographs were useful additions to the mandatory reports sent back to their main offices; they were also absolutely crucial to fund-raising efforts in the Western countries from which the missionaries came.

Reverend Charles A. Killie, a member of the American Presbyterian Mission in Peking, produced the best-known assortment of siege photographs – all of whch he copyrighted. Each print is marked with his copyright stamp. His wife recalled that he had arrived at the British Legation compound on 20 June 1900 with only his 'pocket Kodak'; a large plate camera had been left behind in their hasty departure from the Methodist Mission compound.

Killie used his pocket camera to record daily life within the Legation. Early in August, when it became apparent to the besieged residents that help was finally on the way, Sir Claude MacDonald designated him to take a group of official photographs to preserve for posterity the life they had been leading while besieged. He was relieved of his hazardous work on the fortifications and provided with the camera belonging to a Japanese professional photographer (probably Sanshichiro Yamamoto), who declined to risk his life in this assignment. Killie produced a series of remarkable images, adapting the only available plates to the camera he was given. He developed these plates in an improvised darkroom with the help of his friend, Reverend Courtenay Hughes Fenn, also a member of the American Presbyterian Mission in Peking. (Killie remained in Peking for several years after the siege ended, selling numerous prints to soldiers, diplomats, and tourists.)

Reverend Fenn was also a talented amateur photographer. He had had lost both his own cameras while fleeing from the Methodist Mission compound on 20 June, but had been able to borrow a camera from a missionary colleague, Miss Gowans, who had no glass plates. He cut down some plates which were too large, and took photos during the siege; when the siege ended he carried the plates to Tientsin and developed them in the darkroom of the Isabella Fisher Hospital on Taku Road. He made prints on board ship, and on reaching San Francisco he discovered there was demand for them. Sold to reporters, his photos found their way into newspapers and magazines all over the United States.

Killie and Fenn were not the only photographers operating within the besieged Legation compound. The American tourist Mrs Anna Woodward, who had been visiting in Peking during the spring of 1900, was able to adapt some old-style English plates found in a local camera shop to her Kodak camera. Sir Claude MacDonald gave her a pass which allowed her to photograph anywhere within the Legation compound; she 'went around everywhere, even in places of danger, armed with her camera'. When she returned to Chicago in October 1900 she sold images to publishers and made slides to use in lectures.

Two young British diplomats, Student Interpreters at the British Legation, were also determined to ignore the dangers around them in order to obtain a significant quantity of images which could be sold when the siege ended. Lancelot Giles and W. Meyrick Hewlett were able to accumulate 192 photos by 1 August; Giles planned to obtain a copyright and arrange for publication. They had access to a darkroom in the compound, where Giles developed and printed their photos. Hewlett's published account records their adventures in search of candid photographs.

Photographers were also active in recording the siege in Tientsin. Charles F. Gammon, American Bible Society Superintendent for North China, and Nathan J. Sargent, Clerk in the office of the American Trading Company, were two talented amateurs whose work often appeared in accounts published after the siege. Gammon returned to the USA in the autumn of 1900, providing photographs to missionary publications.

Nathan J. Sargent was the son of Edward A. Sargent, a pioneer American merchant who had settled in Yokohama in 1875. Edward Sargent was the financial backer of the legendary Italian photographer of Meiji Japan, Adolpho Farsari; and Nathan Sargent learned photography from Farsari. In 1898, Nathan joined the family business, working first at their Kobe office before being transferred to Tientsin. He was a member of the Tientsin Volunteers; his photographs record the military aspects of the siege.

With the conclusion of the siege at Peking came the opportunity to record the appearance of the city and the various soldiers who populated it. This chance was seized by the Japanese photographer Sanshichiro Yamamoto, who had lived in Peking for several years prior to the siege, and who also maintained a studio in Tokyo. He took numerous photographs which he published in 1901 in a handsome collotyped album entitled *Views of the North China Affair, 1900*. His photographs of soldiers often appear in contemporary albums.

No account would be complete without mentioning the skilful and artistic photographs taken by Alphons Freiherr Mumm von Schwarzenstein, the Minister Plenipotentiary from Germany who had been appointed to succeed von Ketteler. Mumm arrived in Peking on 21 October 1900, accompanied by his valet, Anton Goebel, who was also an accomplished photographer, and whose job it was to develop and print photos taken by both men. In 1902 Mumm arranged for a selection of their photopgraphs to be privately printed in collotyped format as gifts to friends and colleagues.

Military Photographers: Professional and Amateur

By 1900, the armies of most world powers included a group of professional photographers, normally attached to the Corps of Engineers. The Photo Section of the British Corps of Royal Engineers first came to prominence in 1867 when it was sent to document the Abyssinia expedition. Their success in documenting this campaign, as well as providing maps to the commanding officers, established a model for future British campaigns.

In June 1900 the British government mobilised a China Expeditionary Force, primarily from among troops headquartered in India. Two Photo-Litho Sections were sent from India to China, each consisting of three British non-commissioned officers accompanied by twelve Indian Army men. They did not reach China in time to march to Peking; consequently their work commenced with the occupation.

The Japanese Fifth Army Division had a photographic section which was present during the entire campaign and also much of the occupation. A selection of their photos was published in Tokyo in April 1902 in a collo-typed album prepared by Kazumasa Ogawa, entitled *Souvenir of the Allies in North China: Photos of the 5th Division.*

While the Germans must have had official photographers on hand during the occupation, the most handsome presentation of their efforts was orga-nised by two officers of the First Seebataillon. Marine-Surgeon-Major Dr Wang and Lieutenant Count von Meerscheidt-Hullessem reached Peking on 25 August 1900. They took excellent photos of von Waldersee inspecting the Imperial City on 23 October 1900, and a unique series of photographs documenting the punitive expedition to Kalgan in November 1900. A handsome collection of their photographs was published in Germany in 1902.

The only official photographer attached to the Allied armies whose name is always specifically identified is an American, Cornealius Francis O'Keefe (known as Frank). Each of his pictures was clearly signed with an elaborate oval seal: "US Engineer Office, China Relief Expedition. Photo by C.F. O'Keefe, 26th USV".

O'Keefe was born in 1866 in Burlington, Iowa, USA. In 1882 he left Iowa for the mining camps of South America. By 1892 he was established in Leadville, Colorado as a professional photographer – with a special flair for photographing women. In April 1898 he volunteered to join the fight against Spain and was mustered into the First Colorado Volunteer Infantry as a Lieutenant, Company L. He was sent to the Philippines in June 1898.

Following the capture of Manila on 13 August 1898, O'Keefe was ordered to join the Bureau of Military Information. He worked full-time as a military field photographer, covering the Insurrection battles during the spring of 1899. In July 1899 he was transferred to the 36th US Volunteers when the 1st Colorado returned to the United States. By this time he was designated as 'official photographer of the Eighth Army Corps'. By the end of 1899 he was promoted to captain, 'on Detached Service with Engineer Corps, doing Photographic work, at which he is an expert'.

He covered expeditions on the island of Luzon until 23 June 1900, when he was ordered to report to Colonel Emerson H. Liscum for duty in China. He embarked from Manila with the 9th US Infantry on 27 June and reached Tientsin on 11 July and was present on 13 July at the Battle of Tientsin. When General Adna Chaffee arrived on 30 July to take command of the American troops, he quickly named O'Keefe to his personal staff. O'Keefe remained in China until June 1901. During this time he not only took photos of military action, but also recorded people and scenery – a rich legacy of images of Imperial China.

It would be remiss to close this account of photographic images of China during the period of the Boxer Rebellion without mention of the numerous officers and soldiers who carried their own Kodak cameras into action to record not only their friends on the campaign but also the colourful scenes around them.

The exploration of photography in China during this critical period is a subject which demands further scholarship.

Bibliography

Adamson, Sydney. Reports from China (1900). London: *Leslie's Weekly*, 1900.

Allen, Roland. *The Siege of the Peking Legations: Being the Diary of the Rev. R. Allen.* London: Smith, Elder & Co., 1901.

Andrews, Mary E. Unpublished manuscript journal, June 16–August 15, 1900. Collection of the Phillips Library, Peabody Essex Museum, Salem, MA, USA.

Aspinall-Oglander, Cecil. *Roger Keyes.* London: The Hogarth Press Ltd, 1951.

Atkinson, James J. *Australian Contingents to the China Field Force 1900–1901.* Sydney: New South Wales Military Historical Society, 1976.

Barnes, A.A.S. (Capt.) *On Active Service with the Chinese Regiment: A Record of the Operations of the First Chinese Regiment in North China from March to October, 1900.* London: Grant Richards, 1902.

Bayly, Edward H. Early Proceedings in North China in 1900. Unpublished manuscript. Collection of Jean S. and Frederic A. Sharf, Chestnut Hill, MA, USA.

Bayly, Edward H. General Notes as Regards Tientsin. Unpublished manuscript. Collection of Jean S. and Frederic A. Sharf, Chestnut Hill, MA, USA.

Bigham, Clive C. *A Year in China, 1899–1900.* London: Macmillan and Co. Ltd, 1901.

Brandt, Nat. *Massacre in Shansi.* Syracuse University Press, 1994.

Bredon, Juliet. *Sir Robert Hart.* London: Hutchinson & Co., 1909.

British Foreign Office Publications. China No. 3. *Correspondence Respecting the Insurrectionary Movement in China.* July 1900.

   China No. 4. *Reports from Her Majesty's Minister in China Respecting Events at Peking.* December 1900.

   China No. 1. *Correspondence Respecting the Disturbances in China.* February 1901.

   China No. 3. *Further Correspondence Respecting Events at Peking.* April 1901.

   China No. 4. *Plans Referred to in China No. 3 (1901).* May 1901.

   China No. 5. *Further Correspondence Respecting the Disturbances in China.* May 1901.

   China No. 6. *Further Correspondence Respecting the Disturbances in China.* August 1901.

   China No. 1. *Correspondence Respecting the Affairs of China.* March 1902.

Broomhall, Marshall. *The Chinese Empire.* London: Morgan & Scott, 1907.

Brown, Frederick. *'Boxer' and other China Memories.* London: Murray and Evenden, Ltd, 1936.

Brown, Frederick. *From Tientsin to Peking with the Allied Forces.* London: Charles H. Kelley, 1902.

Casserly, Gordon. *The Land of the Boxers.* London: Longmans, Green, and Co., 1903.

Ch'en, Jerome. *Yuan Shih-Kai, 1859–1916.* London: George Allen and Unwin Ltd, 1961.

Ching-Shan. *Diary of His Excellency Ching-Shan: Being a Chinese Account of the Boxer Trouble*. Published and translated by J.J.L. Duyvendak. Leyden, 1924. Reprinted Arlington, VA: University Publications of America, Inc., 1976.

Chirol, Valentine. *The Far Eastern Question*. London: Macmillan and Co. Ltd, 1896.

Clowes, William Laird. *The Royal Navy: A History* (Vol. 7). London, 1903.

Cohen, Paul A. *History in Three Keys*. New York: Columbia University Press, 1997.

Conger, Sarah Pike. *Letters from China with Particular Reference to the Empress Dowager and the Women of China*. Chicago: A.C. McClurg & Co., 1909.

Crowe, George. *The Commission of HMS* Terrible, *1898–1902*. London: George Newnes Ltd, 1903.

Daggett, A.S. *America in the China Relief Expedition: An Account of the Brilliant Part Taken by the United States Troops in that Memorable Campaign in the Summer of 1900 for the Relief of the Beleaguered Legations in Peking, China*. Kansas City, 1903. Reprint Nashville, TN: The Battery Press, Inc., 1997.

Daily Graphic (London), 1900–1901, *passim*.

Dill, Harry J. Unpublished manuscript letters concerning the Boxer Rebellion. Collection of Jean S. and Frederic A. Sharf, Chestnut Hill, MA, USA.

Dix, C.C. *The World's Navies in the Boxer Rebellion, 1900*. London: Digby, Long & Co., 1905.

Drage, Charles. *Servants of the Dragon Throne*. London: Peter Dawnay Ltd, 1966.

Duyvendak, J.J.L. see Ching-Shan.

Fenn, Courtenay Hughes. Family Archives and Scrapbook. Collection of M.F. Hazeltine, Providence, RI, USA.

Fleming, Peter. *The Siege at Peking*. London: Rupert Hart-Davis, 1959

Graphic, The (London), 1900–1901, *passim*.

Hart, Sir Robert. *The I.G. in Peking: Letters of Robert Hart, Chinese Maritime Customs 1868–1907*. (Volumes I, II). Edited by J.K. Fairbank, K.F. Bruner, E.M. Matheson. Cambridge, MA: The Belknap Press of Harvard University, 1975.

Haven, Ada. See Mateer, Ada Haven.

Hewlett, W. Meyrick. *The Siege of the Peking Legations*. Harrow-on-the-Hill: Harrovian, 1900.

Hooker, Mary. *Behind the Scenes in Peking: Experiences During the Siege*. London: John Murray, 1910.

Illustrated London News, The, 1900–1901, passim.

Jameson, Charles Davis..Unpublished manuscript Journal. Collection of Brown University Library, Providence, RI, USA.

Keown-Boyd, Henry. *The Fists of Righteous Harmony: A History of the Boxer Uprising in China in the Year 1900*. London: Leo Cooper, 1991.

Ker, William P. Unpublished correspondence from the Ker Family Collection.

Ketler, I.C. *The Tragedy of Paotingfu: An Authentic Story of the Lives, Services and Sacrifices of the Presbyterian, Congregational and China Inland Missionaries who suffered Martyrdom at Paotingfu, China, June 30th and July 1st, 1900*. New York: Fleming H. Revell Company, 1902.

Keyes, Roger. *Adventures Ashore and Afloat*. London: George G. Harrap & Co. Ltd. 1939.

Keyes, Roger. Unpublished manuscript letter, 6 September 1900. Collection of Jean S. and Frederic A. Sharf, Chestnut Hill, MA, USA.

Killie, Charles A. Family Archive. Reference Library of Presbyterian Historical Society, Philadelphia, PA, USA.

Kurschner, Joseph. *Schilderungen aus Leben und Geschichte, Krieg und Seig*. Leipzig: Hermann Zieger, 1901.

Landor, Henry Savage. *China and the Allies* (2 vols.). New York: Charles Scribner's Sons, 1901.

Leslie's Weekly (London), 1900–1901, *passim*.

Lucas, Christopher J., Ed. *James Ricalton's Photographs of China During the Boxer Rebellion*. Lewiston, NY: The Edwin Mellin Press, 1990.

Lynch, George. *The War of the Civilizations: Being the Record of a 'Foreign Devil's' Experience with the Allies in China*. London: Longmans, Green & Co., 1901.

Marchant, L.R., Ed. *The Siege of the Peking Legations: A Diary of Lancelot Giles*. Perth: University of Western Australia Press, 1970.

Martin, W.A.P. *The Siege in Peking: China Against the World by an Eyewitness*. London: Fleming H. Revell Company, 1900.

Mateer, Ada Haven. *Siege Days: Personal Experiences of American Woman and Children during the Peking Siege*. Chicago: Fleming H. Revell Company, 1903.

Miller, J. Martin. *China, the Yellow Peril: At War with the World*. Chicago: American Publishing House, 1900.

Miner, Luella. *China's Book of Martyrs: A Record of Heroic Martyrdoms and Marvellous Deliverances of Chinese Christians during the Summer of 1900*. Cincinnati: Jennings and Pye; and New York: Eaton and Mains, 1903.

Mori, Gitaro. Report published in *The Japan Weekly Mail*, July 1900.

Müller, Alfred von. *Unsere Marine in China*. Berlin: Verlag der Liebelschen Buchhandlung, 1901.

Mumm von Schwarzenstein, Alfons. *Ein Tagebuch in Bildern* [A Diary in Pictures]. Berlin: Graphische Gesellschaft, 1902.

Nicholls, Bob. *Bluejackets and Boxers*. Sydney: Allen and Unwin Australia Pty. Ltd, 1986.

Norie, E.W.M. (Maj.). *Official Account of the Military Operations in China 1900–1901*. 1903; reprinted Nashville, TN: The Battery Press, Inc., 1995.

O'Connor, Richard. *The Spirit Soldiers*. New York: G.P. Putnam's Sons, 1973.

O'Keefe, Cornealius Francis. Archive Collection, Colorado Mountain History Collection, Lake County Public Library, Leadville, CO, USA.

O'Keefe, Cornealius Francis. Military Records: O'Keefe File, National Archives, Washington, DC, USA.

Oliphant, N. *A Diary of the Siege of the Legations in Peking During the Summer of 1900*. London: Longmans, Green & Co., 1901.

Paine, Frederick. *With My Own Eyes*. Indianapolis: The Bobbs-Merrill Company, 1933.

Pearl, Cyril. *Morrison of Peking*. Sydney: Angus and Robertson Ltd, 1967.

Peill, J., Ed., *Letters of Dr Arthur Peill*. London: Headley Brothers, 1907.

Powlett, Frederick. Unpublished letter, 27 June 1900. Collection of Jean S. and Frederic A. Sharf, Chestnut Hill, MA, USA.

Purcell, V.W.W. *The Boxer Uprising: A Background Study.* Cambridge: Cambridge University Press, 1963.

Ricalton, J. *China through the Stereoscope: A Journey at the Time of the Boxer Uprising.* New York: Underwood and Underwood, 1902.

Russell, S.M. *The Story of the Siege in Peking.* London: Elliot Stock, 1901.

Ryan, James R. *Picturing Empire: Photography and the Visualization of the British Empire.* London: Reaktion Books, 1997.

S., D.W. *European Settlements In the Far East.* London: Sampson Low, Marston & Company, 1900.

Scheibert, J. *Der Krieg in China, 1900-1901.* Berlin: A. Schröder, 1901–1902.

Schlieper, Paul. Contemporary typescript, Journal of the Seymour Expeditionary Force. Translated from the German original. Collection of Phillips Library, Peabody Essex Museum, Salem, MA, USA.

Simpson, Bertram Lenox. See Weale, B.L. Putnam.

Smith, Arthur H. *China in Convulsion* (2 vols.). Edinburgh & London: Oliphant, Anderson & Ferrier, 1901.

Smith, Polly Condit. See Hooker, Mary.

Steel, Richard A. *Through Peking's Sewer Gate.* New York: Vantage Press, 1985.

Tan, Chester C. *The Boxer Catastrophe.* New York: Columbia University Press, 1955.

Tanera, Carl. *Deutschlands Kampfe in Ostasien.* Berlin: Verlag von Neufeld & Henius, 1901,

Thiriez, Regine. *Barbarian Lens: Western Photographers of the Quianlong Emperor's European Palaces.* Amsterdam: Gordon & Breach Publishers, 1998.

Thomson, H.C. *China and the Powers: A Narrative of the Outbreak of 1900.* London: Longmans, Green & Co., 1902.

Townsend, Alfred Markham (Ed.). *In Memoriam: Walter Ewan Townsend.* New York City: privately printed, 1901.

Tyler, William F. *Pulling Strings in China.* London: Constable and Company Ltd, 1929.

Upham, Oscar. Unpublished manuscript log. History and Museum Division, United States Marine Corps.

Vereschagin, Aleksandr Vasil'evich. *Vidy Mugdena i Pekina 1902* [Views of Mukden and Peking, 1902]. Album of gelatin-silver prints.

Waldersee, Alfred von. *A Field-Marshal's Memoirs: From the Diary, Correspondence and Reminiscences of Alfred, Count von Waldersee.* Condensed and translated by F. Whyte. London: Hutchinson & Co., 1924.

Wang, Dr and von Meerscheidt-Hüllessem, *In und um Peking: Während der Kriegswirren 1900–1901.* Berlin-Schöneberg: Meisenbach Riffarth & Co., 1902.

Weale, B.L. Putnam. *Indiscreet Letters from Peking, 1900.* London: Hurst & Blackett, Ltd, 1906.

Whiting, Jasper. Contemporary typescript journal. Collection of Jean S. and Frederic A. Sharf, Chestnut Hill, MA, USA.

Woodward, Anna Graham. The Personal Side of the Siege of Peking. *The Independent,* Vol. LII No. 2712 (22 November 1900).

Woodward, Ione. Young Girl's Last Word: Miss Ione Woodward Writes to her Father from Peking. *The Sunday Times-Herald*, Chicago, July 8 1900.

Worswick, Clark and Spence, Jonathan. *Imperial China: Photographs 1850–1912*. New York: Pennwick Publishing Inc., 1978.

Wu Yung. *The Flight of the Empress*. London: Faber and Faber Ltd, 1936.

Index

Index

253